The American Exploration and Travel Series

(Complete list on page 214)

THE NEW DEMOCRACY
IN AMERICA

Travels of Francisco de Miranda
in the
United States, 1783–84

Translated by Judson P. Wood
Edited by John S. Ezell

UNIVERSITY OF OKLAHOMA PRESS : NORMAN

LIBRARY OF CONGRESS CATALOG CARD NUMBER: 63–9959

Copyright 1963 by the University of Oklahoma Press, Publishing Division of the University. Composed and printed at Norman, Oklahoma, U.S.A., by the University of Oklahoma Press. First edition.

To the memory of

HENRI AND CHARLOTTE PITTIER

EDITOR'S PREFACE

THE CIRCUMSTANCES under which Francisco de Miranda's diary of his American sojourn came to be translated are, in themselves, unusual. They might go almost unnoted in the normal order of things, for the translator has shown a degree of modesty that has all but kept his role from being known to this and future generations of his countrymen.

As a Harvard undergraduate studying under Professor Samuel Eliot Morison, Judson P. Wood was arrested by one of the suggested readings for the course in the American Revolution and the Making of the Constitution. It was William Spence Robertson's Spanish-language edition of Miranda's diary. Having been born in Venezuela of American parents, Mr. Wood was early bilingual. The reading of Miranda's American journal was therefore doubly attractive to him. From it came a term paper. But he came away from the experience with a deeper conviction, he tells us, occasioned in part by the fact that these materials had been consulted, apparently, only twice in a period of twenty years at the Widener Library. They had an abiding importance to an understanding of the early American republic, in no sense less meaningful than Alexis de Tocqueville's observations nearly half a century later. And they had never been translated in their entirety into English.

After graduation and after a law degree, Mr. Wood settled almost simultaneously into the practice of law and into the challenging task of translating, in his spare time, the commentaries of the Venezuelan patriot of a century and three-quarters ago. By a happy chance, I was invited to prepare an introduction and notes for the completed work. To say that I was delighted for the privilege is understatement.

A double concern confronts an editor in dealing with diary material written in a foreign language: the accuracy of the translator and the verity of the source. The translator has truthfully reproduced the intent of the original diarist without the sacrifice of readability, and his account checks against the two principal printed sources, both in Spanish: William Spence Robertson, *The Diary of Francisco de Miranda* (New York, Hispanic Society of America, 1928), and *Archivo del General Miranda, Viajes, Diarios, 1750–1785* (Caracas, Parra León Hermanos, Editorial Sur-América, 1929), I, 192–351.

Not only was Miranda a broadly educated person, but he also studied English before coming to the United States; thus his orthography was better than that of most foreign travelers during this period. Naturally, however, he committed some errors, and therefore, whenever possible, proper names misspelled in the text are given correctly in the footnotes. It must be candidly admitted that on a number of occasions, when Miranda gave only the last name of an individual without other identifying information, I was forced to make educated guesses concerning the complete identity—guesses based upon the probability of the person's being in the place described at the time assigned. One must also not be misled by the frequent use of dots or periods. Miranda used them (...) to indicate strong feeling, an intentional break, or a greater pause than that provided by the traditional period. Materials which have obviously been inserted, such as mileage charts and the like, usually appeared as marginal notes in the manuscript diary. All pertinent portions of that document are included in this translation, the only major omission occurring in Miranda's description of his voyage from Boston to London. Gaps in the original are indicated at the points at which they occur.

I have departed somewhat from standard scholarly procedure in using the Latin word *sic* ("thus"). Its occasional use in the text or in quotations indicates, as is normally the case, exact reproduction of the original. In the notes, however, I have used it to show the *correct spelling* of a name misspelled by Miranda. Since most of the scores of names mentioned by Miranda are or may be assumed to be spelled correctly, the latter method seemed to me the most plausible and least confusing way of handling variant spellings.

The most useful sources for biographical data concerning Miranda are William Spence Robertson, "Francisco de Miranda and the Revolutionizing of Spanish America," American Historical Association, *Annual Report for the Year 1907*, I, 189–528, and *Life of Miranda* (2 vols.; Chapel Hill, University of North Carolina Press, 1929); Joseph F. Thorning, *Miranda: World Citizen* (Gainesville, University of Florida Press, 1952); and [James Biggs], *The History of Don Francisco de Miranda's Attempt to Effect a Revolution in South America* (Boston, Edward Oliver, 1810). Shorter sketches are numerous and easily found.

I would also like to express my personal indebtedness to Professors Eugene R. Craine and Lowell Dunham and to Dr. Guillermo Morón of Caracas, Venezuela, for their patient assistance in clearing up troublesome points in the diary. Part of the cost of preparing the manuscript for publication was borne by the University of Oklahoma Faculty Research Fund.

J. S. E.

NORMAN, OKLAHOMA
MAY 27, 1963

CONTENTS

ILLUSTRATIONS

THE MAN, THE COUNTRY, AND THE DIARY

Francisco de Miranda and the United States were well matched during the period covered by this diary. The man, thirty-three years old and a fugitive from Spanish justice, had just seen the sudden collapse of a highly promising military career. To build a new life, he had only intangibles: his own unusual talents and the good wishes of a few loyal friends. The country to which he fled had just experienced its own and perhaps equally soul-searching metamorphosis. The initial elation at having cast off old political ties and of setting out to face the challenges of the future upon its own resources was still evident.

Thus in 1783, two unknown quantities confronted each other—a new nation and a new man, both about to begin a new departure. Within the next few decades the man would be known throughout the world as a living symbol of national liberty and the fight against colonialism. The former English colonies, while developing more slowly, would become a major force in the world: a proof of the potentialities of the common man and of democracy. At this time, then, briefly met two identities, each to influence the world for good or evil. Both the man and the country were obviously unique.

THE MAN

In an era when the "great man" could be truthfully said to dominate history, one of the most colorful and attractive, yet enigmatic, figures to cross the world stage was Francisco de Miranda. A hero of three revolutions, he has been variously described as the "Precursor of Spanish-American Independence," "the symbol of an age," "a chronic revolutionist," "a herald of independence," "an avaricious soldier who disposed of his services to the nation which remunerated him most generously," "the St. John the Baptist of Spanish-American redemption," and, finally, "more than a man—he was an idea." His latest biographer[1] has added the accolade "world citizen."

Miranda won military renown on both sides of the Atlantic. He served with distinction as an officer of the Spanish army, yet later became a deserter and was labeled "a conspirator of state." During two important episodes in the American Revolution, he played dominant roles. He became a Russian colonel by order of Catherine the Great. He was a general in the armies of the French Revolution and his services are commemorated on the Arc de Triomphe, yet he was tried for treason before the Revolutionary Tribunal. The victorious forces which made Venezuela the first Spanish-American republic were led by Miranda and he became that country's dictator, but he died, not at the head of his armies, not even as a respected liberator, but as a political prisoner in a Spanish jail.

Born in Venezuela, he lived for many years in Spain and North Africa, yet William Duer of New York could write to George Rose, British "Secretary to the Treasury," that Miranda, after only nineteen months' residence, could give a "much more just account of the Resources, Genius, and State of Politics of the United States than you would be able to obtain from most of its natives." He was also familiar with every corner of the Old World, from Turkey to Scandinavia, from Russia to the British Isles.

An aristocrat and democrat, Miranda was a friend of Alexander Hamilton and General Henry Knox. He sat in the White House with Jefferson and his cabinet, was the confidant of William Pitt, the Younger, and of Addington, Wellesley, and Liverpool, as well as an intimate of Potemkin and the King of Poland. Thomas Paine wrote of first becoming acquainted with Miranda "at New York about the year 1783. He is a man of talents and enterprise,

[1] Joseph F. Thorning, *Miranda: World Citizen* (Gainesville, University of Florida Press, 1952).

and the whole of his life has been a life of adventure." His contemporary the French General Charles F. Dumouriez said of him: "He was a man of capacity and extensive information. He was better versed in the theory of war than any other of the French generals, but he was not equally versed in the practice."

Although a student of military affairs, Miranda was nevertheless a lover of painting and sculpture also, and he discussed music with Haydn. Fond of learning, his diary indicates his broad and catholic tastes in literature. He was a student of the humanities and the natural sciences; while not a university graduate, he was early known as a "walking encyclopedia." He made special trips to Sweden, Norway, and Denmark to study their social institutions, and, viewed as those of a respected sociologist, his recommendations were eagerly adopted by governmental authorities. Colleges seemed to have a special attraction for him: he investigated the methods of instruction at such American institutions as Brown, Princeton, Yale, and Harvard, as well as those at Uppsala and other ancient European universities.

A man who loved the good life, he was a hedonist of hedonists, but was willing to sacrifice comfort for knowledge and to suffer imprisonment for his beliefs. In an amoral century, few could have so justly claimed the title "American Casanova." Faithfully recording in his diary his many conquests, he dazzled women from Charleston to Constantinople. In bed, he was completely democratic, showering his favors upon both the highborn and the lowly alike. A shepherdess could arouse an entrancement equal to that with which he viewed the somewhat mature form of the fifty-eight-year-old Empress of Russia. He captivated the famous beauty Lady Holland and won the heart of Lady Hester Stanhope. There is no evidence that he ever married, but he left at least two sons by his English housekeeper.

This man of contradictions (but singular consistency as far as his primary goal in life was concerned: liberating the Spanish colonies) was born on March 28, 1750. His father, Don Sebastián de Miranda y Ravelo, a native of the Canary Islands, became a prosperous linen merchant and planter in the capital city of Caracas, Venezuela, and a friend and protégé of Governor Josef Solano. The Don's eldest son, baptized Sebastián Francisco, was educated at the Academy of Santa Rosa and the University of Caracas. Although the family had attained high prominence and considerable wealth, it was looked down upon by the native Creoles. The fact that Francisco was not socially accepted at the university may well have been the deciding factor in his decision to complete his education in Spain. Consequently, in January, 1771, he sailed for the Old World.

He did not enroll in any university, however, but spent his time traveling over Spain. His independence of mind during this period is seen in the formal reversal of his baptismal names in 1772 (and finally the dropping of Sebastián altogether) and his decision to become an officer of the king. After carefully searching out his genealogy, in December, 1772, he purchased (for eight thousand pesos) a commission as captain in a proud regiment: the Princess' Own Infantry.

Like many young officers, Miranda was ordered to garrison duty at a frontier post in Africa. Drifting from station to station, he first saw action in 1774–75 in a campaign against the Moslems of Morocco and Algiers. During a lull in the fighting, he was able to visit Gibraltar for two months, where he was an instant favorite with the English officers. This happy experience seems to have made a lifetime impression on him. He later served in Cádiz and Madrid, but was bored with routine and became involved in a dispute with his colonel.

Requests for transfer went unanswered until Spain entered the war against England as an ally of France. In April, 1780, Francisco was ordered to sail for Cuba as a "supernumerary" officer in the Regiment of Aragón and upon arrival was detailed as aide-de-camp to an old friend and admirer, General Juan Manuel de Cagigal, acting governor of Cuba. Soon the two were actively engaged in the campaigns which led to England's defeat and the independence of the United States.

First came co-operation with Governor Bernardo de Gálvez of Louisiana in the siege and final reduction of Fort Pensacola on

May 9, 1781. After the capitulation, Miranda stepped for the first time upon what became the United States. Back in Cuba, he was soon to strike another blow for American freedom. The French fleet under Admiral de Grasse was ordered to the assistance of the hard-pressed Americans. The Count needed funds immediately to resupply the fleet and help finance the bankrupt colonials. Unable to secure them in Haiti, he called at Havana on his way to the Chesapeake; the charming Captain Miranda coaxed the necessary cash and supplies from the Spanish commissary. In this way Miranda was able to contribute, in large measure, to the ensuing definitive victory at Yorktown and the struggle for North American independence.

Despite a claim by jealous rivals that Miranda had allowed a British general to inspect the harbor fortifications at Havana, Cagigal promoted his aide to brevet lieutenant colonel on August 23, 1781, and sent him on a special mission. During the same month, Miranda went to Jamaica, presumably to work out an exchange of prisoners with the British. Whatever the purpose, little could he know that this assignment was to mark a turning point in his life and fortunes.

There is some evidence that his primary function was that of a spy: to pave the way for future operations against the British. Be that as it may, he was furnished with thirty thousand pesos to be used for the care and transportation of the Spanish prisoners and in November he signed an agreement with the British. Apparently to lull the suspicions of the enemy, Miranda also furnished the English with certain information concerning past Spanish operations. When he returned, he brought back not only about one hundred Spaniards but also a cargo of contraband foodstuffs and manufactured goods which would find easy resale in Havana, explaining this as being a favor to an English merchant friend. Later a French general of his acquaintance said that it had been planned and the money furnished to disguise further his character and purpose, but his enemies charged that it was a plot by him and Cagigal to enrich themselves. This, plus a part of the Jamaican agreement which was said to be against Spain's policy, was added to the charges concerning the British general's inspection in Havana and sent to Spain.

On March 18, 1782, King Charles III ordered Miranda arrested and sent a Mexican judge to Cuba to investigate the charges. Before these orders reached Cuba, however, Miranda had sailed as second in command in a successful Spanish-French-American (South Carolina) attack on New Providence, the capital of the Bahamas. Here he played a conspicuous role and was chosen to draw up the terms of capitulation which on May 8, 1782, gave the islands to Spain.

Upon his return, he was arrested, but paroled in custody of Cagigal. The judge handed down a heavy sentence: deprivation of his commission, a heavy fine, and ten years' imprisonment. (The case dragged on from 1782 to 1799, when the Council of the Indies completely exonerated both Miranda and Cagigal of any wrongdoing.) Despairing of justice, Miranda decided to flee and make a personal appeal to the King. Planning to work his way to Europe via the United States and with a glowing letter of introduction by Cagigal to General George Washington, he deserted from the Spanish army and on June 1, 1783, slipped aboard an American whaler.

Regardless of what Miranda's original plans may have been, when he arrived in the United States, his intentions quickly took another form. The accusations of his enemies that he was "passionately fond" of the English were not completely unfounded. In 1782 he was actually in correspondence with dissatisfied Creoles in Venezuela, and once he was in the United States, it became clear that his intent was to escape all Spanish control. He himself later wrote: "In the year 1784 in the City of New York I formed a project for the liberty and independence of the entire Spanish-American Continent with the co-operation of England." In the United States he found fresh ideas and friends. An American named James Biggs, who served under Miranda in his expedition of 1806, wrote that he had talked with many Americans who knew Miranda during his earlier tour and "they say his mind was full of the ideas of reform and innovation, of liberty and philosophy."[2] Not only was Miranda a social success, but William Duer and Stephen Sayre lent him money to continue his journeys. General Henry Knox helped him plan the number of men, muskets, and cannon he needed and suggested where these might be obtained. Alexander Hamilton listened to Miranda's plans with more enthusiasm than he cared to remember when he wrote fourteen years later: "Several years ago this man was in America much heated with the project of liberating S Am from the Spanish Domination. I had frequent conversations with him on the subject and I presume expressed ideas favorable to the object and perhaps gave an opinion that it was one to which the U States would look with interest."

In December, 1784, Miranda left the United States and began a long and personally successful tour of Europe. In June of 1789 he became a resident of London and a few months later submitted a plan for the liberation of the Spanish colonies, with English aid, to Prime Minister William Pitt. At this time England's relations with Spain were poor because of the Nootka Sound controversy, and the situation seemed propitious for Miranda's scheme. However, the successful settlement of the issue left the British unwilling to co-operate. In despair, when the French Revolution broke out Miranda hastened to offer his services to the rebels. As a successful general, he quickly attracted popular acclaim until the unfortunate defeat at Neerwinden. For this he was accused of treason, but triumphantly won acquittal. Early in 1798 he returned to England to renew his campaign for British help in a South American revolution.

Until October, 1810, with exception of the years 1805–1807, when he was attempting to liberate Venezuela by means of an expedition from New York, Miranda lived in London. There he spent his time with his beloved books, cultivating influential friends, carrying on propaganda through the press, corresponding with South American radicals, and pressing his plans upon English governmental officials. At this time he was described as

[2] [James Biggs], *The History of Don Francisco de Miranda's Attempt to Effect a Revolution in South America* (Boston, Edward Oliver, 1810).

being about five feet, ten inches tall, with a stout and active frame and well-proportioned limbs. He was of dark complexion, florid and healthy, with intelligent, piercing, and quick hazel eyes. Unusual for that time, he had good teeth, "which he takes much care to keep clean." His nose was large and handsome, "rather of English than Roman cast . . . without saying he is an elegant, we may pronounce him a handsome man." He was described as a "courtier and gentleman" in his manners, with dignity and grace in his movements, and even while sitting he was never perfectly still. Conversant on all subjects, his excellent memory prevented his ever being at a loss for names, dates, and authorities.

This was the man about to enter the final act of his personal drama. In April, 1810, Venezuelan natives overthrew the local captain general and refused to recognize the Madrid regency. They dispatched three emissaries to London, including the young Simón Bolívar, to seek British support. There was, of course, the old revolutionary Miranda, who immediately used all his connections to insure their success. Furthermore, he decided upon the sacrifice of a comfortable home, growing children, friends, the social whirl—which he dearly loved—and a comfortable English pension in order to return with Bolívar to Venezuela, even over the protest of British officials. On October 10 he sailed from London.

Arriving in Venezuela in December, 1810, Miranda was soon in the throes of organizing the revolutionary government and prominently promoting the 1811 Declaration of Independence from Spain, which established the first Hispanic-American republic. Few who signed this document realized that it was also a declaration of war. Counterrevolutions soon broke out, and General Miranda was called to take command of the Republican troops. When peace was restored, as vice-president of Congress and a member of the Constitutional Committee he sought to establish a government based upon that of the United States, but was dissatisfied with the final result. Soon, too, the Spanish forces were in the field, and Miranda, at the request of Congress, assumed absolute power in the new nation. Despite his best efforts, with the refusal of foreign nations to aid him and his government disintegrating around him, in July, 1812, he was forced to surrender. After several vain attempts to escape from various Spanish prisons, he died in a cell at Cádiz on July 14, 1816.

Although the liberation of South America came on a later day, Miranda made his contribution. To the vision of Latin-American freedom he had dedicated his extraordinary abilities wholeheartedly and would be remembered by later generations in three ways: as a gallant hero who fought for human liberty, as the vital London hub of all Spanish-American independence activities, and as eloquent spokesman of this cause before the world.

THE COUNTRY

Miranda's shift in political allegiance in the 1780's, occurring when he decided that as a Latin-American he could not expect justice under Spanish authority, had come earlier for most citizens of the thirteen English colonies of North America. Convinced that they had hopes, aspirations, and legitimate interests which could not be gained or protected within the British Empire, they gradually began thinking of themselves primarily as Americans and only secondarily as Englishmen. This rise of American nationalism reached its culmination in the Declaration of Independence on July 4, 1776.

Against frightening odds in what has been described as not one but thirteen revolutions and having only the unity of a common dream, the new nation reluctantly broke with the old. Americans were not a military people, and although they were eager for a fight, sustained warfare was unappealing. Steady service in Washington's ill-fed, ill-paid, and ill-clothed army was consequently unattractive. The nature of the government also contributed to the general disorder. The Continental Congress had no legal authority and could only issue requisitions, instead of orders, to member states. If Americans had really been as united and resolute as the Declaration of Independence suggested, the war might have been won in a year. As it was, outside assistance was the determining factor, and but for French and Spanish aid the

Patriots would have had to give up complete independence in 1778 or take a bad beating.

The Colonies' defeat of General John Burgoyne in October, 1777, at Saratoga set the stage for a new appeal for French aid. The time was ripe. Ever since 1763, France had been spoiling for revenge. Moreover, the French intellectuals were captivated by the possibility of seeing their philosophical speculations put into practice, while the royal authorities were eager to see England humbled and the balance of power redressed in France's favor. On February 6, 1778, France signed treaties of commerce and alliance with the United States, promising to make common cause until American independence was recognized. Since Spain was bound firmly by the "family compact" in an alliance with France, her entrance was practically insured also, an event which occurred in 1779. Still another significant development came when, after five years of wrangling often characterized by high purpose and low motives, in March of 1781 the Articles of Confederation and Perpetual Union were ratified.

Drafted by John Dickinson, the charter had been earlier adopted by Congress in 1777. All states but Maryland ratified it by 1779, but that state held out for two years; on the same day Maryland announced ratification, Congress proclaimed the new government to be in effect, an event attracting small notice outside of Philadelphia. The change of government actually did little more than legalize what Congress had been doing since 1775. The Confederation had the same powers, or lack of them, and Congress was organized in the same fashion as formerly.

Yet 1781 was a turning point. The new men coming into power would at least temporarily give new drive to the government. October saw a combined French and American army run Lord Cornwallis to ground at Yorktown, Virginia. His surrender, with his army, gave Americans new hope, brought about the fall of the North government in England, and promoted the rise to power of the Rockingham Whigs, who were friendly to peace and independence. Thus ended six years of fighting, in which the Americans had lost most of the battles but won the war. After Yorktown, English military men gave up, abandoning their southern posts the next year. Only New York was held as the peace negotiators carried on their work, culminating in the signing of preliminary articles of peace in the fall of 1782.

In their elation at their successful political revolution, few Americans recognized certain changes then in progress would constitute, in some respects, radical social and economic revolutions. Not only was there the necessity of establishing a new government to replace that established by England, but in eleven colonies new state governments would have to be devised. Here was an opportunity for Americans to give legal expression to their political ideals and to remedy some of their former grievances. Although the war could not be said to have resulted from democratic fervor, that struggle released democracy as a major force in American life. The downfall of the Colonial aristocracy was far more than a political phenomenon. With many exceptions, the Patriots represented in the main the common people, and the Loyalists the upper strata of society. The victory of the former, together with the active persecution of the latter, made it possible for men formerly considered to be of low degree to hold high offices and enjoy important privileges. The trend toward small, independent landholdings was greatly accelerated when confiscated Tory property was thrown on the market, and it was a sorry man indeed who could not acquire fifty acres or a forty-shilling freehold, either of which would entitle him to the vote. Old legal restrictions, such as primogeniture, entails, and quitrents, went into discard. The period also saw progress in the achieving of complete religious freedom, with separation of church and state, and a concerted attack upon slavery and the slave trade. Emancipation societies were common, even in southern areas.

On the other hand, the transition to freedom did not come without difficulties. Religion, in the more formal sense, suffered disastrously, for churches were destroyed, religious ties loosened, traditional beliefs swept away, and standards of morality lowered. Colonial schools, such as they were, had been virtually destroyed by the years of revolution, and new systems had to be devised.

The Treaty of Paris was satisfactory neither to England nor to the United States. Not only was it to breed future disputes, but there were also immediate controversies over claims that one or the other party had failed to fulfill its obligations, such as those regarding debts, Negroes, Loyalists, and the removal of garrisons.

American political leaders were faced with what seemed to be insoluble problems at the end of the war. The army was discontented: promises had not been kept and with the return of peace it was unlikely that they would be. Delegates from the army were demanding an advance on back pay, some provision for the payment of the remainder due, and some settlement of the promise of half-pay for life to the officers. Threats of mutiny filled the air. Altogether the United States had incurred an indebtedness of well over forty million dollars during the war. About six million had been borrowed from France, perhaps another two million from other foreign sources. The remainder, mostly in the form of back pay for soldiers and certificates of indebtedness to those who had furnished supplies for the army, was owed to citizens of the United States. All were clamoring at the doors of Congress, which lacked the means to satisfy them, and politicians feared that the public creditors might try to achieve by force what persuasion had not gained.

The means by which the government could raise money to meet these obligations were strictly limited. Paper-money issues, the principal support during the war, had been dried up by overuse. The government could indulge in further borrowing, provided creditors could be found—an unlikely prospect. Small sums were realized from sale of public lands and post-office receipts, but in the main, Congress would have to rely upon requisitions to the states for the money it needed for every kind of operation. In the past this had proved entirely inadequate. States, faced with war damage, economic depression, and declining incomes of their own, honored these requests only to the extent they chose.

To view the new nation through the eyes of angry politicians, clamoring debtors, and disgruntled soldiers gives a distorted concept of the spirit of the times. Underneath and overriding was a spirit of exuberant optimism, a belief in the great destiny of the country. Americans were convinced that, freed from the traditions of the Old World, they could do anything. After years of despair, there was room now only for optimism. The United States would become the hope of the world!

This, then, was the nation which Miranda saw and recorded. A people emerging from one era, confronted with great problems, but sure that the future would be theirs. Economically, they faced an unknown future; politically, democracy was still in swaddling clothes. At the time of his visit, the last battle of the Revolution had been fought; the preliminary treaty between England and her rebellious colonies had been signed on November 30, 1782, and two months later, preliminary articles of peace were ratified by England, France, and Spain. On April 11, 1783, President Elias Boudinot had issued a proclamation announcing cessation of hostilities between England and the United States, and during the month Miranda decided to flee Cuba, the first American soldiers were receiving furloughs.

The new nation stretched from the Atlantic to the Mississippi and from Canada to Spanish Florida—a million square miles: 589,000,000 acres of land and 51,000,000 acres of water. More than a third of this area was unoccupied, except by Indians. The United States had approximately three million people, about half a million of whom were Negroes, mostly slaves. The vast majority of its inhabitants lived in a narrow band of settlement along the Atlantic Coast from Maine to Georgia, but already a westward movement had reached proportions sufficient to stir awed comment. The five "great" cities were Philadelphia, New York, Boston, Charleston, and Baltimore, and the largest, Philadelphia, had less than forty thousand inhabitants at the time of Miranda's visit. Even most towns seemed merely collections of farmers in this basically agricultural nation. To a traveler from the Old World, the United States had many of the earmarks of a frontier civilization, and few could help being impressed with the latent possibilities for growth and development and, especially, the spirit of high adventure and optimism which characterized the citizens of the new United States. Certainly a visitor such as Miranda could not miss the prevailing spirit of the day.

THE DIARY

Miranda early showed the instincts of a historian and a strong sense of history. Even before leaving his home in 1771 he began a collection of personal papers which he believed might be important, and one of his stated reasons for wishing to go to Spain was a desire to secure documents concerning his family. There, with the added incentive of supporting his application for a military commission, he not only gathered family material but also began the practice of filing with them personal comments on what he had seen and materials of a historical nature. He also saved copies of his personal correspondence and letters addressed to him. Before leaving Spanish service he expanded his personal collection to include a wide range of documents dealing with the Spanish colonies in America.

Soon his collection amounted to a veritable archive of materials which reflected his broad and catholic interests, as well as an extensive library. In a protest to the French National Convention in 1795, he stated that among his manuscripts one could find "an exact diary of his life since adolescence." His collecting proclivities and his care to preserve anything that touched him personally have resulted in the fortunate circumstance that his papers, although not now intact, have become literally a treasure-trove for historians. In 1805, Miranda expressed the desire that if Venezuela ever became independent, it should have his documents as proof of "the sincere love of a faithful citizen and the constant efforts which he had exerted for the welfare of his beloved compatriots." During his many travels, he took his collection with him or stored it with friends, but was always careful to have it near at hand. Upon his return to South America, his archives went with him. When his government fell, one of his first thoughts was their safety. To prevent their falling into Spanish hands, he put them aboard an English vessel bound for Curaço. British officials there then sent them to the Secretariat of War and the Colonies in

London. Here they remained for a number of years, then disappeared and were presumed lost.

In 1902, William Spence Robertson, after a search of the English archives for Miranda material, got an idea: Miranda's collection had probably ended up in the private collection of Lord Bathurst when he went out of office in 1828, since it was customary for English ministers to view official papers accumulated during their terms of office as private. Twenty years later, after rumors that the Miranda papers had indeed been found in this collection, Professor Robertson made a trip to the ancestral home of the Bathursts. In his own words: "At once I identified the mysterious collection as the long-lost Miranda manuscripts. I found that these manuscripts, which were bound in sixty-three folio tomes, contained a veritable legion of diaries, letters, squibs, newspaper clippings, and intimate memoranda in their original form."[3] After remaining in the family archives of Lord Bathurst for nearly a century, the collection was purchased by the Venezuelan government and returned to Caracas in 1926, fulfilling Miranda's wish for its final disposition.

Miranda's diary, a portion of which is the subject of this work, was begun in 1771, before he left Venezuela, but entries for these early years are spasmodic. Apparently, it was not until he fled Cuba in disgrace that Miranda undertook a continuous narrative of his life. The section dealing with his experiences in the United States was written on unruled sheets of papers of various sizes and later bound into volumes, along with various letters, cards, brochures, and memoranda. Miranda did not always write from day to day, but sometimes composed his diary in sections after the occurrences described had taken place, probably from notes taken at the time. This method seems almost certainly to have been employed in the part dealing with the journey from Havana to New York, while the sections dealing with New England were apparently composed from day to day or after the lapse of only a few days. The care taken in composing much of the diary would

[3] William Spence Robertson, *The Life of Miranda* (2 vols.; Chapel Hill, University of North Carolina Press, 1929), I, x.

make it seem almost certain that Miranda had a future audience in mind.

The failure to provide an English translation of such an important work before now is well in line with what appears nearly to have been the perverse fate of obscurity for all of Miranda's archives. It seems almost incredible that for more than thirty years his penetrating insights into one of the most fascinating, but critical, periods in American history has been available only to those who could read Spanish, and therefore largely unknown. This journal should have the broadest of appeals. For the antiquarian it is a detailed account of the day-to-day life of Americans, great and small. To the student of Hispanic-American history this work gives information concerning an important formative period in the life of one of that region's most illustrious sons and additional material upon which to base an intellectual and moral characterization of him.

Scholars of United States history will find in the diary an instructive and highly suggestive description of the new nation during its natal period. Coinciding in the brief span of months covered in Miranda's account are the closing days of an old era and the opening of a new one. Here is pictured the beginning of reconstruction after the Revolution, the leading personalities in that epic struggle, and the social and economic conditions which ensued as a result of that upheaval, all viewed at firsthand. Here, too, is to be found the impact, destined to shape Miranda's whole life and career, that young America made upon this educated and discerning citizen of ancient Spain. Even the most casual reader should, in many respects, find this as fascinating as Alexis de Tocqueville's *Democracy in America*, which appeared half a century later.

Translated with a literary flair, Miranda's diary is one of the better travel accounts dealing with the United States. Aside from its entertaining qualities and insights, it has the additional merit of filling an important gap in our firsthand knowledge of the period. This nation has been fortunate in the number and high quality of foreign visitors who have commented upon the American scene, but the years 1783 and 1784 were notably slighted. J. Hector St. John Crèvecoeur, a Frenchman chiefly noted for his *Letters from an American Farmer*, wrote only of the years between 1770 and 1780. Thomas Anburey, *Travels through the Interior Part of America*, spans the years 1776–81, but since he was a captured member of the Burgoyne expedition, his account is shallow and has a British bias. The letters of François de Barbé-Marbois described briefly and superficially the period from 1779 to 1780; and more famous, because it was more irritating, was an account by the Marquis de Chastellux, *Travels in North-America in the Years 1780, 1781, 1782,* a work so careless and condescending that fellow Frenchman Jacques Pierre Brissot de Warville condemned the Marquis in 1788 as being unfair.

Besides Miranda's account, only three others touch on this period. J. F. D. Smyth, *A Tour in the United States of America* (London, 1784), was an Englishman who had come to America before the war. He was a Loyalist, and his journal of a tour in 1784 clearly shows his disgruntlement and anti-American bias. Robert Hunter, Jr., was a twenty-year-old boy from an English merchant family; his description of his trip from Boston to Charleston, September, 1785, to June, 1786, is commonplace, naïve, and smug. Best of the three, *Travels in the Confederation,* was written by Johann David Schoepf, a thirty-two-year-old German physician who came to America with Hessian troops in 1777. This narrative of a trip through New Jersey, Pennsylvania, Delaware, Virginia, and the Carolinas during 1783 and 1784 suffers from his overriding interest in the fauna, flora, and mineral resources of the country, but makes a good parallel to the account of Miranda.

Miranda enjoyed the special advantage of having no ax to grind, was predisposed to like the Americans, and had unusual opportunities to make observations. Not only did his travels take him to most of the major cities and into ten states, but he was highly personable and with his good contacts he met almost every person of importance in the new nation. However, his intellectual interests were so broad that he has left more than merely an early

American *Who's Who*. In spite of occasional crudities, errors, and misconceptions, his charming and enlightening narrative deserves recognition and companionship with the small number of outstanding accounts of American life which have been left to posterity by foreign visitors to American shores. In terms of modern scholarship, his picture of life in the United States in 1783–84 is well substantiated and will buttress many conclusions which have heretofore been educated guesses.

PART ONE

The Carolinas

☆

THE CAROLINAS

June 1, 1783, Havana, Cuba. At nine o'clock in the morning I sailed on the American sloop *Prudent,* Captain J. Wilson.[1] My good friend Don Ignacio Menocal came to see me, saying his farewells until the last moment. His conduct offers me each day more reasons for admiring his honesty and sound judgment in this, the home of vice and corruption. . . . Pleasant notion in my memories!

Setting sail at the same time was the entire Spanish squadron and convoy bound for Cádiz under the command of Lieutenant General Don José Solano[2] and carrying most of the field forces and about sixty million pesos in specie and products, stored in our America since the declaration of war.

On awakening, we saw El Pan de Matanzas[3] and, because the wind and currents have been so favorable, only two small vessels out of the entire squadron and convoy. We directed our route to the mouth of the Bahama Channel and early the next day sighted Cape Cañaveral.[4] A fresh wind continuing to blow from the west, on the fifth we crossed the latitude of Charleston, where I intended to go ashore, but the good Captain Wilson, either because the wind was not very favorable or, as was more likely, because it did not suit him, proceeded immediately to North Carolina in spite of our agreement and the promise he had made

[1] Miranda left Cuba under a cloud because of apparent complicity in contraband trade.

[2] Solano was in command of the Spanish forces sent to the West Indies to cooperate with the French against the English during the American Revolution.

[3] A peak on the northern coast of Cuba.

[4] On the east coast of Florida.

my friend James Seagrove[5] to take me to Charleston. Apparently he is not fastidious in these matters.

In the afternoon of the eighth we took on a pilot, passed through Ocracoke Inlet,[6] and anchored in the sound, hard by a hamlet which is the abode of the pilots who conduct the ships arriving there.

The people boarding our ship from the pilot's boat seemed extremely robust and corpulent; I observed the same qualities in the women and children I saw later. The natives attribute this to the food, which is nothing more than fish, oysters, and some vegetables (which they grow in small gardens near their homes and comprise the only agriculture of these people that I know of). The people of the sea oppose always any idea of agriculture. The sea air is the largest contributor, I think, to the health of the region, and I have no doubt that fish, prepared in their simple way, contributes to the extraordinary procreation, as the same can be observed in the case of the poor people of Málaga and other seaports.

The smallpox would seem to be their principal enemy because before we could disembark they required us to make a thousand protests that such disease was not with us on board.

Their boats, being of excellent construction, are taken out to sea in all weather and do not appear to differ much from those used by our warships except that the former, in place of a stern, have another bow, with the result that they can sail in all directions without tacking and are, therefore, extremely fast. The joining of the keel and hull seems to me also different from ours. Construction is so cheap in these parts that the owner of one of the best asked only eighty pesos[7] for it, and I have no doubt that had we come to an agreement, he would have given it to me for seventy.

[5] An American who told Miranda of the United States while in Cuba and helped him escape.

[6] Eastern entrance to Pamlico Sound, North Carolina.

[7] The peso, or Spanish dollar, was widely circulated in the Colonies. Its value differed, however, as measured by pounds, in the various states. An approximation would be eight shillings.

At ten o'clock in the morning of the ninth we set sail for New-bern and during the remainder of the day and night went about forty miles through this very dangerous sound. (A few years ago more than sixty merchant vessels, composing a large convoy at anchor here, were lost, perhaps through a lack of good pilots, although I will not assume this because those there are to my mind the most careful and capable I have seen.)

Early the next day we entered the river Neuse and, going fifty miles with a fresh wind from the northeast, arrived at twelve-thirty at Newbern, capital of the state.[8] Its agreeable location is at the flowing together of the rivers Trent and Neuse; the latter in particular is large, its navigation pleasant, and its shores here and there covered with thick, luxuriant forests and some dwellings with little agriculture in their vicinity.

At five o'clock in the afternoon I landed and took a room at the tavern of Mr. Oliver, paying one peso duro[9] daily for room and board, which seemed to me very cheap considering the cleanliness and good behavior at this lodging.

The principal inhabitants present at that time were Mr. Ogden, Mr. Blount, Le Marquis de Bretigney (a French officer in the service of this state), Mr. Oram, Mr. Cooke, Mr. Sitgreaves, Mr. Ellis, Mr. Schilbeack, Mr. Goff, Monsieur Heró, Dr. McClure, Dr. Halling, Mr. Johnston, Monsieur Mayoli, etc.[10] These came to call on me and honored me with the greatest hospitality, and this good treatment has continued throughout my residence here even though their ideas are generally not very liberal and the social system is still in its swaddling clothes. The married women main-

[8] New Bern, thirty-five miles from the ocean, was founded in 1710 by German and Swiss Palatines under the leadership of Swiss Baron Christopher de Graffen-ried. It was the seat of the royal governors from 1770 to 1774. After the Revolu-tion it was important for shipbuilding, timber, iron, rope, and exports of tobacco, molasses, lumber, and naval stores. The town was quite famous for its gay social life.

[9] The peso duro, or "hard dollar," was a silver coin equivalent to ten silver reals, or eight British shillings.

[10] Titus and Thomas Ogden were merchants; Blount was probably William Blount, land speculator, member of Congress, and later governor of the territory south of the Ohio River (1790); John Sitgreaves represented New Bern in the

tain a monastic seclusion and a submission to their husbands such as I have never seen; they dress with neatness and their entire lives are domestic. Once married, they separate themselves from all intimate friendships and devote themselves completely to the care of home and family. During the first year of marriage they play the role of lovers, the second year of breeders, and thereafter of housekeepers. On the other hand, the unmarried women enjoy complete freedom and take walks alone wherever they want to, without their steps being observed. The men dress carelessly and grossly. All smoke tobacco in pipes and also chew it, with so much excess that some assured me they could not go to bed and reconcile sleep without having a cud in the mouth.

A few days after my arrival in this region I met Mr. Nash and Colonel Spaight,[11] who live in country houses on the river Trent, two and three miles, respectively, from the city. The former is an excellent jurisconsult and was governor of the state in the past emergencies; his manner and conversation, and also those of his family (including the young Witherspoon), gave me many moments of pleasant company and instruction. The Colonel is a young man with good ideas and an excellent disposition for outstanding education who should continue in his plan of studies and travel. Both men are delegates to Congress for the coming year.

The population of this city is composed of five hundred families of all classes. The houses are middling and small as a rule, but comfortable and clean; almost all are made of wood. The church and the assembly house are of brick and are suitable to the town. The finest building of all and one which really deserves the atten-

---

North Carolina House of Commons, was speaker in 1787, and was a member of the Continental Congress; Ellis and McClure probably were Richard Ellis and Dr. William McClure; and Samuel Johnston was one of the state's most prominent citizens: a member of the Continental Congress (1781–82), governor (1787), and later United States senator. A month later, Dr. Solomon Halling wrote a friend that Miranda was a "most agreeable" person with the "most liberal Sentiments."

[11] Abner Nash settled in North Carolina in 1762, was a member of the Continental Congress, and served as governor (1779–81). Richard Dobbs Spaight, the first native-born governor (1792–95), was killed in a duel in 1802.

tion of an educated traveler is the so-called "Palace," built eighteen years ago by an able English architect, Mr. Hawks, who came from England with Governor Tryon for this purpose and still remains in the city.[12] I have conversed with him very particularly, and he possesses an admirable character. The building is entirely of brick, and its construction is in the pure English styling; the ornaments are very simple and placed with much taste and intelligence. In the great audience, or assembly room, there is the decoration of a marble fireplace of good taste, wrought in England; one infers from an inscription over the interior door of the portico that this fireplace is a gift from Sir William Draper, who was here on his return from the expedition to Manila in 1763, visiting his friend Tryon.[13] The building is situated on the banks of the river Trent in a somewhat elevated spot, which gives it the command of a prospectus of more than twelve miles over the river Neuse and makes its location quite pleasing.

June 17. Today, to the sound of drums and a volley from four small campaign pieces brought up beforehand for this purpose, with a company of militia under arms (each soldier and officer with uniform and musket of different type), the cessation of hostilities and the preliminary treaties with England were announced in the field.[14] By way of celebration for this event, starting at one o'clock there was a barbecue (a roast pig) and a barrel of rum, from which the leading officials and citizens of the region promiscuously ate and drank with the meanest and lowest

[12] The "Palace" was built by John Hawks for Governor William Tryon (1765–71). It was begun in 1767 and completed three years later at an approximate cost of sixteen thousand pounds. Serving as the governor's residence and as a meeting place for the assembly and council, it was regarded as the most beautiful structure in British America, but its cost led to a popular outcry over the waste of tax money. Partly burned in 1798, it has now been restored.

[13] Draper commanded the British expedition which captured Manila on April 6, 1762. Early in 1770 he landed at Charleston and made a tour of the Colonies.

[14] A preliminary treaty between England and the United States was signed on November 20, 1782; on January 20, 1783, preliminary articles of peace were signed by England, France, and Spain; and on April 11, 1783, the president of the Continental Congress issued a proclamation announcing the end of hostilities between the United States and England.

kind of people, holding hands and drinking from the same cup. It is impossible to imagine, without seeing it, a more purely democratic gathering, and it confirms what the Greek poets and historians tell us of similar concourses among those free peoples of Greece. There were some drunks, some friendly fisticuffs, and one man was injured. With that and the burning of some empty barrels as a *feu de joie* at nightfall, the party ended and everyone retired to sleep.

A few days later I went to the home of Mr. Green,[15] twelve miles away. He is one of the leading farmers of the state, and his character, sincerity, and age are remarkable; he is more than eighty-five years old, and one is not able to note the least decadence in his health, vigor, and activity. His spirit is always festive and pleasing. The house is located on a small rise, at the foot of which are two or three springs providing extremely crystalline water in abundance. The agriculture one sees in the vicinity amounts to little and consists mainly of corn, potatoes, and fruit trees, which form an extensive orchard.

The country houses are generally comfortable and clean, although, as has already been noticed in the case of town dwellings, somewhat small. The industry of the inhabitants cannot be denied; because of the war and the general scarcity of manufactured goods, every citizen set up a loom in his country house and made cotton and woolen clothes to dress his entire family (and I have seen some of very good cloth and design). With apples, pears, and peaches, they make excellent cider and brandy.

Among the animals this old man had, I noticed a swan of very handsome shape; it appeared to be very young, although according to its owner's calculation it was more than sixty years old. A rare constitution indeed in such a small individual!

At sunset I returned to Newbern with my friends Oram and Cooke, who had given me the pleasure of joining me on this excursion. My plan had been to spend a few days there, but the happenstance of a swarm of bedbugs coming forth to greet me in

[15] It is possible that this was James Green, a former clerk of the Provincial Council (1775).

bed when I lay down for a moment after dinner made me change my mind immediately. This insect is so abundant here that all the houses are generally contaminated, to which condition their wooden construction is no small contributor. Throughout the length of my stay I was obliged to sleep on the floor in the middle of a room, as there was no way of getting them out of bed. They are of such extraordinary size that a single one is the equivalent of three or four of those found in Europe. There is another large contributor to nocturnal discomfort; the quantity of frogs (of different species) is so large that their music is heard at a great distance, and since this region is covered with rivers, marshes, and moors, there is no lack of musicians in any part. There are some in particular, called bullfrogs, whose song resembles perfectly the roar of the bull. Their size is about four times that of European frogs.

Among the song birds there is one which certainly is admirable and deserves special attention: the mockingbird. Its melody and variety of tones are so excellent they elude description, and what is best is that this bird is so common that every citizen who has a tree near his home can be sure of an interlude of music during the course of the day. A splendid contrast to the night music of the frogs! Its shape and color are similar to those of the *sinsonte*[16] of New Spain.

Another day I went to see the plantation of Mr. Ogden, in the company of the owner himself, Colonel Blount,[17] Mr. Sitgreaves, and the young Ogden. I saw fields of corn, barley, wheat, and potatoes; the fruit-bearing trees were so laden with apples, pears, and peaches that any tree that was not propped up had its stalks broken and branches hanging down with the weight of the fruit. The inhabitants do not observe this spectacle with the pleasure of the traveler, because they know through experience that in the year of much fruit, agues[18] abound everywhere, which disease is

[16] *Sinsonte* is a mockingbird; the word derives from the Aztec *censontli*.

[17] Colonel Blount was Thomas, brother of William and Thomas Gray Blount.

[18] Ague was probably malaria, a serious problem in the low coastal areas of the southeastern United States. Although the residents were not aware of the

very predominant in the region and callously ruins their health and turns pallid the most dazzling European complexions.

Some ladies nevertheless retain their beautiful coloring and are in excellent health. My favorites and acquaintances are Mrs. Oram, Mrs. Ellis, Mrs. Nash, Mrs. Ellis, Sr., Mrs. Schilbeack, Mrs. Cooke, Mrs. Cooke, Sr., Mrs. Oliver, Mrs. Egliston (her manner is somewhat pusillanimous, but her society, when one has obtained some confidence and familiarity, is gracious and jocose), Mrs. Stanley (whose husband was absent and is the leading businessman of the region, is a lady of very good manners and circumstances, but I did not have the pleasure of engaging her attention at close range), and her sister, Miss Cogdell (one of the best-looking and most florid complexions I have seen in America).[19]

July 12. At ten o'clock in the morning I parted from all my friends in Newbern and, crossing the river Trent on the ferry, took the road to Beaufort. At two o'clock in the afternoon I arrived at the Allways Inn, twenty-three miles from Newbern. The road is quite good, as they generally are in this region, the ground being hard, gravelly, and level everywhere, but the happenstance of much rain in the previous days resulted in all the wooden bridges being destroyed and it was with much effort that I continued the trip, for I had to do without the horses and sulky. This was just a little bit tiring, but a moderate and clean meal and the company of Comfort and Constance, daughters of the innkeeper, fifteen to eighteen years old and very good looking, soon made me forget the excursion. That evening there was a good supper and better conversation with the girls; after all had retired

role played by the mosquito in this disease, it is interesting to see that they had noted that the rains which brought abundant fruit also brought an upswing in agues.

[19] See notes 10 and 11 above for identification of these ladies, with the exception of Mrs. Stanley and Miss Cogdell. The former was Mrs. John Wright Stanly (*sic*), the wife of a wealthy merchant who lost fourteen privateers during the Revolution. In their home, which is still standing, such notables as Washington, Lafayette, and Nathanael Greene were entertained. Miss Cogdell was probably a relative of Richard Cogdell, a New Bern merchant.

for the night, one had no embarrassment in coming at my request to continue the conversation in my bed.

At six o'clock in the morning I continued my journey and, having gone twenty-one miles on roads similar to the one of the day before and crossed a swamp which must be more than a mile wide and had millions of mosquitoes, I arrived four hours later at Beaufort. I took lodging at the home of Mrs. Cheney, who treated me and took care of me grandly. Her gracious company mitigated to some extent the aridity and unsociableness of the town. Here I found all my baggage, undamaged (I had sent it by river from Newbern the day before), and also my friend Schilbeack, who had come here to help some French businessmen who, on their way from Havana, had been shipwrecked on the shores of Cape Lookout. With his society and company and by playing the flute a little, I was able to diminish slightly the discomforts caused by the mosquitoes and the heat; the latter is so excessive that I cannot remember having gone through a similar unpleasant situation, even on the coasts of Africa and in the Spanish province of Estremadura.[20] The affairs of the Frenchmen were settled with such good order, justice, and equity that all withdrew satisfied. I am very happy to see myself among people who, although poor, are benevolent and generous. According to the laws of the region, every individual who, through his presence and assistance, saves any effects of a ship wrecked on said coasts has for his own the fourth part; and that is where the boats of the pilots which I mentioned above, or whaleboats, as they call them here, are of the greatest usefulness and prove their dexterity. The ship carrying the Frenchmen having run aground on the shores of Cape Lookout, the blows of the sea covered it and passed over it from stern to bow, at which time the whaleboats, without the least hardship, cruised over the irritated waves, protected the ship, and picked up whatever objects were floating about. (They even salvaged the copper sheathing and brought it to Beaufort.)

Beaufort[21] is located on a sandy beach that, except for some

[20] Miranda had been in Africa in 1774–75 and in Spain from 1776 to 1780.
[21] Beaufort, established in 1722, was first known as Fishtown.

sandbanks, which act as a barrier against the sea and form the sound, is quite unsheltered. It has about eighty inhabitants, and the houses are very miserable. Despite the fact that its location is much more advantageous than that of Newbern (even frigates can enter the sound), there is no commerce and, as a result, the inhabitants are poor. Mr. Parrat and Mr. Dennis are the educated persons of the town and favored me with their company while I was here, waiting for a ship to take me to Charleston. The first is a surveyor general and gave me a very good map of the state.

I made an excursion for a distance of twelve miles into the region, going up the little Newport River to the homes of two Quakers: one was rich and ignorant and the other, Mr. Williams, poor, educated, and generous. The latter wrote me a long letter,[22] sending me the exalted apology of Robert Barclay for those of this persuasion and inserting a document as an example of the peculiar way they have of writing.[23] Never before have I suffered similar discomfort from heat, bedbugs, and mosquitoes to that which I went through in these two days of Quaker study. The agriculture one sees around here amounts to very little (mostly corn, and potatoes), the earth being sandy and very poor. On the shores there are many windmills of very good construction and design. They are of wood and nevertheless last between twelve and twenty years. There are others on the creeks which fall into the rivers; by means of a causeway and locks they collect water and generally form two mills: one to saw wood and the other to grind grain. Of this type there are an infinity in this region, as lumber is one of the principal branches of commerce.

At two o'clock in the afternoon of the twenty-second, I said farewell to my few friends and boarded a small schooner, Captain J. Adison, to continue my journey to Charleston. The wind blew favorably, and at three o'clock in the afternoon of the next day we arrived at Cape Fear. We entered the river by the New Inlet

---

[22] This letter is still to be found among Miranda's papers.

[23] Robert Barclay wrote *An Apology for the True Christian Divinity*. A Latin version was published in Amsterdam in 1676 and it appeared in English two years later.

THE TRAVELS OF FRANCISCO DE MIRANDA IN THE UNITED STATES, 1783–84

and passed on our left Fort Johnston, which is in front of this entrance.[24] Ten miles up the river, on the left, is the town of Brunswick, perfectly situated for both commerce and the enjoyment of life, but completely ruined and demolished during the last war.[25] A mile farther up, on the same bank of the Cape Fear River, is the home and estate of the American General Howe.[26] While he amuses himself in dissipation elsewhere, his unfortunate family lives here; the wife has the manner of a divorcée, and one lovely daughter, eighteen years old, has just had two sons by one of the Negro slaves. God help nature and the unjust laws which afflict it!

We continued twenty miles farther up the river, with little wind, and at eleven o'clock in the night arrived in Wilmington.[27] It surprised me much to see here ships of six hundred tons and more, which can go up the river with all facility, and to learn that frigates of war reach Brunswick; the reason is that the principal mouth of the river is more than three fathoms deep at its entrance. Consequently it is not strange that there is much more commerce here than in Newbern and other towns of this state and that these should thrive more than the others.

The location is advantageous, pleasant, and very abundant in springs of crystalline water, which gush everywhere; the buildings, although not many in number, are comfortable, clean, and generally better than those in Newbern. There is much more commerce than in the places already mentioned, and the inhabitants appear to be more sociable, more generous, and better dressed.

Major Walker, for whom I brought a letter of recommendation, and Mr. Blount, a businessman—both were men of respect

[24] Fort Johnston, authorized in 1745 and completed in 1764 for protection against pirates, was on the Cape Fear River south of Wilmington.

[25] Brunswick was settled in 1725 by emigrants from South Carolina. It later suffered from competition with Wilmington, pirate attacks, and mosquitoes and had gone into a severe decline even before the Revolution.

[26] Robert Howe was a friend and aide to George Washington. His plantation was plundered by Lord Cornwallis' troops in May, 1776.

[27] Established in 1730 and originally called New Liverpool, Wilmington quickly became the commercial center of North Carolina. It was seized by Cornwallis on June 29, 1781.

in the town—showed me the interior. Afterwards we went to the billiard house, where we played a few games until noontime. This game has taken such strong roots in the country that none of the towns I passed through lacked two or three billiard tables. The wives complain that their husbands spend too much time at this French custom, introduced during the war.

Early in the morning I went to the market, which is very good, relatively speaking, and among the fruits I noticed some peaches so large and beautiful that, without exaggeration, they were like oranges, their color mostly incarnate and on one side yellow.

I also noticed, in the most elevated and commanding places in the vicinity of the town, the remains of field fortifications, erected by the British in the recent war when they took possession of this place.

This state, situated between 34° and 36°33′ north latitude, is populated about 300 miles into the interior and 150 along the coast. Agriculture is a small matter generally; animal husbandry is much more considerable, particularly swine and cattle. The winter is short and cold, the summer very hot; thunderstorms are quite frequent. Corn, wheat, and a variety of vegetables are produced; likewise much fruit, and the fruit-bearing trees are twice as large as those in Europe. Horses, the husbandry of which is not small, are of English breeding and very good.

Deer are plentiful, and deer hunting is the favorite sport of the gentlemen and country folk. I went on some of these excursions and assure you that at every moment I expected one of the participants to have a leg, arm, or head broken. The fashion is to dash forth on horseback behind the discovered buck through a forest covered with branches, the horse sometimes barely having room. The horse is already accustomed to this and, happen what may, charges after the game and acts as the guide; the rider bends down, grasping the neck of the horse. There is no lack of mournful reminders of this sport in the region.

The towns are small, since the great number of sounds and narrow passages prevents them from growing. Except for the Cape Fear and Clarendon rivers, there are none which permit the navigation of ships of more than eighty tons. The principal branches of commerce are tar, pitch, turpentine, staves, lumber, small masts, and furs. For the year 1770, entries and exits of ships of all tonnages in this state were calculated at close to 990, and the number of inhabitants at 150,000.

Governor of the State: His Excellency Alexander Martin, Esq.[28]
Principal Towns: Newbern, Brunswick, Wilmington, Edenton, Halifax, Beaufort, Bath, Hillsboro, Hartford, Winton, Exeter, Tarboro

July 25. At one o'clock in the afternoon we set sail and, descending the river, passed on our right the well-located town of Brunswick and Fort Johnston, both ruined; before the sun set we disgorged into the sea through the large inlet, or principal mouth, which, as I have mentioned, has sufficient depth to admit ships of major burden. With a fresh wind from the northwest we continued our trip and between ten and eleven o'clock that night, cast anchor on the banks forming the mouth of Winyah Harbor.

As the twenty-sixth day [of July] broke, we raised anchor and with all safety entered the Waccamaw River by the mouth called Town Entrance, which has a depth of two fathoms. The wind blew softly from the northwest and we continued our navigation up river until eleven o'clock in the morning, when we tied up at the wharves of Georgetown, situated on the northern bank of the Waccamaw River twenty miles from its mouth.[29] The site is pretty and on slightly elevated terrain. The population appears to be decent and there are some very good houses, although some of these are burnt and others completely in ruins as a result of the last war. I jumped on shore immediately and, accompanied by Captain Anderson [*sic*] and Mr. Tucker, a passenger from Boston, went to the only inn of the town, where my lodging was rather poor. In the evening I had an argument with the housekeeper and finally convinced her that a terrible bed, which she had intended

[28] Martin was governor from 1782 to 1785 and from 1789 to 1792.
[29] Georgetown, at the head of Winyah Bay, was established in 1735 and became a shipping point for rice and indigo.

This crayon portrait of Francisco de Miranda, executed at Zürich in
1788, was Miranda's favorite likeness of himself.

On July 29, 1783, Miranda arrived in Charleston, where "we tied up at one of the wharves of the city, amid a large number of merchant ships."

Phelps Stokes Collection, The New York Public Library

for Mr. Tucker and myself to occupy together, should be for only one of us.[30] Nevertheless, she thrust two other guests into another small bed in the very room that had been set aside for us, no doubt believing that the privilege of separate beds naturally excluded that of the room, which she had granted us first and of which she now deprived us without further ceremony or civility.

The bread we ate here was in the form of small cakes made of rice (the same thing happened to us in Beaufort); the taste is very good and the nourishment healthful.

The next morning I took a horse and rode through the neighboring plantations, observing the fields of rice and indigo.[31] The soil is very good throughout this area and the agriculture very advanced and flourishing (various persons of this locality have assured me that it is the best in the entire state). On the commanding places in the neighborhood of the town are the remains of field fortifications built by the British during the course of the recent war. The country houses here are handsome, comfortable, and spacious, reflecting thereby the wealth, sound taste, and love of rural life which characterize the inhabitants.

I spent the twenty-eighth in the same manner, visiting the environs of the town and some of the very few persons of distinction there. I called on Miss N—, who owns the best house of all and a great deal of property. Her manner is gracious and she is a middling musician. To her misfortune, she had given her delicious private favors to a married individual, the consequence of which was a son, who lives with his doting mother as a monument to her unjust infamy, either because she did not have sufficient discretion or perhaps does not wish to hide him.

Here is an anecdote which I tell so that you may see that crass superstition is present in all peoples of the earth, even the most civilized. One of the days I spent in this town was a Sunday. Finding myself indoors and being unable to go for a walk because of a heavy rain, I picked up my flute and began to play a

[30] As will be seen, the practice of sharing beds was common during the period and a sore trial to Miranda.

[31] In 1775, South Carolina produced 1,170,000 pounds of indigo.

piece of music as a diversion, whereupon the surprised and scandalized master and mistress of the house ran to Mr. Tucker, asking him to intercede and tell me to let the flute alone and not play on Sunday. Mr. Tucker came to me immediately and related the event, and I had to let loose loud laughter and, of course, the instrument. With this the entire family quieted down, and I made my apology for this carelessness from which they had suffered. Another such instance had occurred in Newbern when, through forgetfulness, I started to play cards on a Sunday. I did not have to do little to give satisfaction to those people and recover my reputation, which otherwise would have been lost irretrievably.

At six o'clock in the morning of the twenty-ninth we again set sail, went down the river in a matter of two hours with a fresh wind from the north, and then entered the sea. Passing the river Santee on our right, we doubled Cape Romain and then went past the small islands of Bull, Capers, Dewees, Long, and Sullivan. At four o'clock in the afternoon we came in sight of Fort Moultrie, located on the south end of the last of these islands at the entrance to the Bay of Charleston. Fort Johnston, which is on the opposite side, on the north end of James Island, signaled us with a flag.[32] We sent the boat, and after the commander had informed himself of where we came from and charged us one peso fuerte,[33] we proceeded and crossed this handsome bay. At five o'clock we tied up at one of the wharves of the city, amid a large number of merchant ships, which enter and leave this port constantly.[34]

We immediately jumped on land and, without anybody saying a word to us and no guard or revenue agent (there is no scoundrel

[32] Fort Moultrie, about one hundred yards offshore, was an incomplete fortification of sand and palmetto logs when it was attacked by eleven British vessels on June 28, 1776. After the British commander, Sir Peter Parker, was wounded, the British withdrew. The fort was then named for its commander, Colonel William Moultrie. Fort Johnson (*sic*) was Charleston's oldest fort. Built in 1708, it was seized by Americans from the British during the Stamp Act controversy.

[33] The peso fuerte was the silver coin, worth eight reals, which became known as the "piece of eight" and was the equivalent of the original American dollar.

[34] Charles Town was settled in 1670. The name was changed in 1783 in the

of this species here) attempting to examine our baggage, proceeded to look for lodging. Fortunately, I encountered, upon disembarking, Mr. Bourdeaux, a merchant of this city whom I had met in Newbern; he was so attentive that he immediately helped me find a good inn. At his recommendation, I took lodging at the inn of Mrs. M. Stone, No. 13 Trade Street, paying little more than one peso for food and lodging. I remained there until the twenty-third of August, when, in order to improve my rooms and in the expectation of obtaining the benefit of an agreeable amorous enterprise, I moved to No. 80 King Street, Miss Melar, occupying the quarters vacated by Colonel of Artillery Carington and Major Edwards.[35]

⚭ *August, 1783.* The next day I went to visit Thomas Bee, Esq.,[36] for whom I brought a letter of recommendation from Mr. Seagrove in Havana. He received me with the greatest politeness and attention and accompanied me on a visit to His Excellency Benjamin Guerard, Esq., the present governor, to whom I presented a letter from General Cagigal.[37] In consequence of this, the Governor has conferred upon me honors and kindnesses during my entire residence in this capital.

I was involved in these matters and was receiving various persons of character who had come to visit me the next morning when lo and behold, the famous lawyer, counselor, and major, Edward Rutledge, Esq.,[38] arrived, carrying a sword in military fashion;

belief that "Charleston" was less British. The city was attacked in 1776 but finally fell in May, 1780, after a siege of two months. It was held by the British for two and a half years and was in a partially ruined condition when evacuated. It served as the state capital until 1786. Its wealth was based on rice and indigo.

[35] Colonel Edward Carrington (*sic*) was quartermaster general to General Greene during his southern campaign; the major was probably John Edwards, aide-de-camp to General Marion.

[36] Thomas Bee was a pre-Revolutionary leader, member of the Continental Congress, and lieutenant governor of South Carolina.

[37] Benjamin Guerard was governor from 1783 to 1785. Juan Manuel de Cagigal was a Spanish general and governor of Cuba. Miranda had formerly served as his aide-de-camp.

[38] Edward Rutledge was a member of the First Continental Congress and a signer of the Declaration of Independence.

he called me to one side and turned over to me, after a courteous and studied prelude, a sealed letter from William Brailsford. I opened it immediately and found therein an absolute challenge, expressed, notwithstanding, in very ambiguous terms, naming Mr. Rutledge as second and arranger of the preliminaries: "To Lieutenant Colonel F. de Miranda: Wishing to forget your illiberal reflections on my country, I shall make no mention of them and only demand satisfaction for the pointed insult offered to myself. My friend Mr. Rutledge, who is so obliging as to be the bearer of this, will settle every preliminary respecting our meeting and his arrangement be positive and binding by me. I am, with due respect, your most obedient servant, William Brailsford."[39]

[Miranda's letter to Brailsford]

Ayant reçu vottre lettre datée jeudi 9 heures, par M. Rutledge, à qui vous avez commissionné pour arranger des certains préliminaires sur une affaire qui vous était de la plus grande conséquence en honneur, j'ai bien voulu arriver à un éclaircissement là-dessus avec ce monsieur, le résultat duquel, arrangé par lui-même dans sa propre langue, je vous envois ci-joint une copie. Je désire que cela puisse satisfaire vos souhaits, par-ce-que rien n'a changé la considération avec laquelle je suis monsieur. . . .

[Rutledge's memorandum]

Mr. Rutledge having called on Colonel de Miranda with a letter from Mr. Brailsford respecting the ill treatment which Mr. Brailsford received on the Island of Providence and which Mr. Brailsford conceived himself entitled to attribute to the Colonel, particularly his having occasioned Mr. Brailsford's confinement in the Castle, Colonel de Miranda was pleased to say that he had long had

[39] An Englishman by this name visited George Washington in 1786. However, internal evidence would seem to indicate that the man who challenged Miranda was an American. On May 6, 1782, a Spanish force, aided by South Carolinians, seized New Providence, the capital of the Bahamas; Miranda arranged the terms of the capitulation. Later, bad feeling developed between him and the Americans, who claimed he was responsible for their failure to receive sixty thousand pesos which they believed had been promised for the use of their ships. This incident may have had something to do with the challenge.

an opinion of Mr. Brailsford as an honorable gentleman and still entertained it, that so far from intentionally reflecting at America he had always respected and preserved a friendship for her, that he bore no enmity to Mr. Brailsford as he did never imagine Mr. Brailsford ever intended to reflect on him the conversations which had passed between them, that the imprisonment which Mr. Brailsford suffered on the Island of Providence was entirely by the General's orders and that he, Colonel de Miranda, went from his sick bed to the General and used his best endeavors with that officer to obtain Mr. Brailsford's release, which was accordingly effected. If the foregoing should not be satisfactory to Mr. Brailsford, Colonel de Miranda authorizes Mr. Rutledge to say that he will give Mr. Brailsford any other satisfaction which a man of honor has a right to require from another.

Mr. Rutledge in consequence of the conversation which had passed between himself and Colonel de Miranda waited on Mr. Brailsford, who declared that the treatment which he had received on the Island of Providence had exceedingly wounded his sensibility and that it had been attributed to the Colonel. Wherefore as a man of honor, if therefore the Colonel would answer his letter and convey to him the sentiments which he had expressed to his friend Mr. Rutledge, he should consider it as satisfactory.

~~~~~

These circumstances obliged me to open conversation and discuss the matter with the emissary, who then asked my permission to talk in the meantime with Mr. Brailsford, who undoubtedly proceeded mistaken in the matter. It caused me no embarrassment to grant him this request, with the clear understanding that Mr. Brailsford should know beforehand that he would never lack from me, should he not be satisfied, whatever other satisfaction one gentleman gives another in similar circumstances. While I awaited my splendid adversary and was prepared, with arms in hand, to receive the satisfaction which he indicated in his letter, he informed me that afternoon, through Mr. Rutledge, that he had been mistaken and that he would be completely satisfied if I assured him in a letter that his character did not become unworthy in my judgment. But since the foundation of his letter to me was false and its contents ambiguous, I forwarded to him a copy of the conversations and messages, which Rutledge himself put in writing, hoping that this would put to rest his displeasure. It apparently had the desired effect because the instance was not repeated.[40] Indeed, the next day we ate together at the house of Mr. Bee, and, greeting me in a cordial manner, he offered his hand, with demonstrations and expressions of friendship! Thus was concluded this grand, chivalrous affair, the cause of it all showing me, in what followed, that his character does not lack a large measure of quixotism.

The Governor, at a large reception he gave for me four days after my arrival, introduced me to the principal persons of the region and officers of the Army of the South who were there at the time. These came to visit me and I owe them great attentions and kindness. I will record here some of their names in grateful memory and recognition: General Green,[41] General Moultrie,[42] Thomas Bee, Intendant Hutson,[43] Mr. Chief Justice Burke,[44] Colonel Washington,[45] Colonel Lewis Morris, Colonel Walton White, Dr. Turnbull,[46] the Messrs. Penman,[47] Colonel Pickney,[48]

[40] Dueling became very popular during the Revolution and was blamed on the French influence. It was outlawed in South Carolina after 1880.

[41] Nathanael Greene (*sic*), a native of Rhode Island, assumed command of the Army of the South in October, 1780, and forced the British out of the Carolinas and Georgia in 1782. After the war he lived on a plantation near Savannah, Georgia.

[42] William Moultrie, brigadier general and lawyer, was the hero of the 1776 invasion; he was a British prisoner of war from 1780 to 1782 and served as governor from 1785 to 1787 and 1794 to 1796.

[43] "Intendant" is an administrative title. Richard Hutson was a lawyer, the son of a former minister of the Congregational Church in Charleston, and a member of the governor's council. He was arrested by Cornwallis and sent to St. Augustine in exile, and his estate was confiscated. He became lieutenant governor in 1782.

[44] This was Aedanus Burke. For additional information, see note 74. below.

[45] Colonel William Washington, a kinsman of George. His home still stands.

[46] Andrew Turnbull, a physician. For additional information, see note 76 below.

[47] E. and J. Penman were merchants of Charleston.

[48] This was almost certainly Charles Cotesworth Pinckney. He served in the Battles of Brandywine and Germantown and was captured at the fall of Charles-

Major Butler,[49] Mr. Medliton,[50] Major Pearce,[51] Colonel Eustace,[52] the Reverend Mr. Purcel, Dr. Ramsay,[53] former Governor Matthews,[54] Collector General Hall,[55] Mr. Jones, Judge Heyward,[56] Dr. de la Howe,[57] Dr. Flag,[58] Mr. Colleton,[59] Mr. Morris, Mr. Banks,[60] Monsieur la Canterie, Mr. Bethune, Mr. Ewen, Treasurer Black, Mr. Campbell, Mr. Smith, Mr. Marshall, and Attorney General Moultrie.

The inhabitants of the region are generally rich and love the countryside and rural life, as a result of which one sees here very fine country houses. Hunting, dancing, and smoking tobacco in pipes are the favorite diversions. Society is not very animated in the city, despite the fact that there is no lack of educated and knowledgeable persons. The youth are generally vain and igno-

ton. He was later a member of the Constitutional Convention, a diplomat, and candidate for vice-president and president of the United States.

[49] Pierce Butler, adjutant general of South Carolina, was later delegate to the Constitutional Convention and one of the first senators from the state.

[50] Cannot be identified, but probably a member of the socially and politically prominent Middleton (*sic*) family.

[51] Probably William Pierce (*sic*), Jr., aide-de-camp to General Greene.

[52] Probably Jean S. Eustace.

[53] David Ramsay, M.D., later a noted South Carolina historian. He described Miranda as loving liberty "with an ardor that would do honor to the freest State in the world."

[54] John Mathews (*sic*), former member of the Continental Congress; elected governor in 1782.

[55] George Abbott Hall, who was in South Carolina at that time to receive, for the United States, South Carolina's quota for national expenses and other national funds.

[56] Thomas Heyward, judge of circuit court (1779–89), one-time member of the Council of Safety and of the Continental Congress; signer of the Declaration of Independence.

[57] John de la Howe, a physician of French Huguenot extraction. By his will in 1797 he gave his plantation to become one of the first agricultural schools in the nation for poor boys and girls.

[58] Dr. Henry C. Flagg (*sic*) was chief medical officer in Greene's army and stepfather of the artist Washington Allston.

[59] The Colleton family held one of the original baronies in South Carolina. The reference here may be to John Colleton.

[60] Probably John Banks, who held a government contract to clothe and feed Greene's army. He became involved in a trading scandal which touched even General Greene.

rant. The women are more agreeable although somewhat shy when one first meets them, and they dress with the greatest taste (except for the hairdress, which they do themselves with much carelessness). The number of this sex is very large compared to that of the men; there is no lack of those who make the computation of five to one, and the reason they give is the large number of Tories killed by the Whigs in the past war and of the latter which the Tories and British likewise destroyed. In District No. 96 alone (and I know this from good authority) there are twelve hundred widows.[61] Whoever wants to choose a wife, therefore, should come to this land of abundance!

The principal ladies with whom I had the pleasure of becoming acquainted during my residence here are these: Mrs. Eliot, Mrs. Pinckney, Mrs. Purcel, Mrs. Moultrie, Mrs. Turnbull, Mrs. Bee (antonomastically Queen Bee), Mrs. Ward, Mrs. Colleton (sings very prettily in the English style), Mrs. Sawyer (merry coquette), Mrs. Dubose (remarkable for her beautiful and majestic person), Mrs. Jones, Mrs. Hall, Miss Townsend (my inamorata), Miss P. Turnbull, Miss Marshall and Miss Glower (the two reigning beauties), Mrs. Bay, Mrs. Marshall, the Misses Thibault, Miss Eliot, Mrs. Butler, Miss P. Smith, Mrs. Ramsay, Miss Magot (one of three famous travelers who, unaccompanied by any man what-

[61] For nearly three years there was no semblance of government in South Carolina. Whig and Tory fought each other in small detachments with the fury of civil war, and lynch law and plundering became a habit. In all, 137 battles, actions, and engagements took place in South Carolina between the British, Tories, and Indians on one hand and the American patriots on the other. Of these, 103 were fought by South Carolinians alone, and they took part in twenty others. In no state was there more fighting or suffering during the Revolution.

The town of Ninety-Six was the oldest white community in the upcountry and was important as an Indian trading post. The British erected a unique star-shaped redoubt there, the outlines of which are still evident today. It was besieged for twenty-seven days by General Greene in 1781. The Ninety-Six area was the center of the bitterest sort of internecine struggle between patriot and loyalist bands. Approximately forty battles of various magnitudes took place there. The name apparently derived from traders' estimates of the distance from the first Cherokee town in the foothills.

soever, journeyed through France, Italy, etc.), Miss Feneque, Mrs. Matthews, Mrs. White, and Mrs. Haleston.

The city is quite large and contains very good houses of brick and wood, the number of which is calculated at fifteen hundred, although a large section is in ruins as the result of a fire which occurred three or four years ago. Among the burnt buildings is the House of Assembly, the ruins of which reveal that it was one of the best and most spacious. It is incredible how many times history tells us the city has suffered from this voracious element. The location is pleasant and very advantageous for commerce, as it is exactly at the flowing together of the rivers Ashley and Cooper, both of which are spacious and navigable; the ocean breezes refresh it and make its habitation more bearable in the summer, when the heat and diabolic multitude of mosquitoes exceed all exaggeration. The most remarkable buildings are the House of Assembly, the New and Old churches, and the Exchange;[62] their architecture is simple and passably well designed. The steeple of the New Church is quite high and can be seen at a considerable distance, not only from the sea but also from the interior, since the surrounding land is extremely low and flat. The streets are straight and spacious, with brick pavements on both sides for the comfort of those who go on foot; the most conspicuous of these are Meeting, Broad, and Church streets. Near the House of Assembly is the statue of Pitt, standing on a marble pedestal with an iron fence around it. The execution is of average merit, the size natural, and the costume Roman (a strange idea). It is in the attitude of orating, the right hand resting on a book on which one reads "Stamp Act," and this, one infers, was the motive for the erection of the monument in honor of this great man.[63] He lacks, at the present time, part of his right arm, taken away by a cannon ball during the last siege.

There is no theater or spectacle whatsoever.[64] The only place

[62] The Exchange was begun about 1767 as an exchange and customhouse. Finished in 1771, it is a good example of Colonial English Georgian architecture.

[63] William Pitt denounced the Stamp Act in the House of Commons. The statue was erected July 5, 1770.

[64] The theater burned in 1782, but drama had a long history in Charleston.

women are seen in large numbers is in church on Sundays, and so it happens that the congregation is always large and very brilliant. The interiors of the churches are plain and very clean, which makes them more pleasant and adds luster to the gathering. The hours of service are ten-thirty in the morning and four o'clock in the afternoon. There is no lack of congregation at the latter hour, as the object of youth is not only the zeal for religion but also other advantages which only the church provides here, there being no walks or public gathering places. Proof of this is that the old people and heads of families scarcely attend at all, and only accidentally is one of these seen in church!

A few days after my arrival I was indebted to General Green for the favor of sending me his aide-de-camp, Major Edwards,[65] to show me from a military point of view the local fortifications. We took our horses at the break of day and with much scrupulosity examined the fortifications in their entirety. Those that surround the place (which are quite extensive) and its avenues are built provisionally and, one cannot deny, with good judgment and great intelligence, particularly two large advance redoubts on the land side, which, like almost all the others, are the work of the famous British engineer Moncrieff.[66] All are rushing to their decay, and there is not even one cannon mounted on their slopes. This is certainly a shame, because, even though the construction is provisional, the foundations of the principal bulwarks are of brick and the rest well supported with wooden unions, so that with a little care they could last a long time.

About six miles farther on is another fieldwork. This is composed of several redoubts, which formed a complete line of protection for a British camp established there and were sort of an advance post to impede access to the place and to protect, doubtlessly, the above-mentioned installations at the time they were under construction. In my opinion, this is one of the best forti-

---

[65] Miranda may have been in error; F. B. Heitman does not record a Major Edwards as an aide to General Greene in his *Historical Register of Officers of the Continental Army . . . April, 1775, to December, 1783* (Washington, 1914).
[66] Major Moncrieff designed the Charleston fortifications in 1780.

fied field positions imaginable—and it was accomplished in an original manner. The ground in front is covered with a thick pine grove, protecting therefore all approaches of the enemy. So what did Moncrieff do in these circumstances? He commandeered a large number of slaves and had them cut down all the trees over a considerable area, letting them fall on the ground in an interpolating manner and in the greatest disorder possible; in this way he formed an abatis almost two miles long and a half a mile wide, which made the position completely inaccessible, except for a narrow path which serves as a connection with the countryside. The flanks rest on the rivers Cooper and Ashley. Thus was this capable engineer able to fashion the greatest and surest defense—with the very disadvantages of the terrain.

Forts Moultrie and Johnston, like the others, are rapidly decaying. In the latter there remain only two poor artillery pieces, used to signal vessels entering the bay. The former, so famous for its repulse of the sea attack led by Admiral Sir Peter Parker in 1776, does not have a single piece remaining; its construction, nevertheless, deserves attention. The parapets are extremely high, for which reason the superior firepower of the ships did not make the least impression on those manning the artillery; the timber of the parapets, etc., is palm, very well joined and filled in with earth. The terrible fire of five British men-of-war, which lasted more than ten hours, was not able to demolish a single merlon.[67] The cannon balls striking the palm, as one can still see, were blunted and fell away, without having penetrated five inches or caused splinters. This wood is without doubt the best for this type of fortification, but, unfortunately, with the earth and humidity, it soon rots. Next to this fort is a fortification of elliptic shape, which can mount thirty-five artillery pieces and has small furnaces in the center to heat the cannon balls until they are red. (It seems this idea occurred to Moncrieff before the commander of Gibraltar put it to use against our floating batteries!)[68] All these are built with that taste, firmness, intelligence, and simplicity which char-

[67] The merlon is the solid part of a parapet between the embrasures.
[68] Floating batteries were used by the Spanish at Gibraltar in 1782.

acterize British works. In two or three places one can still see
where the British tried to burn this work, intending to destroy it,
when they evacuated the place; but the rain put the fires out, pre-
serving for us through this happenstance a monument to the
ability and intelligence of the military genius who erected it. It
was otherwise for an installation which appears to have been somewhat larger than this one and was built by the same engineer; it
was located on the bank called Shute's Folly, in the middle of the
bay exactly opposite its entrance and surely the only point from
which artillery can contain a naval force decisively attacking the
port. The fire reduced all the woodwork to ashes, ruining the
parapets and outer works, but the foundations, which are the
masterpiece and undoubtedly the best of their kind in this America, will remain for a long time. This visit to the forts I made one
pleasant morning, accompanied by Mr. Young of Savannah and
by my good friend Mr. J. Penman, whose generosity and civilities
I experienced throughout my stay here. Colonel Senf,[69] the commander of Fort Johnston, was supposed to have accompanied me
on this excursion, but, as he was obliged to go to Georgetown on
official business, turned the matter over to Captain Bellevue, who
is in charge of the installation in the Colonel's absence and conducted himself with civility and courteousness.

Another day I went on an excursion with Colonel Lewis
Morris[70] (aide-de-camp of General Green and one of the Continental officers best instructed in his profession that I have
known); his wife; his sister-in-law, Mrs. Huger;[71] Miss Elliott
[sic]; and his mother-in-law, Mrs. Elliott [sic]. We spent the day
pleasantly, walking in the shade of the copped pines and enjoying the sensitive and merry conversation of Mrs. Elliott and Mrs.
Huger, who do not lack information or a taste for literature.
Accabee, the country house where this delightful family lives,
is on the banks of the river Ashley, eight or nine miles from

[69] John Christian Senf was a Hessian captured at Saratoga who then gave
allegiance to the United States. He became one of South Carolina's most noted
engineers.
[70] Of New York; half-brother of Gouverneur Morris.
[71] Probably the widow of Major Benjamin Huger, who was killed in 1779.

Charleston; it is well situated with respect to the configuration of the area, which, being flat, does not offer pleasant vistas to the eye. In the afternoon we returned to the city, and the young ladies accompanied us on horseback; this is the favorite diversion of the ladies in this region, and one can always see groups of them on horseback in the streets and avenues of the city. An incident occurred on this occasion which I do not want to omit. Walking with my friend the Colonel around said country house after dinner and noticing a small brick building close by, I asked him what it was, and he answered that it was the repository of the family bones. I reproached him for the impropriety of placing it right in front of a spot for recreation, pleasure, etc., and urged him to remove it from there forthwith, but he assured me that if he did such a thing, not only would he be regarded as impious but his people would consider themselves unfortunate.[72] Good God! How far extends yet the dominion of superstition and error!

One of the most original personalities I met here was General Gadsden.[73] He is close to eighty years old and nevertheless is learning the Hebrew language. He built a very long wharf over the river Cooper (from which the British troops embarked, protected by two batteries on the flanks, when they withdrew from this city), despite the disapproval of most of the intelligent people, who doubted very much that it could be executed. While I was here, fire spread from a near-by rum warehouse to the wharf, and although everybody gathered immediately with fear and surprise at such a terrible and dreadful spectacle, the General gave his orders and took the necessary measures with the greatest serenity. A man of unusual fortitude and presence of mind!

Mr. Chief Justice Burke, author of the pamphlet entitled *Considerations on the Society or Order of Cincinnati*, which, under the name of Cassius, was published in Charleston on the tenth of October, is a man of intellect, ability, and good judgment.[74]

[72] Because of the rural nature of the South, the practice of burials in family plots, rather than churchyards, became quite common.

[73] This was Christopher Gadsden, a leader of South Carolina Radicals and the Liberty party; he was a delegate to the Stamp Act Congress.

[74] Aedanus Burke published a pamphlet entitled *Considerations on the Society*

It cannot be denied that in the inclinations of individuals is discovered the analogy of genius, talent, etc., because never before have I found a person so passionate an admirer of the excellence and good taste of our inimitable Miguel de Cervantes.[75] I owe him particular friendship and esteem, having profited immensely from his conversation and knowledge during my entire residence in this city.

Dr. Andrew Turnbull, the Penn of Florida,[76] is a person of vast erudition, great accomplishments, and good judgment, combining with these traits a pleasant manner and winning ways. In a word, he is a complete citizen of the world. He favored me with his valuable friendship and conversation and finally honored me with letters of recommendation to Lord Shelburne, Colonel Barré, General Haldimand, Dr. Priestley, etc.—individuals of the first order in England.[77]

Dr. David Ramsay, author of the famous oration concerning the advantages of the independence of the United States of America, read before a public assembly in Charleston in 1778; an active nature, just ideas, love of civil liberty, and somewhat austere habits form the sketch of this republican character. Several letters of recommendation with which he favored me at the approach of

---

or Order of Cincinnati in 1783. The Society of the Cincinnati was formed early in that year, at the suggestion of Henry Knox, to perpetuate the friendships formed among officers of the American army.

[75] Miguel de Cervantes (1547–1616), the Spanish novelist and author of Don Quixote.

[76] A reference to the Crown's efforts to revoke Penn's charter to Pennsylvania. Because of alleged disloyalty during the Revolution, Turnbull lost control of large grants of land made to him in Florida by the English government. He had established a colony of Greeks at New Smyrna.

[77] Sir William Petty, Earl of Shelburne, was an English statesman and friend of the Colonies who had opposed the Stamp Act; Colonel Isaac Barré was a British officer, member of Parliament (1761–90), and friend of America during the Revolution; General Sir Frederick Haldimand was a lieutenant general in the British army who served in America and Canada (1758–60) and as governor and commander-in-chief in Canada (1778–85); Joseph Priestley, an English minister, chemist, and physicist, is known for the discovery of oxygen. He migrated to the United States in 1794.

my departure served me as introductions to various men of letters and members of Congress in Pennsylvania and New Jersey.

Judge Heyward is the famous member of Congress who, when the difficult matter of declaring independence was discussed on the fourth of July, 1776, with resolution and heroic spirit cast the decisive vote and settled the affair, probably forever. Austerity of habits and manner, just ideas, and unalterable fortitude comprise the principal part of his character.

General Moultrie: marked in the glorious annals of America for the obstinate defense he made of Fort Sullivan (renamed Moultrie, in his honor) against the orders of General Lee,[78] who at the time was in command at Charleston and whose opinion it was that the fort should be evacuated because it was incapable, he thought, of resisting so strong an attack. The enemy committed a thousand errors and blunders and, as chance would have it, was repulsed. So see you here Moultrie raised to the clouds and the famous Lee fallen to the extreme, for the very reason that the latter deserved the greater applause! Nothing reveals more the small abilities of the one and the accomplishments and military ability of the other than this event, for which the multitude has characterized them so falsely and unjustly. Good judgment and a kind, sociable, and impartial disposition adorn the character of this man of good will.

Intendant Hutson—this post was created for him in September, while I was in Charleston. His spirit and resolution manifested themselves later in the suppression of the mobs incited by the great rogue Gillon and led by Dr. Fagan. These two personages, *caudillos* of the rabble, had, two months before, insulted countless inhabitants, persons of respect and reputation, whom the said Gillon wished to have thrown out of the country, by calling them, odiously, "Tory" or "British," in order to carry out his mercantile transactions without competition and to his advantage. The Governor and leading citizens attempted to contain the damage at first, but with all their authority they could not prevent

---

[78] General Charles Lee, a British-born officer who was suspended by Washington for disobedience during the Battle of Monmouth.

many persons from being "Pumped & Ducked." Shortly after the election of Mr. Hutson these people tried to rally again for the same purposes. The Intendant sent a guard to the designated area with orders to arrest every individual who for that reason should assemble there; in this way the evil which an irresolute and timid leader had thought incurable was ended at a stroke. Never again have the tumultuous bands or their *caudillos* appeared. Good judgment, considerable education, and a love of the sciences, society, and humanity are the qualities of this affable person.

During this time I often attended the courts of justice and I cannot exaggerate the contentment and pleasure I received from seeing the admirable method of the British constitution in action. Good God! What a contrast with the Spanish system!

These were outstanding among the individuals who shone at the bar: Edward Rutledge, Colonel Pinckney, Attorney General Moultrie, and Major Pinckney.[79] The first possesses an average knowledge of the law and brilliant, facile exposition, together with a very pleasant manner and a commendable person. The second is a man of good judgment, profound knowledge in his profession, and force in his argument; his eloquence, however, is neither as brilliant nor as sonorous as that of the first. Moultrie has firmness, judgment, and very good elocution. The last is finished in nothing as yet, though many think him a prodigy in everything. He has received a good education in Europe, is still young, and gives very good hopes, without his progress showing as yet anything out of the ordinary.

The terrain of this state, like that of North Carolina, is sandy and very poor its entire length for a distance of more than one hundred miles from the ocean, at which extension it changes entirely, and the quality of the earth is good and the surface wooded. Rice and indigo are the principal products of the region, and their value constitutes South Carolina the richest state of this America. The first, as we know, is cultivated where there are marshes and fresh water, which are provided here by the abundant rivers and

[79] The Pinckneys are C. C. and Thomas, members of a well-known South Carolina family.

Miranda described Philadelphia as "the most beautiful [city] on this continent" and "one of the most pleasant and well-ordered cities in the world."

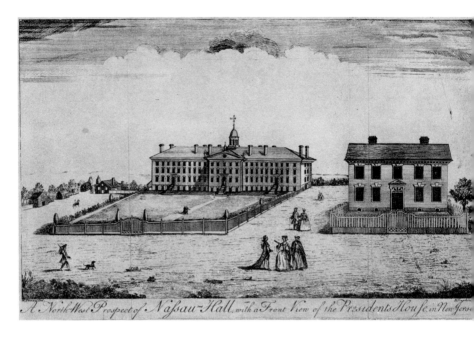

A North-West Prospect of Nassau-Hall, with a Front View of the Presidents House in New-Jersey

"This town," said Miranda of Princeton, "combines the advantages of being healthful and merry. It has a well-regulated college for the education of youth."

Lenox Collection, The New York Public Library

tides. At a distance of twenty to thirty miles from the mouth of a river, the native selects his land in the lowest place. The tide, which twice daily makes the waters at the mouth rise four and a half feet, completely inundates the ground and makes it very suitable for said cultivation. Indigo does not need as much water, so it is planted in more elevated ground, although always in a humid and level place.

The whole region is infested with the ague and to such an extreme in the summer—when the effluvia of the stagnant waters increase and penetrate the atmosphere more—that, even though people of some ease are always able to go to the city or seaports to preserve themselves from the contagion by breathing the pure air of the breeze, almost all suffer more or less. The doctors have made a very singular observation, which is that if in this season one changes air (that is, those who live in the country go to the city, or vice versa), the fever attacks unfailingly. Similarly, it has been observed that the effects of this contagion upon the stranger, and especially upon the balsamic European blood, are much more violent and marked than upon the natives. The latter are so accustomed to the evil that if, in greeting them, one asks, "How are you?" they answer, their teeth chattering with the cold of the ague, "Pretty well, only the fever!"[80]

In the year 1729 it happended that a brigantine proceeding from Madagascar stopped at Sullivan Island on its way to England and its captain offered a small sack of rice to the governor, from which source this plant propagated throughout the region.[81] Oh, with how much reason did the introducer of this benefit deserve the remembrance and applause of these people! But see how difficult it is to destroy a habit and preconception: it was only after much time and great efforts on the part of the most prudent men that the cultivation became general and the people realized the incomparable advantage it offered them. To a similar chance the

---

[80] A German traveler, Johann David Schoepf, wrote in the same year: "Carolina is in the spring a paradise, in the summer a hell, and in the autumn a hospital."

[81] It is now believed that rice was introduced prior to 1686 by Captain John Thurber and Dr. Henry Woodward.

island of Jamaica owes the introduction of the valuable pasture called guinea grass.

In addition this region produces a great deal of corn, some wheat, very good fruit, pomegranates, nuts, cotton, mulberries, and grapes. Grapevines are found wild and in great abundance in virgin and remote forests, and as a result, several individuals make wine, but neither is the juice suitable nor does the climate permit the grape to acquire a good taste; several experiments confirm this opinion. The pine, called lightwood, abounds; it produces turpentine, pitch, and tar, which form a considerable branch of commerce. The inhabitants boil a small, round fruit which the bayberry shrub produces in bunches and extract therefrom bayberry tallow, with which they make very good candles. This tallow is green and exudes a certain delicate and fragrant odor when it burns, which makes it preferable to wax; yet its consistency appears to be harder than that of wax.

The commerce of the state commences with vigor, but as yet there are no exact figures; for this reason we give those compiled with most accuracy just before the general revolution:

Ships	Sailors	Imports from England	Exports
140	1,680	£365,000	£395,666

The population, including whites and persons of color (the latter comprise more than half), is believed to amount to 225,000. The city of Charleston has about 16,000 inhabitants, who have been in imminent danger on various occasions. In the year 1752, among others, a terrible hurricane blew in, with the result that the water rose ten feet above the highest tide, ships broke from their moorings and ran aground, sloops and schooners rendered themselves into pieces against the houses on Bay Street, and the inhabitants, despairing of their lives, took refuge on the roofs. Miraculously the wind veered to the west and the waters went down five feet in ten minutes. The wooden pest-house[82] on Sullivan Island was taken by the sea for some miles up the river Cooper with fifteen people inside, nine of whom drowned. While

[82] Probably a hospital or quarantine station for those with infectious diseases.

I was here, at the beginning of October, the same scene began to develop; luckily the wind changed to the north, and only the lower rooms of the houses on South Bay were inundated. Acquaintances meeting on the streets the next day congratulated each other as if they had survived a great danger. Bad jests for certain!

The government of the state is entirely democratic, as are those of the other United States; a governor, senate, and house of representatives are a weak supplement to the three bodies which organize the admirable equilibrium of the British constitution. The salaries of the magistrates and officials of the state are quite moderate and do not, I believe, amount to three thousand pounds sterling. All the public expenses of the state before the war, according to a very accurate calculation, did not amount to eight thousand pounds.

Beaufort, situated on Port Royal Island about fifteen miles farther up from the mouth of Great River, is a town of the same size, with little difference, as Georgetown and the only other that merits such a denomination in the entire state.

I saw a list in the possession of Colonel Pinckney of all the persons who, by the law of the state, had been proscribed or fined: 230 was the number of the former and 48 of the latter.[83]

November, 1783. At ten o'clock in the morning of the second of November, I said my final farewells to my friends in Charleston and set sail for Philadelphia on the brigantine *James*, Captain Benjamin Darell. The passengers were Monsieur Macorell, a businessman from Port-au-Prince, Hispaniola; Mr. Focke, a Prussian by birth and former secretary to Mr. Van Bramme, consul of Holland in South Carolina; Mr. Nealson, a Jersey farmer; his daughter, Miss Jane, seventeen years old and very good looking; and his niece, Miss Sally Singleterry, twenty years old (both girls were merry, in the American fashion).

---

[83] In South Carolina the refusal to take an oath of allegiance to the Patriot government made a Tory subject to banishment. If he did not sell his estate within a fixed time, it was forfeited.

At six o'clock in the afternoon we anchored outside the Bar of Charleston. At seven-thirty in the morning of the third we set sail; at nine the pilot left and we observed that a brigantine which had sailed with us had run aground on the bar. On the fourth, fifth, sixth, and seventh we sailed, with variable winds from the northeast, toward Cape Fear. On the eighth we had a fresh wind from the southwest and on the ninth, at eight o'clock in the evening, we found ourselves off Cape Lookout, so embayed by the reefs that only by great good luck we escaped. When the Captain saw, by the moonlight, the danger and gave the order to turn about, we were only two ship's lengths from the reefs and the ship was in full sail, doing seven knots. It was one of the most imminent dangers I have ever seen myself in! After having run over these shallows of three and less fathoms for about ten knots (luckily the wind was blowing from the coast), we extricated ourselves from the danger and gave a thousand thanks to the Captain for the peril in which his lack of prudence had placed us.

On the tenth we had a strong wind from the northwest; increasing more and more, it became a violent storm, which lasted without intermission until the seventeenth, obliging us to lay to almost all this time, as the vessel could not bear the sail. In my opinion two circumstances preserved us from this danger: first, the wind blew from the coast and thus carried us away from the reef; second, the quality and condition of the ship, for, even though the sea and wind wished to devour us (the sailors admitted they had never before seen such a storm), it neither sprang a leak nor strained a mast with the rolling.

At five o'clock in the morning the wind changed to the north, and, the sea becoming peaceable, we sailed for the Delaware River.

PART TWO

Pennsylvania and Delaware

☆☆

PENNSYLVANIA AND DELAWARE

〜〜〜 *November 19, 1783.* At eight o'clock in the morning we saw clearly the lighthouse on Cape Henlopen, which, with Cape May, forms the mouth of the Delaware. We immediately signaled for the pilot. He came on board at eleven o'clock, and, with a fresh wind from the southeast, we went up this splendid river, the banks of which are very pleasant, full of attractive cottages and country houses (particularly so the left bank, which forms the province of Delaware and is fertile; the right, part of West Jersey,[1] is arid, as one can tell from the abundance of pines covering it, this tree being the most positive sign of land that is sandy and of little substance). At five o'clock in the afternoon we anchored off Reedy Island, sixty-five miles from the mouth of this river, where we found several ships riding at anchor, waiting for favorable weather to go out to sea. On the bank opposite said island is a small town called Port Penn.

At seven o'clock in the morning of the twentieth we set sail in pursuit of our course and at ten o'clock anchored, for lack of wind, at the town of New Castle, fifteen miles up river.[2] The passengers, except for the women, went ashore and were provided with an excellent dinner at the tavern of Israel Israel. The building that houses this tavern was erected by a Dutchman and predates Philadelphia, as does this town, which was the first Euro-

[1] In 1644 the Duke of York gave New Jersey to two favorites, hence the division, which was formalized by a line drawn in 1676. Most of West Jersey eventually passed into Quaker hands, and William Penn and associates bought East Jersey in 1682. Two capitals, Perth Amboy and Burlington, were maintained until 1790.

[2] New Castle, Delaware, was settled by Swedes and Finns, who were taken over by the Dutch in 1655.

pean settlement on this river. After dinner we took a walk around the town, which has a pretty location, good houses, and about seventy inhabitants, and at one o'clock went back on board and set sail with a fresh wind from the northwest. Two hours later we passed Wilmington, six miles farther up on the left bank and located on a beautiful hill. Ten miles farther is the small town of Marcus Hook and four miles farther up on the same river the town of Chester.[3] Anchored at Chester, which has sixty houses, were a Dutch ship, the sixty-four ton *Overissel,* and a thirty-six ton frigate, which, with another vessel that had separated itself during the trip and was later known to have been lost, composed a squadron under the command of Commodore Rimersmar which had brought over the minister plenipotentiary of Holland. At five-thirty in the afternoon we anchored at the spot where the first chevaux-de-frise[4] had been placed in order to obstruct navigation during the war when the British gained control of Philadelphia in 1777; they were protected by a fort located on the Jersey shore at a place called Billings' Point.

At eight o'clock in the morning we set sail with a favorable tide and very carefully passed the second chevaux-de-frise (there is just barely an opening for the passage of a ship), located three miles farther up in front of Mud Island, where there are remains of the fort which made the island famous by its defense and helped contain for a long time the efforts of the British squadron to pass. Perhaps the enemy would not have succeeded, had not some ships, which stole through the small west channel (thought to be very shallow), enfiladed it from the rear. It cannot be doubted that the chevaux-de-frise are one of the firmest and happiest inventions in fortifications of this sort. It could have been the sublime and universal genius of Doctor Franklin that produced this remarkable invention! The new system of chimneys, by means of which it is possible to give more heat to an apartment

---

[3] Chester, Pennsylvania, lies fifteen miles southwest of Philadelphia and is the second-oldest settlement in the state. It was founded by Swedes in 1644.

[4] Chevaux-de-frise are defenses consisting of barriers covered with spikes; first used against cavalry.

or room with a third of the firewood or charcoal commonly used; the famous shaving soap sold under his name in Boston; the conductors for the preservation of lightning . . . together with numberless other inventions and minor discoveries which, although not so brilliant as those of the laws of electricity and others of this character, are much more useful to humanity—all these have been the product of this great friend of society. A battery on the Jersey shore in the place called Red Bank likewise protected it. Six miles farther up on the same shore is the small town of Gloucester.

~~~ *November 22.* Two miles past the small town of Gloucester is Philadelphia, where we arrived at ten o'clock in the morning, tying up at the wharves amidst the multitude of ships of all nations which frequent this beautiful, free, and commercial city. We disembarked immediately, without ceremony or inspection. The women and Mr. Nealson went their way, and Mr. Macorell, Mr. Focke, and I went to the Indian Queen Inn,[5] belonging to Mr. Thompson, on Fourth Street, where we took lodging, paying one peso fuerte for room and board (not including liquors). I must certainly admit that at no other inn have I seen more cleanliness, abundance, regularity, and decency; it is the best I have known.

Mouth of the Delaware to Philadelphia	
to Reedy Island	65
New Castle	15
Wilmington	6
Marcus Hook	10
Chester	4
Billings' Point	9
Mud Island	3
Gloucester	6
Philadelphia	2
	120 miles

This city is indisputably the largest and most beautiful on this continent. Its streets are straight and are cut at right angles; their

[5] The Indian Queen was a famous inn. Jefferson stayed there and is supposed to have written the Declaration of Independence while a resident.

width is generally fifty feet (and Market Street one hundred feet), with brick sidewalks on both sides so that people on foot may pass, for which reason little use is made of coaches and carriages. At intervals in front of the houses, forming pillars on the sidewalks, are wooden pumps, which with the greatest convenience and cleanliness supply the inhabitants with all the water they need.

Philadelphia is located at the confluence of the Delaware and Schuylkill rivers, in a dry and dominant spot. Nine streets, which run from one river to the other, intersected perpendicularly by nineteen others, form the center. The houses are comfortable, clean, and in good taste, although somewhat small; they generally have gardens and their architecture is plain and simple, like the dress and habits of the first inhabitants.

It has numerous very good wharves for the facility of commerce; the principal one is two hundred feet wide. The market, the House of Assembly (where the Congress almost always convened for the great work of independence), the hospital, the jail, and the barracks are the principal buildings, constructed with middling skill and with no ornament or decoration whatsoever. The beef market is the best, cleanest, and most abundant I have ever seen; decent women are wont to go to it in the morning and bring home pieces of beef in their hands, without soiling themselves or giving off any bad odor . . . such is the propriety and cleanliness with which everything is regulated!

Christ, St. Peter, and St. Paul are the best churches,[6] and their architecture judicious; the interiors are clean and have iron stoves, which are of infinite help in winter. The church of the Papists is small, but clean and well regulated.[7]

The cleanliness, evenness, and length of the streets, their illumination at nighttime, and the vigilance of the guards, posted at each corner to maintain security and good order, make Philadelphia one of the most pleasant and well-ordered cities in the world.

---

[6] These churches were erected in 1724–54, 1758–61, and 1761, respectively. All three were aided by the grant of a lottery in 1765.

[7] There was a strong anti-Catholic feeling in Philadelphia until a much later date.

Among the curiosities in this city is the Peale Collection, consisting of some one hundred portraits of middling merit done by this artist of the leading citizens and foreigners who contributed to the American Revolution.[8] It not only offers entertainment and pleasure to the curious and educated traveler but also sheds light on history and forms patriotic and virtuous ideas in the youth, to whom it presents the worthiest monument which could be erected to the glory of an entire people! Certainly this example should be imitated by all other nations which value virtue and good taste!

Shortly after my arrival I went to see our envoy, or agent, Don Francisco Rendón,[9] for whom I brought a letter from General Cagigal; he received me with the greatest courteousness and hospitality, offering me his home, table, and facilities in such an obligatory manner that I was obliged to accept and so have lived at his house throughout my stay in Philadelphia. A very sociable nature and residence of more than four years in this city have given him a general acquaintance with all the inhabitants. Through this circumstance and the great number of letters of recommendation with which my friends in Charleston had favored me, in a very few days I was introduced to and receiving invitations and courtesies from the leading people of the region. I will record their names here in gratitude and recognition: General Thomas Mifflin,[10] president of the Congress; Robert Morris, Esq., superintendent of finance and of the Department of the Navy; John Dickinson, Esq.,[11] president of the state; Le Chevalier Anne-César de la Luzerne, minister of the court of France; Peter John

[8] Charles Wilson Peale, a major American artist, was a native of Maryland and a student of John S. Copley and Benjamin West. In 1784, Peale opened a museum in Philadelphia. He was also one of the founders of the Pennsylvania Academy of Fine Arts, the first art museum in the United States.

[9] Rendón became Spanish agent to the United States in 1780.

[10] Mifflin, a Philadelphia merchant, was active in pre-Revolutionary affairs and was chosen president of Congress on November 3, 1783. He was later a member of the Constitutional Convention.

[11] Dickinson, a lawyer, was at first an advocate of conciliation with England and voted against the Declaration of Independence. Later he served in the Continental army, was president of the Supreme Executive Council of Pennsylvania, and a member of the Constitutional Convention.

Van Berckel, minister of the Netherlands; Don Francisco Rendón, agent of the court of Spain; Monsieur François de Barbé-Marbois, consul general of France; William Moore, Esq.,[12] former president of the state; John Penn,[13] former governor of the province and a direct descendant of the founder; Joseph Read, Esq.,[14] former president of the state—

General Washington; General St. Clair;[15] General Anthony Wayne;[16] Dr. Benjamin Rush;[17] David Rittenhouse,[18] secretary of the state and astronomical genius; Colonel Charles Pettit;[19] George Meade, Esq.;[20] Jacob Read and J. Beresford,[21] members of Congress for Charleston; James Wilson;[22] Jacob Jarvis; Thomas Hutchins, Esq.,[23] geographer general of the United States and a man of great ability in this line; Mr. Coxe;[24] Mr. Ross;[25] Mr.

[12] President of Pennsylvania in 1781-82.

[13] Son of Thomas (a brother of William) Penn. He came to the United States in 1783.

[14] President of Pennsylvania from 1778 to 1781.

[15] Arthur St. Clair, a former British soldier, became an American patriot. A major general in 1777, he fought in the Battles of Princeton and Trenton. He became the first governor of the Northwest Territory.

[16] General Wayne won the nickname "Mad Anthony" because of his daring exploits during the war; later famous as an Indian fighter and for his role in the Battle of Fallen Timbers.

[17] A noted Philadelphia physician, signer of the Declaration of Independence, and professor of chemistry at the College of Philadelphia.

[18] Treasurer of Pennsylvania (1777-84), but better known as an astronomer. He built two orreries and what was probably the first American telescope.

[19] Assistant quartermaster general; later a member of Congress.

[20] Prominent Philadelphia merchant (George Meade and Company) and shipowner.

[21] Congressmen from South Carolina. Beresford, however, was undoubtedly Richard, elected March 15, 1783.

[22] Lawyer and long-time member of the Continental Congress; re-elected in 1782.

[23] An American cartographer born in New Jersey. Appointed "Geographer to the United States" by Congress in 1781, he was in charge of the Northwest Territory survey.

[24] Possibly Tench Coxe, a Philadelphia merchant, member of the Continental Congress, active promoter of manufacturing, and author of works on political economy.

[25] Perhaps either George or James Ross, sons of the signer of the Declaration of Independence.

Shippen;[26] Mr. Hill; Mr. Powell;[27] Mr. Holker;[28] Dr. Vankroff; James Benezet,[29] author of a small, well-written tract on the doctrine and religion of the Quakers—

Mr. Chew;[30] Dr. Shevet,[31] a celebrated anatomist, who has several anatomical parts in his school or cabinet made by himself out of paste, which demonstrate singular knowledge and ability in the art; Peter S. Duponceau, Esq.,[32] interpreter of foreign languages for the state, is a young man of very good intellectual disposition, application, and extensive knowledge in the living languages, which he speaks with singular facility and good dialect; Major Moore;[33] John Vaughn;[34] Monsieur Barrière, one of the very few Frenchmen I have known on this continent who is capable of recognizing, notwithstanding his native prejudices, the advantages of a free government as compared with any other despotism, and who is a good republican!—

Monsieur Sarsnau, secretary of Rendón; Don Joaquín de Quintana, companion of Valois in Havana, who came here from England and lost his ship, cargo, and part of the crew (among them a lovely Quaker girl, eighteen years old, who drowned in the cabin for lack of someone to give her a hand and bring her out over the roundhouse of the ship, where Quintana was with those who

[26] Probably Edward, jurist and chief justice (1799–1805) of the Pennsylvania Supreme Court.

[27] Possibly Samuel Powel (*sic*), Philadelphia's last pre-Revolutionary and first post-Revolutionary mayor.

[28] John Holker was consul general of France.

[29] This must be Anthony Benezet, who came to Philadelphia in 1731. As a reformer, he was active in the causes of antislavery, Indians, and temperance. In 1780 he published a tract entitled *A Short Account of the Society of Friends*.

[30] Benjamin Chew was a prominent lawyer and chief justice of Pennsylvania.

[31] Almost certainly a reference to Abraham Chovet (*sic*), a Philadelphia physician at this time.

[32] A learned Frenchman, formerly on the staff of General von Steuben. He became a United States citizen in 1781.

[33] Probably Major James Moore, who served with distinction under General Anthony Wayne in the First Pennsylvania Regiment throughout the war. Later he went into the drug business, with great success, and moved in fashionable society, entertaining Washington in 1787. He moved to Virginia in 1800.

[34] A Philadelphia physician.

saved themselves) off the coast of Jersey, near Monmouth, and is one of the very few of my countrymen who have penetrated the marvelous arcanum of the British constitution and is a good sectarian, but I will never forgive him the incident of the unfortunate Quaker girl!—

Mr. Gouverneur Morris,[35] the lively intellect of the town, and it seems to me he has more ostentation, audacity, and tinsel than real value; Chief Justice Thomas M'Kean[36] of the Supreme Court, a man of considerable accomplishments in his profession, but he is of a deceitful character and not very good heart! Chief Justice Smith[37] of Jersey, a man of ingenuous spirit and many accomplishments, has mastered drawing, music, etc., and in the house of Mr. Rutherford[38] in New York one sees several pieces in the antique style, drawn with middling taste and great skill! Mr. William Hamilton,[39] a person of pleasing nature, elegant manner, generosity, and good taste; General Frederick A. Muhlenberg,[40] member of the Council of Censors and a person of consequence in the area, his origin German, as is that of a great many in this region, descendants of poor Dutch and German settlers; Baron von

[35] Member of the Continental Congress, state constitutional convention (1776–77), and land speculator. He became a member of the Constitutional Convention, a leading Federalist, minister to France, and an important backer of the Erie Canal.

[36] Thomas McKean (sic), signer of the Declaration of Independence, lawyer, governor, member of the Stamp Act and Continental congresses, and chief justice of Pennsylvania.

[37] Frederick Smyth (sic) was appointed chief justice in 1764 at the age of thirty-two. He died in 1815.

[38] This was probably John Rutherford, a leading lawyer, son-in-law of Lewis Morris, and United States senator (1791–98).

[39] One of America's earliest collectors of pictures and cultivator of ornamental gardens. He was a country gentleman, and his home, *Woodlands*, with its trees and shrubs from around the world, was one of the show places of Pennsylvania. Because of his association with British officers, he was accused of treason but acquitted; in 1787 he was host to George Washington.

[40] Frederick A. C. Muhlenberg was trained as a minister but became a merchant. Active in politics, he was speaker of the Pennsylvania House of Representatives, a member of the Continental Congress, and first speaker of the United States House of Representatives. Miranda, however, is in error. It was Frederick's brother Peter who was the general.

Steuben,[41] former inspector general of the American army; General Armand;[42] General Steward;[43] Major Segond;[44] and Major Du Pointy.[45]

The women: Mrs. Robert Morris, called antonomastically Queen Morris, for her vain, haughty, and somewhat affected character; an obscure birth and no foundation of formal education give a shadow of quite unfortunate position to this refined personage. . . . Mrs. Powell, rival of the former in occupying first place at the public concourses, as her qualities are very different; she is of genteel birth and has received an excellent education, the beginnings of which she has carried forward with unusual progress, through application and ability. If a magisterial tone and pedantic affectation did not mar her discourse, she would be the most delightful conversationalist one could wish. . . . Mrs. Penn: this personality causes no small amount of envy in the preceding two, because, possessing a conspicuous moderation, a middling education, and polished manners, together with being the wife of the Big Chief of the region, she is wont to receive the principal attentions at public gatherings, to the obvious mortification of the other two. . . .

Mrs. James Allen, an attractive and elegant manner, frank conversation, generosity, good countenance, and no little coquettishness form the character of this pleasant widow—Miss Polly Vining, an outstanding education, sharp intellect, and fluent,

[41] Baron Friedrich Wilhelm Ludolf Gerhard Augustin von Steuben, a Prussian, by act of Congress in March, 1788, became volunteer inspector general; in May he was made major general and inspector general. He was given a congressional vote of thanks for his services upon his resignation in 1784.

[42] Charles Armand was the assumed name of Armand Tufin, Marquis de La Rouërie. He became a colonel of cavalry, Pulaski Legion, on May 10, 1777. In October, 1779, he was put in command, and in October, 1780, the Legion's name was changed to Armand's Partisan Corps. He became a brigadier general in March, 1783.

[43] He is not identified in Heitman; it might possibly be a reference to Charles A. of South Carolina.

[44] Major James Segand, or Segond, was attached to the Pulaski Legion from 1778 to 1783.

[45] This was probably Louis de Pontiere (*sic*) of France, aide-de-camp to General von Steuben from February, 1778, to April, 1784.

47

elegant locution render her manner and conversation extremely pleasant and sought after by foreigners and men of taste. A mixture of mettle and spontaneity in her actions often produce a contrast almost incompatible with her singular accomplishments and good ideas—Miss Peggy Chew, a gracious, pleasing girl—Miss Sally Shippen,[46] clear undersanding, very good education, elegant manner, and a disposition constantly festive and jovial make her extremely pleasing; added to this is the most noble, sensitive, frank, and generous heart, with its small share of coquettishness, forming all together the most beautiful combination I have known—

Miss Moore, an elegant figure of the second order, and knowledge of French and Italian, which she speaks so-so, together with a good share of coquettishness, make her manner amusing, and often delightful; Mrs. Moore[47] (my *querida*), very good looking and born in the West Indies; Mrs. Crook, Mrs. Coxe, and Miss Molly Coxe, all three very good looking; Miss Molly Shippen,[48] lovely graciousness; the Misses Bond,[49] Miss Sitgreaves,[50] and Miss Miller, four of the graces of Philadelphia, although without extraordinary merit; Miss Hicks, celebrated for the incident involving La Case; the Misses Jane and Margaret Marshall, gracious persons—

The Misses Susan and Rebecca Morris, two Quaker girls, sisters-in-law of General Mifflin; their education, good humor, and simple, elegant manner and dress are certainly very particular and give a more favorable idea of the Quaker system than the writings of Fox, Barclay, Whitehead, etc.[51] They favored me

[46] Member of a prominent Philadelphia mercantile family; sister of Molly and "Peggy."

[47] Possibly the wife of William Moore. See note 12 above.

[48] See note 46 above. Margaret, or "Peggy," Shippen married Benedict Arnold.

[49] Probably the daughters of Dr. Thomas Bond, prominent physician of Philadelphia.

[50] Probably the daughter of John Sitgreaves of North Carolina, a member of the Continental Congress.

[51] George Fox was the founder of the Society of Friends in England; George Whitehead and Robert Barclay (see note 23 of Part One) were also active English Quakers.

greatly with their friendship and conversation. . . . Miss Isabella Marshall, another Quaker girl, good looking, well educated, and speaks French middlingly; Mrs. Lawrence,[52] mother of Mrs. James Allen, a matron of majestic bearing and extremely good looking; Mrs. Shippen, sister of the former, a woman of very good judgment, agreeable society, and excellent heart; Mrs. Rush, good looking and sensitive. . . . Mrs. Vaughn and her daughters; this family has recently come from England and is one of the most consequential in this city. Their conversation, education, and elegant manner distinguish them particularly. . . . Mrs. Rutledge and Miss Rutledge, wife and daughter of the famous Governor John Rutledge of Charleston;[53] the former is a woman of much respect and good judgment; the girl has education and is moderately good looking. . . . Mrs. Moore, wife of the Major; Miss Jones, presumptuous know-it-all; Miss Footman, a very good girl, of gentle manner; Mrs. Craig.[54]

Here I will reflect upon some characters who seem to me to have some particularity. Robert Morris, superintendent of finance,[55] etc., seems to me, without doubt, the official of greatest capacity and performance in his line that the United States has had during the past strife, in any department! It is nevertheless said that the extraordinary assistance of Gouverneur Morris has contributed principally to this, but only one reflection that occurs to me now will I offer in vindication. Morris himself related to me one day after dinner that in 1761, sailing in a small schooner off Punta Maisí of the island of Cuba, a French corsair from Le Môle de St. Nicolas, Hispaniola, pursued them and made them run aground on the coast of Baracoa; in this way they escaped, leaving

[52] Probably Mrs. John Lawrence. He served as mayor of Philadelphia and was a justice in the Colonial supreme court. The family entertained Washington in 1787.

[53] John Rutledge was a Charleston lawyer, president of South Carolina (1776–78), governor (1779–82), and later a justice in the United States Supreme Court.

[54] Probably the wife of Major Isaac Craig, shipbuilder.

[55] Morris served in this capacity throughout the war and until November 1, 1784.

49

the ship for lost and taking refuge in that town with what baggage they were able to save. From there they attempted to flee to the Bahama Islands in a fishing boat, but, having been discovered, were forced to go, under arrest, to the fortress, where they remained some time. Through lack of assets and reputation, he was reduced to selling his shirt, leaving himself naked, in order to buy oranges, which are in great abundance there and on which he subsisted for three days. Finally, Bishop Morel, passing through there on his visit, learned of this accidentally and they were sent to the island of Providence. How then can we imagine that a man who was in these circumstances twenty-two years ago and who, through intelligence and ability alone, has been able to accumulate a fortune of about one million pesos, as I was assured, should lack capacity to direct his affairs with the help of all the authority which the Congress could give him? I, at least, do not conceive it.

Le Chevalier de la Luzerne,[56] minister of the court of Paris, a man of lucidity, generosity, and gentle manner, but feeble and without ability for his employment; from this it results that Monsieur de Barbé-Marbois,[57] recently appointed consul general of his country, is the counselor who runs everything. Neither the latter's talents nor his ability are remarkable in any way, much less in politics, although his presumption, boldness, and ignorance persuade him to the contrary. When Miralles, our agent, died, he claimed to be full of certainty and confidence that Spain would name him to that post. When the last peace was being rumored about and the independence of America was believed certain, he wrote a letter to the ministry of France, advising it that it would be very expedient for the Newfoundland fishing not to be granted to the Americans and that the war should continue some time more so that the Americans, being well whipped, would remember better the favor they owed to France. The letter was intercepted and read publicly in Congress (although under oath

[56] Anne-César de la Luzerne was French minister plenipotentiary to the United States from 1779 to 1783. The Countess was very active in relief drives for American soldiers.

[57] François de Barbé-Marbois was a former secretary to the Chevalier de la Luzerne.

that none of the members would mention the matter outside for a period of two years), and see you here how, in one day, Monsieur de Barbé-Marbois caused more injury to the interests of his nation than the good his services are capable of producing in one hundred years! Intrigue is his dominant passion and the channel through which he attempts to conduct all his public and private transactions, using at times the lowest means for the achievement of his ends, and I will not deny that if in some branch he possesses accomplishments, it is in this. Another personage is Monsieur Otto, secretary of the Minister. He serves as marshal at the balls His Excellency presents, goes about corseted, plays the fop and perhaps the confidant; I do not believe he serves for much else. These are the principal actors on the Gallic stage, if we exclude the Agent of Spain, who, through the damned concomitance and our ignorance (despite which there is not one person who in his heart does not detest it) plays the role of subaltern, in all the force of the term.

P. J. Van Berckel,[58] minister plenipotentiary of Holland; judgment, moderation, broad experience, and quiet manner form the principal part of the character of this good man. I do not doubt that with time, considering the line of conduct which he follows and the great similarity between his people and those of this region (many of them came from Holland), he will acquire a larger retinue and greater popularity than the French Party, as they call it. Two young sons, not very prudent, and an able secretary, Mr. Taucker, compose his modest family.

To come back to the city, it should be observed that neither theaters nor houses of assembly have been built yet, this type of diversion being unconstitutional in the Quaker system.[59] This

---

[58] Peter John Van Berckel became Dutch envoy extraordinary to the United States in 1783.

[59] It is true that the Quaker-dominated legislatures had passed laws against the theater, but these were not strictly enforced. Plays were being performed by 1749, although usually just outside the city. In 1766 the first theater in Philadelphia proper was built. It was closed during the Revolution until reopened by the British when they occupied the city. Schoepf also discussed the state of the theater in Philadelphia.

religious persuasion has been predominant in the region despite the fact that every religion and sect is permitted: Quakers, Anabaptists,[60] Church of England, Methodists (their way of singing psalms is extremely pleasant), Presbyterians, Moravians, Lutherans, Catholics, Reformists (a newly composed sect of those Quakers who took up arms in the war and consequently were expelled from their old church), Winchesterites (a recent doctrine, being preached now by its author, Parson Winchester, and consisting substantially of the very humane and rational dogma of universal salvation),[61] etc. All praise God in the language and manner that seem to them best!

At the time of my arrival a short play was presented here in a small theater fashioned for the occasion. Neither were the actors tolerable, nor did the government protect them in any way; rather they had to flee in order not to fall into the hands of the sheriff, who was already pursuing them for the offense. The stratagem was used of every actor's holding a sheaf of papers, which they pretended was the play being presented, in order to evade the literal meaning of the law, considering the performance a reading and not a representation; but here sophisms are of no value, and the safe thing to do was to pack off bag and baggage. The gathering was numerous, which is not strange, as these were perhaps the first dramatic pieces shown in the area. The costume of the actors was the most miserable and indecent I have ever seen.

One circumstance contributed to dividing our attention as spectators. Some boys, by dint of throwing rocks and with the help of a rabble, having forced their way into the pit, we were able to see three scenes at the same time: a comic one upon the stage; a compassive one in the boxes, with the languishing ladies leaning their pale bosoms upon the railing and near-by athletes; and a tragic one in the pit, with whacks and blows administered. The gathering was so large that one could neither leave nor, what was

[60] A group (originating in Switzerland) which opposed infant baptism and advocated separation of church and state.

[61] Elhanan Winchester, an American clergyman, was a Baptist until his unorthodox beliefs cost him his pastorate. He was a successful preacher in England (1787–94) and a pioneer in spreading the Universalist message.

worse, even move. Four hours of being fixed in one place quenched my curiosity concerning the first concourse Philadelphia offered me; furthermore, my feet swelled up so much (as a result, no doubt, of having been on board ship twenty days without taking exercise and also of the cold, which was already beginning) that I had to take two purgatives to recover.

The principal church of the Quakers (there are four or six in the city) is on Market Street near the City Hall. Its architecture is greatly lacking in elegance and ornament. There are benches in all parts for the comfort of the congregation; a small tribunal, or gallery, for the patented preachers (known by the congregation to be pious and instructed men, they have a patent for it and enjoy a certain degree of prominence in this line); a section for the women; and on the walls and pillars some tin-plate candle-holders with wax candles, which give a dark illumination when the night services are celebrated. These are the only ornaments one sees in the interior of the temple: all with neglect, little taste, and not much cleanliness.

I attended the night service, which begins at six o'clock and ends at eight, at one of the Quaker churches. The entire congregation was seated on the benches, their hats on, heads inclined, in the greatest silence. Suddenly the man on my left stands up and in an emphatic tone says, "My spirit says that God shall not always tread upon earth! Because he is in heaven!" Shortly thereafter one of the principal preachers (my neighbor, one supposes, was only a beginner), taking as his text the proverb that says "Think twice and lead once," thrust upon us a sermon lasting more than an hour and a half, in the style of our hebdomadary monks. Another lugubrious and emphatic voice, seemingly that of a woman, recited the Common Prayer; then, all standing up, they shook hands, using the expression "friend," and we all left the church, men and women promiscuously. I noticed that some of the latter also shook the hands of men and called them "friend." I did not observe (although the congregation was large) any of those convulsions or the quaking which are supposed to affect these people in church when they feel moved by the Divine

Spirit; nor did I observe any other ceremony deserving the title of ridiculous. I confess, nevertheless, it seemed strange that people remarkable for their religious spirit, judgment, and personal cleanliness should pay so little attention to the architecture, ornamentation, and cleanliness of the temples!

January, 1784. The diversions of the city were reduced to a dance, or assembly, as they call it, every fifteen days at the City Tavern, in a room that is quite long but narrow. The expenses are paid for by a subscription arranged at the beginning of the winter; the management is given to four persons elected by the subscribers, and they direct everything with order and decency. The ladies, and the strangers arriving in the city, then receive a letter of invitation and are admitted without its costing them anything; not so the inhabitants, because if they are not subscribers, it is presumed they do not care for the diversion and so are not invited. The dance begins at seven o'clock and lasts until two or three in the morning. Those who do not like to dance play cards on tables prepared for that purpose in near-by rooms. Between eleven and twelve the whole gathering ascends to the hall on the second floor, where tea, coffee, and chocolate are served, with biscuits and toast, at different tables. This finished, the dance starts again and lasts as long as one wants. Everyone comes or goes, plays or dances, talks or keeps quiet as he pleases.

The Bentley Concert[62] is also held every fifteen days, and the hall where it takes place is not badly decorated; among the performers the flautist Brown, of middling merit, distinguishes himself. The German Concert[63] is held in the same hall every fifteen days, in alternation with the preceding, but as the performers are almost the same for both concerts, there is little difference between them.

The Minister of France gives balls frequently and is the only person who has a suitable room. For the parties he gave two years ago celebrating the birth of the Dauphin,[64] he built in the garden

[62] The Bentley Concert was established by John Bentley.

[63] Germans were numerous in Pennsylvania and very active musically.

[64] This was the title given the first-born son, hence heir, of the king of France

next to the house a wooden structure, the capacity and proportions of which are combined with middling skill and effect. It holds from three to four hundred people and has an interior gallery, which runs along the four sides of the parallelogram (the shape of the building), where those who are not dancing can stroll, enjoying at the same time the diversion of watching those in the center play cards and dance. This gallery is rather narrow, with the result that couples walking in opposite directions do not have enough room to pass when they meet, making it necessary for them to turn to one side.

(It cannot be denied that the Chevalier behaves at all these functions with dignity and sincerity, appearing at the gatherings as one of many and without subjecting anybody in the least. On the other hand, some ladies observe him carrying the *sans façon*[65] to the extreme, for at times he goes outside to visit his favorites, leaving the entire gathering occupied with dancing and card playing.)

Our Rendón also gives balls in the wintertime. These are not as frequent or brilliant as the foregoing, for the reason that his room is much smaller (it is nevertheless the best and most spacious of all the others in Philadelphia). The garden is without doubt the most pleasant in the city for taking walks and has come to be the resort of the leading people in the afternoons and evenings of the summertime. Several persons of discernment informed me that a function given by Rendón in honor, I believe, of the birth of the Dauphin was the most elegant and enjoyable they had attended in Philadelphia. His conduct and his manner are proper in his circumstances and make him worthy of having had better education and more accomplishments.

Mrs. Robert Morris and Mrs. James Allen are also wont to give nocturnal functions, limited to dancing and card playing, which they call "private parties" and are extremely pleasant. The company is select, the people know each other, and consequently there

from 1349 to 1830. In this case, news of his birth was formally announced to Congress on May 18, 1782.

[65] Without regard to fashion or manners.

is more assurance and satisfaction. At those of Mrs. Allen one notes in addition a certain sincerity and friendliness, inspired by her elegant manner and the graciousness with which she conducts everything at her house, thus elevating the character of her parties and distinguishing them from all the rest.

Mrs. John Penn has a private concert in her home once a week, at which the best musicians in the city gather. The room is small, and, necessarily, the orchestra and company.

These were all the diversions which took place in Philadelphia during my residence there and they indicate sufficiently that its inhabitants love and cultivate society and, also, that the dance is their favorite entertainment. In the home of Mrs. Allen, I have seen mother (Mrs. Lawrence), daughter (Mrs. Allen), and two granddaughters (the Misses Allen) dancing together in the same country-dance, and persons more than fifty years old are regularly seen dancing until daylight with fifteen-year-old girls.

Notwithstanding strangers complain that the people here are diffident and not hospitable, I myself have noticed only a certain reserve and humility at the beginning of their conversation, particularly in the women; this is characteristic of the American system and has its origin, perhaps, in their not being introduced from the first years to the general intercourse of people and in their not frequenting thereafter public gatherings, at which the contrast and variety of manners and customs broaden the outlook and create in us an open, frank, and generous manner—a quality sometimes much more valuable in society than those which stem from wealth and vast knowledge. From this very failing, many individuals are wont to derive advantages in their education, especially women; segregated from the general society of people, they dedicate themselves to reading and cultivating the mind and, if by good fortune they find someone to guide them well, make singular progress. Miss Vining, Mrs. Powell, Miss Sally Shippen, Miss Moore, Miss Molly Coxe, Miss Peggy Chew, and the Quaker Misses, Susan and Rebecca Morris and Isabella Marshall, etc., are incontestable testimonies to this.

These distinguish themselves among the men of letters: Mr.

Rittenhouse, whose advances in astronomy and the orrery machine have made him famous; Dr. Rush, professor of medicine in the college of this city;[66] President Dickinson, author of "Letters from a Farmer in Pennsylvania to the Inhabitants of the British Colonies";[67] the Reverend Dr. Smith, director of Princeton College in New Jersey;[68] John Armstrong, author of two discourses addressed to the American army concerning half-pay and commutation (worthy of Junius);[69] Mr. Gouverneur Morris; the Reverend Dr. White, the best speaker in the pulpit;[70] Mr. Duponceau, former aide-de-camp of Baron von Steuben and secretary in the Department of Foreign Affairs.

The men are almost always immersed in their business affairs and in political intrigue, which inclination, planted and cultivated with the greatest care by France, is stronger here than in any other part of this America.

On the eighth of December, General Washington entered Philadelphia on his way to Congress, which was assembled at Annapolis,[71] in order to effect its submission completely, having already taken possession of New York and disbanded the army.

[66] This was the College of Philadelphia, later the University of Pennsylvania. For Rush, see note 17 above.

[67] John Dickinson's first letter was published in the *Pennsylvania Chronicle* on December 2, 1767. He was elected president of Pennsylvania in 1782.

[68] Dr. Samuel Standhope Smith was the son-in-law of President John Witherspoon and succeeded him, becoming president of Princeton in 1795.

[69] Major John Armstrong, an aide to General Gates, wrote the anonymous "Newburgh Address," which appeared about March 10 and 12, 1783, urging the officers of the army to compel Congress to treat them fairly in regard to back pay. He was secretary of war in 1813–14. "Letters of Junius," author unknown but probably Philip Francis, began appearing in the *Daily Advertiser* in November, 1768, and were bitter attacks on the King and members of the British government.

[70] William White was rector of Christ Church, Philadelphia (1776–1836), and a leader in the organization of the Protestant Episcopal church in the United States, drafting its original constitution and becoming the first Bishop of Pennsylvania (1787).

[71] In June, 1783, disgruntled soldiers marched on Philadelphia and began demonstrations against Congress. President Boudinot changed the meeting place of Congress to Princeton and then scheduled it to meet on November 26 at Annapolis under a plan, adopted October 21, calling for alternate sessions there and at Trenton.

He made his entrance at noon in the company of the following: his two aides-de-camp, Colonel Humphreys[72] and Colonel Benjamin Walker, who came with him from New York; the Minister of France; President Dickinson; Mr. Robert Morris and some other American officials who were in Philadelphia at the time; and a company of cavalry militia, which had gone out for a distance of four or six miles to receive him. Children, men, and women expressed such contentment as if the Redeemer had entered Jerusalem! Such are the excessive fancies and sublime estimation which this fortunate and singular man enjoys in the entire continent, although philosophers are not lacking who examine him in the light of reason and conceive a fairer idea than that which the high and low multitude imagines. It is certainly remarkable that, considering the many illustrious personages in America who through their vigor and talents have accomplished the great and complicated work of this independence, none have either a general approbation or the popularity of this leader (better said, nobody has it but him). Just as the rays of the sun, shining upon the burning glass, concentrate in the focus and produce such an admirable effect in physics, so do the achievements and deeds of so many individuals in America reflect upon the independence and concentrate in Washington! A usurpation as capricious as it is unjust.

The next day I visited the General in the company of Rendón and delivered a letter of recommendation from General Cagigal; in consequence of this I owed him much kindness and had the pleasure of dining in his company the entire time he was in Philadelphia on this occasion. His manner is circumspect, taciturn, and has little expression, but tranquility and great moderation make him tolerable. I was never able to see him set aside these qualities, despite the fact that the wine flowed with humor and merriment after dinner and that, when drinking certain toasts, he would

[72] David Humphreys was also a poet and one of the Hartford Wits. He became minister to Spain (1796–1801), introduced the first merino sheep into the United States (1801), and was recognized as a leader in the manufacture of woolens.

stand up and give his three cheers with the rest of us. It is not easy to form a definite opinion of his character, and so we will suspend judgment for now, until an occasion or time provides better grounds for it.

At the end of December so much snow began to fall that in the city streets and adjacent roads it was more than two feet in thickness. In such circumstances the means of transportation are changed, the wheel being replaced by the "skate." (I call it thus, because the operation of the sledge on snow and ice is none other than that of a person moving about on skates.) In the country, in the city—everywhere—one sees nothing but sledges, and these move with such great speed that at times it seems impossible for the horses to endure it. The machine is entirely of wood and is built very lightly; the feet, which have the exact shape of skates, are lined with a thin plate of iron. If the road is level and beaten by carriages that have passed before, the sledge slides over the snow and the horse pulls hardly any weight at all, for the continuous repetition of small thrusts is sufficient to maintain movement. Two horses (the number commonly used) can pull six or eight people with the greatest ease in the world at the rate of nine to ten miles an hour.

Desirous of trying out this favorite diversion of the region, I resolved to visit my *amiga querida*[73] Miss Polly Vining, who had retired for the Christmas holidays to Wilmington on the Delaware, where she usually resides with her mother and brother, Mr. John Vining[74] (a young man about twenty-four years old who practices law and does not lack mental power and acuteness). The latter, Captain Hoops[75] (officer in the Continental army), Mr. Hamilton (a young English businessman), Cornet Taylor[76] (officer in the Horse Guards of His Britannic Majesty), and I left Philadelphia in two sledges at one o'clock in the afternoon. At two-thirty we arrived at Chester, fourteen and a half

[73] Roughly, "darling" or "darling friend."

[74] John Vining of Delaware was later a member of Congress from that state.

[75] This was probably Robert Hoops of New Jersey.

[76] "Cornet" is an obsolete military title, formerly the fifth grade of commissioned officer in the British army and usually a standard-bearer.

miles away, where we ate very well at the General Washington Inn,[77] and at five o'clock reached Wilmington, twenty-seven miles from Philadelphia. We were all given lodging at the house of Mrs. Vining and were treated with the greatest warmth and generosity possible.

From Philadelphia to Wilmington

to Schuylkill	2
Darby	3½
Chester	9
Wilmington	12½
	27 miles

On the following day there was an assembly dance, and, as strangers, we were all invited. Mr. Taylor, Mr. Brown (an English businessman who was also a visitor at the house of Mrs. Vining), and I accompanied Miss Polly Vining, who out of kindness to us attended this gathering. This was the first diversion of the sort to take place in said town. The settlement being Quaker, there had never been any thought of dancing, but, with the revolution in the government, the customs, like true daughters, manifested the change immediately. The assembly, although small and in a very compact hall, was decent and pleasing, and for the first time I saw Quaker men and women taking part in this type of diversion, even though they themselves did not dance. We had a very good supper of tea, coffee, chocolate, cold tongue, ham, wines, etc. The country-dances and cotillions lasted until three o'clock in the morning, when most people retired. I had the pleasure of meeting there Mr. Beresford, the attorney general; Dr. White, a noted physician and a man of judgment and accomplishments; some officers of lower rank in the American army; and William Geddes, Esq., a man of respect in the town, for whom I brought letters of recommendation from the governor of Charleston, Mr. Guerard. I also had the pleasure of meeting and, later, conversing with Captain of Engineers Mr. Rutherford (in the service of His Britannic Majesty), who had been present at the siege of Gibraltar

[77] This was probably the inn where Washington stayed following the Battle of Brandywine.

from beginning to end. For this reason there developed in both of us curiosity and desire of informing ourselves thoroughly of the various events and circumstances of this famous and extended military spectacle. We exchanged observations, comparing them with care and accuracy, and I can assure you I received singular gratification upon seeing confirmed, by his, my principal ideas relative to this extraordinary siege, especially in the branch of artillery, which appears to be his favorite study and in which he really manifests more accomplishments comparatively. He delayed his trip two or three days for this purpose, and we passed the time in the afore-mentioned talks and visiting and examining the places the British occupied and fortified in the environs of this town when they took possession of the area in consequence of the defeat at Brandywine. He also gave me news of several friends and acquaintances I had left in Gibraltar in 1775–76. (I was there for three months for the purpose of seeing the fortification, its garrison, and the Hanoverian troops, which had arrived to relieve part of the British.) We bound ourselves in good friendship, and he left for Wilmington, North Carolina, where he had a plantation; he had gone to Europe at the beginning of this revolution to continue his education and had remained there in the capacity of officer at the siege of Gibraltar, for which reason his property had not been confiscated.

I also took advantage of the good company and the proximity to see the site of the famous Battle of Brandywine.[78] We mounted our horses after breakfast and, in the company of Mr. Geddes and two American officers who had participated in the action, went to see this place, so exalted, which is about twelve miles away. We arrived at noon and with the greatest care examined all of it, observing especially the positions and movements of both armies. I did not understand why Washington exposed himself to such an obvious danger; nor why General Howe did not cross the river

[78] On September 11, 1777, Washington and twelve thousand troops met eighteen thousand British and Hessian soldiers under Generals Howe and Knyphausen in an effort to halt their march on Philadelphia. The Americans were flanked and suffered a major defeat.

at Chadds Ford[79] and attack him immediately with his entire army; nor why Cornwallis marched ten miles to Trimble's Ford and Jeffery's Ford, having to retrograde some more miles to meet the enemy, leaving all this while the left flank of his army exposed, when by having gone three or four miles he could have executed the same movement; nor why, finally, the American army, completely defeated at eight o'clock in the evening, should be permitted to reunite and form again the next day in Chester, Philadelphia, etc. I certainly did not understand it, nor could I fathom the reasons these *caudillos* advanced. At three o'clock in the afternoon we returned, by another road, which was a bit closer, and at five o'clock arrived in Wilmington.

That night we had our game of comet,[80] in the delightful company of Miss Vining, who entertained us immensely with her never-failing humor and repartee.

Early the next day Mr. Taylor and I prepared for our return to Philadelphia and at eight o'clock mounted our horses, with the intention of stopping for breakfast at the home of Mr. Geddes, who lives on the road to Philadelphia a quarter of a league from the environs of the town; but the cold was so intense (the first time in my life I had been in an agony of this sort) that we had to ride at full speed and, upon arriving at the home of Mr. Geddes, neither had sensitivity in the feet, hands, ears, nose, etc., nor could we dismount (notwithstanding we had been exposed to the air for only about ten minutes).

A good fire and an excellent breakfast soon restored to us our feeling, and we decided not to leave the house while the weather continued so severe. The affability, good conversation, and hospitality of Mr. Geddes made us adopt this plan with all the more pleasure. The weather having been restrained considerably around two o'clock in the afternoon, we resolved to return to Wilmington after dinner, although not on horseback; for just as Sancho,[81]

[79] Chadds Ford was the center of the Battle of Brandywine, occupying the east bank of Brandywine Creek.

[80] Comet is an old game in which sequences are formed and the winner is the person first playing all of his cards.

when he was tossed in a blanket at La Venta, acquired such a grudge he did not even wish to see it afterwards when he happened to pass by there, likewise for us, with the tossing the wind had given us upon our *Rosinantes*![82] So we availed ourselves of the phaeton[83] of Mr. Geddes, which was going to the town for the youngsters, who were in school; well covered with woolen blankets, we ventured forth . . . just like scalded cats!

The next day was also very cold, and we again postponed our journey. The weather having moderated, we started out for the second time, in the phaeton of Mr. Vining and protected by woolen stockings over our boots, thick gloves, heavy baize cloaks, blankets, etc. At seven o'clock that night we arrived in Chester, and I assure you it was with no little satisfaction, because, with the setting of the sun, the cold began to afflict us in such a way that neither of us could hold the reins for more than ten minutes without suffering immense pain in the fingers. Good tea, good supper, good bed, and a robust and not bad-looking servant girl soon repaired these damages. Early in the morning we had our breakfast, served well and with much cleanliness, and then took a walk through the town, which has about eighty small and generally poor houses. Tied up at the wharves were some vessels, which, with the cold, were entangled in a mass of ice covering almost all the surface of the water. Curiosity induced us to walk upon the ice, and thus it was that here for the first time I had the pleasure of observing this phenomenon of nature.

We resumed our journey in the phaeton and, by the same road, still covered with snow, returned to Philadelphia. Shortly before reaching the Schuylkill, we passed the country house of William Hamilton, Esq., located on a very well selected height; it is in very good taste and of sound architecture.[84] At noon we arrived

---

[81] Sancho Panza is the name of the squire in Cervantes' *Don Quixote*.

[82] Rosinante was Don Quixote's horse—very lean, bony, and full of blemishes but highly admired by the owner.

[83] A phaeton is a light, four-wheeled carriage with an open body.

[84] See note 39 above. The house, *Woodlands*, was constructed about 1770 and is still standing. It is one of this country's finest late Georgian Colonial houses revealing the Adams influence.

at the wooden bridge over the Schuylkill and found it broken with the weight of the ice that had formed on the river; only one barge served for passing (through a narrow channel cut in the ice). Because of the innumerable carriages detained there, we left ours, that it might cross in its turn, and went on foot to Philadelphia, where we arrived at one o'clock in the afternoon. The streets were still covered with snow, and the inhabitants were enjoying their favorite diversion of going about or, better said, dashing about in sledges.

The principal products of the region are wheat (in the greatest abundance and of very good quality), corn, barley, hemp, and wood for shipbuilding (although as the country gets closer to the tropics the quality of the wood is heavier and not as solid as in the north); plentiful and good fruit, among which the pippin apple stands out for its taste and delicacy; and equally abundant vegetables. In a word, nothing can be said to be lacking in the Philadelphia market, except for fish, which, although in truth not absent, is scarce and not of the best quality; but the beef and butter are the best I have known in these parts.

The commerce and traffic in the city are considerable and produce so large a number of carriages in the streets that, the latter not being too wide, I should think confusion and vexation would result. This demonstrates at the same time that the internal commerce of the region must be conducted on roads and does not enjoy the convenience and advantage of water transportation.

The population of the state is estimated at 350,000 inhabitants, and that of Philadelphia in particular at 30,000. The most exact calculations made before the recent revolution are as follows:

	Ships	Seamen	Imports from England	Exports to England
Pennsylvania	35	390	£611,000	£705,500

The expenses and disbursements of this province before the revolution were only £4,500, which circumstance indicates the happy government and wise system that alone could produce such admirable and flourishing establishments. The so-called "Civil List" is now as follows:

	Pesos Fuertes
President	4,000
Chief Justice	2,000
Two Puisne[85] Judges (1,500 pesos each)	3,000
Delegates to the Congress; the number varies yearly but ordinarily there are two (from 3 to 6 pesos daily each)	3,650
Senators (10 shillings daily)	495
Total	13,145

The other officials receive their remuneration through their perquisites and fees.

Having seen as much of the buildings, cleanliness, commerce, and government of this city as is offered to public observation, with some scrutiny into the character of the leading inhabitants and persons of consequence, I decided to proceed to New York. To this contributed equally the fact that the Minister of France and especially that ridiculous fool Marbois, as a result of some conversations we had had after dinner and in casual meetings, became alarmed, seeing that their political machinations and entanglements were not concealed from me and that I was now going to reveal, to the conspicuous detriment of their pompous character and influence, the false dogmas they had infused into the generality of people concerning the Jamaica expedition[86] and the shameful conduct of Spain in all the operations of the last war (their favorite doctrine, which with great vigor they try to inculcate in the spirit of the Americans). They began to fabricate a thousand tales and hatch dark plots to find a way to induce me to let them cackle in their hen-houses and continue my trip to

[85] Subordinate.

[86] After the Battle of Yorktown ended the fighting in the United States, the Caribbean became the final battleground of the fleets, with the British islands as the prizes. Jamaica became the unsuccessful object of a Franco-Spanish attack, the "Battle of the Saints," on April 9, 1782. Miranda was emotionally involved in the failure because he had earlier spied out the area for the Spanish.

another part. Rendón, the poor man, was out of his wits, not knowing what to do in such circumstances, but I penetrated the whole mystery, acquainting myself with all its aspects, and informed him of all I understood regarding it and of what he did not know in respect to me, General Cagigal, etc. I proposed the expedient of his writing me a letter in answer to the one I would send him explaining the matter extensively, in order that he might protect himself on both sides. So I abandoned to scorn these Gallo-political rivals, without giving myself the satisfaction of combating them nor them the glory of fleeing, and my friend Rendón avoided a very difficult situation, for which he gave me a thousand thanks. It was this circumstance which in truth was the principal motive inducing me to adopt the plan.

I said good-by then to all my friends and acquaintances, who with tender expressions of friendship and kindness promoted in me the liveliest anxieties or the most agreeable inconsistent feelings of absence!

PART THREE

New Jersey and New York

☆☆☆

NEW JERSEY AND NEW YORK

January 16, 1784. At three-thirty in the morning we left for New York on the so-called "stage." This is a coach which leaves periodically almost every day of the week and in which the passengers enjoy the advantage of promptitude in traveling and the cheapness and convenience of taking their baggage with them; the price from Philadelphia to New York is three pesos fuertes for each passenger and one for each hundredweight of baggage. For these reasons the leading people of the area generally travel in these carriages. Owing to the entire region being covered with snow more than two feet thick and the weather being extraordinarily cold, the stage was fitted with skates rather than wheels, forming a great sledge, covered with a painted canvas for protection. Ten passengers, two coachmen, and twelve hundredweights of baggage—all went on the one sledge, drawn by four horses and traveling nine to ten miles per hour. Had it not been for the excessive cold, which forced us to stop many times at public houses (found at every step on the road) to warm our feet and hands, which were numb and pained us considerably in spite of our wearing two pairs of gloves and baize socks over boots and stockings, we would have completed the journey in very good time. At seven o'clock we arrived, dead with cold, at the town of Bristol, very well situated on the Delaware River, opposite Burlington, the capital of Jersey.[1] Stopping at an excellent inn there, we had a good breakfast and warmed ourselves at the fireplace for about an hour. After breakfast I took a walk through the town in the company of Dr. Craiggie, one of the passengers,

---

[1] Founded by Quakers in 1677, Burlington was one of the two capitals of New Jersey.

who seemed to me a man of merit, moderation, and education. Around nine o'clock we continued our trip. The morning was clear and beautiful, but the cold so intense it did not permit us to put our heads outside the windows of the sledge to see with pleasure the countryside and forced us to halt from time to time in order to warm our feet and hands, which afflicted us terribly.

At ten o'clock we passed over the Delaware, completely frozen over, at the same spot, we were informed, that General Washington crossed it on Christmas Eve of 1776, when he surprised and captured the brigade of Hessians which, under the command of the German Colonel Rall,[2] was quartered in Trenton, garrisoning one of the most important posts of the British army cantonment. At twelve o'clock we arrived at Princeton and were given a very good meal at a tolerable inn. This town is well situated and combines the advantages of being healthful and merry. It has a well-regulated college for the education of youth, the advantages and benefits of which are well known in all this America. Its illustrious president, Dr. Witherspoon, is now in England.[3] There is an orrery[4] here, perfected by the celebrated Rittenhouse, which, although out of order at present, is known to be a work of the greatest ingenuity. After the meal and a walk through the town with my companion Dr. Craiggie, we continued our journey, passing through the towns of Brunswick (situated on the Raritan River) and Woodbridge.

At seven o'clock we arrived in Elizabeth, very happily, because not only did the cold afflict us too much but some of the passengers who had most enjoyed the bottle at mealtime became of such a humor that we could no longer endure them. There was abuse of words to the limit, and we feared they would come to blows at any moment. Finally, a good meal, better company, and comfortable lodging repaired our disgust and weariness. The next day, after breakfast and a walk through the town with the Doctor, I

[2] Johann G. Rall was leader of the Hessian troops mentioned here.

[3] This was the College of New Jersey, later Princeton. John Witherspoon, a Scotch Presbyterian clergyman and signer of the Declaration of Independence, became president in 1768.

[4] A type of planetarium.

continued the journey in the sledge, crossing frozen marshes and rivers. This activity is quite dangerous, for if by chance the ice should break (as very often happens where there are "wind-holes," that is, where the wind has gotten into the ice), it never fails that the horses and what people are in the carriage drown. Therefore the passengers will get on their feet on such occasions and walk behind the sledge, certain that if the larger weight does not break the ice, much less, then, the lesser. Such is, nevertheless, the cold that many, so as not to leave the shelter (and I was one of them), stay inside the sledge; many misfortunes result from this.

At eleven o'clock we arrived at Paulus Hook, on the Jersey shore of the North River. Here there is a very good fortified position, built by the British during the last war, which certainly deserves special attention, as much for its advantageous location as for the good judgment, intelligence, and knowing manner with which its defenses were arranged. It was, nevertheless, surprised and captured by the famous American officer Colonel Lee, who, having taken possession of it and spiked part of its artillery, had to withdraw.[5]

At three o'clock in the afternoon, when the ice floating on the river permitted the passage of the boat, we embarked and in a quarter of an hour were on the opposite shore, having had the felicity of not being dragged by the cakes or masses of floating ice which dashed over the surface of the river. These had caused several misfortunes during the preceding days, sinking, or running aground in dangerous places, vessels that hazarded this navigation. At the direction of Dr. Craggie I took lodging at the private inn of Mrs. Mary Turner on Water Street, paying eight pesos fuertes for myself and three for my servant, weekly.

[5] Paulus Hook, present site of Jersey City, was the location of a fort held by the British during the occupation of New York. On the night of August 18, 1779, Major Henry "Light-Horse Harry" Lee led three hundred men south from the American camp on the Upper Hudson River in a bold attack on the garrison. Crossing the moat at low tide, Lee's men stormed the fort at 3:00 A.M. and captured about one-third of the defenders. He had only two killed and three wounded, and escaped before the British could organize pursuit. For this exploit he was given a gold medal by Congress, his men a cash award.

New Jersey is divided into East and West Jersey; the capital of the former is Amboy, of the latter, Burlington, at both of which the Assembly convenes alternately. The surface and cultivation of the region are so delightful that it is commonly called the Garden of America. In all parts one can see flowing rivulets and springs of crystalline water, directed with an industrious hand through the gentle slopes and hills and beautifying the surface of the land, nourishing the earth, and forming a series of the most delightful vistas in all this region. The ravines are covered with luxuriant woods, preserved with intelligence and care for a thousand very useful purposes. These present to the eyes the most beautiful variety and contrast with the neighboring fields of wheat, hemp, etc., and, at the same time, shelter the prodigious quantity of songbirds which resort to their shade and coolness in the summer and with their melody add no little brightness to this beautiful rural scene.

From Philadelphia to New York	
to Frankford	5
Sign of General Washington	5
Bristol	10
Trenton	10
Princeton	13
Brunswick	17½
Woodbridge	9½
Elizabeth	10
Newark	6
Paulus Hook	8
New York	1
	95 miles

The healthfulness of the region is another of the great riches which New Jersey enjoys. The complexion and robustness of the inhabitants, the large number of children one sees everywhere, and, above all, the population and agriculture of the region (for one can hardly find a corner or ravine where there is not a house) are convincing proofs of the truth of this. At the same time, I can assure you that in all this region (not a small area), I have not encountered an individual who was ill clothed, hungry, sick, or idle. Nor have I seen any other place in which the people in general appear happier and on more of an equality than here.

The land is generally divided into small portions, called farms, with the result that the earth is much better cultivated and the number of houses is much greater. Although the latter are not of sumptuous appearance, as in other regions (Havana and South Carolina, for example), still, they have a rural comfort and are happy.

Among the inhabitants of Jersey are a large number of families of German and Dutch origin, whose ancestral languages and customs one hardly notices any more (only dining at eleven or twelve o'clock in the day is still practiced).[6]

The land is indifferent rather than good and on the coast is extremely poor and sandy. However, as we have already observed, it is irrigated everywhere, is in the hands of an industrious people, and, above all, under the influence of a free government, and these circumstances make it prosper despite all its difficulties. Its principal products are wheat and all other grains, a variety of excellent fruit, vegetables, good lumber, and an abundance of livestock (the cattle are small in size). There are iron and copper mines, which in other times have been worked profitably.[7] Commerce has been carried on, until now, through New York and Philadelphia, for which reason it has not prospered yet. At present the inhabitants think of establishing it in Amboy, accepting thus the counsels the learned Abbé Raynal[8] gives them, and I do not doubt they will accomplish it in a short time.

[6] The Dutch once owned the area, and large numbers of Germans early migrated into the region from Pennsylvania and New York.

[7] Copper was mined extensively near New Brunswick, and the first iron-ore mine was opened in 1676. By the time of the Revolution, forges and furnaces dotted the northern part of New Jersey, supplying much of the nation's iron. The New Jersey furnaces were the mainstay of Washington's army. The German traveler Johann David Schoepf, who visited New Jersey in 1783, has left an extensive account of mining operations in that state.

[8] Guillaume T. F. Raynal edited the four volumes entitled *Histoire philosophique et politique des établissments et du commerce des Européens dans les deux Indies* (1770).

The population of the region is, according to some, 100,000, and according to others, 150,000; the proportional middle is more likely the true number.

A general tolerance forms the foundation of its government in the spiritual branch. Everyone can pray to and glorify God in the form and language his conscience dictates! There is no dominant religion or sect—all are good and equal![9] May the same dogma and liberal principles reign in the political sphere!

The civil expenses of this province under British dominion amounted to twelve hundred pounds sterling, and the present ones, little different, are as follows:

Governor	salary	£550 or 1,466⅔ dollars
	perquisites	400
Chief Justice		350
Other Judges		300 and 250
Treasurer		150
Attorney General		30

There are thirteen counties, which annually choose one counselor and three assemblymen; their wages are two dollars a day (formerly six).

The Governor (at present His Excellency William Livingston, Esq.)[10] is elected annually and can be re-elected indefinitely. (See the memorandum[11] I received from Mr. Rutherford, a landowner in this state and a man of judgment, truthfulness, observation, and accomplishments.)

Tired from the toil of the trip and having formed some acquaintances in New York, I thought I would visit Boston and then return to New York, whence I would embark for England. The harshness of the winter held me suspended for some time and finally made me change this plan. The sound and the rivers

[9] New Jersey was one of four colonies which successfully resisted attempts to establish an official religion. Tolerance, however, did not extend to the Catholics: they numbered only one thousand in 1785.

[10] Member of a prominent New York family, Livingston was a delegate to the Constitutional Convention and governor of New Jersey (1776–90).

[11] This memorandum has not been found.

remained frozen for a long time, obstructing all navigation, and the roads, although covered with snow, became impassable with the frequent thaws—neither sledge nor wheels could attempt them. So I decided to remain here until the weather improved and I moved to better lodging, at Maiden Lane No. 9, the home of Mr. Ellsworth and an excellent private inn, paying seven pesos fuertes weekly (not including fire and liquor) for myself. The servant I had brought from Philadelphia, who was obligated to serve me for two and a half years, escaped a few days after my arrival here. I had bought him for ten guineas in Philadelphia, on board an Irish ship bearing a cargo of more than three hundred male and female slaves. John Dean (his name) was born in Scotland and was about sixteen years old; he seemed to me honest and without mischievousness, but the event proved the contrary.[12]

A trip to Kings Bridge[13] on the island of New York was my first sally into this region. I wished to see the fortifications there and at the same time pay a visit to my friend Colonel Lewis Morris,[14] who, with his wife, was living in a country house named Courtland House, where his parents and family reside. At nine o'clock in the morning I left New York in the phaeton of Mr. D. Parker,[15] who, without there being motive of particular friendship, offered me carriage, servants, and horses in a manner so obliging and sincere that I had to accept them. At eleven I arrived at said fortifications, located upon two heights quite difficult of access; the one on the left, falling to the North River, is called Land Hill, and that on the right, falling to the East River, Laurel

[12] There is an indenture dated Philadelphia, December 19, 1783, between Miranda and John Dean whereby, in consideration of ten pounds paid Captain A. Osborn for Dean's "freight from Ireland," the latter was bound to serve Miranda for two years. Dean was apparently recaptured or returned.

[13] Kings Bridge, now the Marble Hill area, was the site of a toll bridge built in 1693 across the Harlem River. Washington's troops crossed here in their retreat to White Plains after the Battle of Harlem Heights.

[14] Member of a famous New York family and half-brother to Gouverneur Morris. At one time he tried to sell his estate as a site for the national capital.

[15] This was almost certainly Daniel Parker. In 1783 he was appointed a commissioner by Congress to see that no American property was carried off by the British during their evacuation of New York.

Hill.[16] On the former is Fort Washington (later called Knyp-hausen, in honor of the Hanoverian general who took it from the Americans, with a garrison of three thousand men),[17] and on the latter is Fort George, built entirely by the British. The pass through these two small mountains is extremely narrow and is exposed to immense fire from the heights; in addition, it was com-pletely closed by means of trenches, very ably and very wisely built, which run from one fort to the other and rest upon the two rivers already mentioned. The trenches are twelve miles from New York. I could not examine them leisurely because the cold was excessive. Three miles ahead is Kings Bridge.

Traveling two miles past Kings Bridge, a small wooden bridge over the Harlem River, or "Spuyten Duyvil,"[18] as it is commonly called, a small arm of the North River which flows through this cleft, and forms the island of New York, opening communication here with the sound, or East River, as it is called, I arrived at Courtland House, where I found my friend the Colonel, who was immensely pleased to see me (our friendship had been formed in Charleston). I spent the rest of the day very graciously in his company and that of his wife, his sister, and two younger brothers, one an ensign of artillery in the service of America and the other a businessman. The next day I wished to see White Plains,[19] but this was not possible, as much because of the excessive cold oblig-

[16] The Land Hill mentioned here is actually Long Hill, which borders the Hudson River; Laurel Hill is on the Harlem River.

[17] On withdrawing into Westchester, across Kings Bridge, Washington left behind at Fort Washington a garrison under Colonel Robert Magraw. The fort was west of what is now Fort Washington Avenue and about in line with 183rd Street. The battle was fought on November 16, 1776. The fort was surrounded by troops under General William von Knyphausen and General Cornwallis and bombarded by warships on the Hudson. Magraw finally surrendered, losing 54 killed and 2,634 captured.

[18] A Dutch term meaning "in spite of the Devil." Spuyten Duyvil Creek is now a ship canal connecting the Hudson and Harlem rivers. The name derived from the legend of a Dutchman who vowed he would swim it—but the Devil got him!

[19] The area to which Washington and his men retired October 21–26, 1776, after the retreat from Manhattan. A brief skirmish with General Howe took place on the twenty-eighth, but Howe did not press the attack.

ing us to stay by the fireside the entire day as for the three feet of snow which had fallen the night before; by the same token it was impossible to return to New York.

The morning of the next day was clear, and I undertook my return to the city. With great effort, for the roads were not yet beaten and there was still much snow, I reached a tavern in the vicinity of the afore-mentioned fortifications; here I drank a glass of wine and, while the horses were being fed, decided to examine slowly all these works with the help of a hunter I encountered there, an inhabitant of the vicinity who knew all the ground (he had been taken prisoner in the attack on Fort Washington, the sixteenth of November, 1776). With considerable difficulty we began to climb the mountain, at times burying ourselves in the snow up to our necks, but, in about two hours, we visited all of it. Fort Washington is a small pentagon with five bulwarks and a solid storehouse for the powder, but without water or moat; it can maintain a garrison of three hundred men for its defense. Its location dominates all the neighboring heights, and the view it commands in all directions is one of the most delightful and extensive that can be imagined. Fort George is a very well built parallelogram with four bulwarks, solid storehouse, barracks, and cistern; it can easily shelter a garrison of four hundred men. Not only this fort, but the redoubts, trenches, etc., built here by the British manifest the discernment, firmness, and good judgment this ingenious and wise nation reveals in all its works; it seems Colonel of Engineers Montrosel is their author, together with Captain of Engineers Fryers.

This military inspection concluded, we descended, frozen, to the tavern, where I warmed myself internally and externally with a glass of wine and a good fire, and then continued my journey to New York. All the ground from these fortifications to New York is highly defendable; at McGowan Pass,[20] about three miles away, the difficulty increases and a small number of well-led troops can

[20] McGown's Pass (*sic*) saw the retreat of the Colonial army on September 15, 1776. It was subsequently occupied by the British, who built breastworks along the northern ridge. They evacuated the pass on November 21, 1783.

detain the largest army (the defenders being masters of the waters, it is understood).

February, 1784. A few days later, the weather clearing up a little more (although the cold each time more oppressive and the sound and rivers frozen), I resolved to make another foray upon Long Island. At noon I boarded the ferry in the company of Jack McEvers, a youth about eighteen years old, who with the greatest civility had offered to accompany me. After watching for a favorable occasion to cross the sound through a great quantity of floating ice, we went over in less than a quarter of an hour, without mishap, to Brooklyn, a small town located on the opposite shore of Long Island, having about 150 small houses, mostly of poor people. There we ate at the leading tavern, which is quite good, and took a sledge to continue the foray, for the whole countryside and the roads were covered with at least two and a half feet of snow. At two o'clock we left Brooklyn, passing through Bedford, another small town four miles farther on the Jamaica Road, and at three-thirty stopped at the Half Way House[21] two miles ahead to warm ourselves a bit, for already our feet, hands, ears, noses, etc., were almost frozen.

Feeling somewhat restored after drinking a glass of wine, we went on, dashing like a thunderbolt, and at five o'clock arrived in Jamaica at the home of Mr. Charles McEvers, uncle of my young companion, who received us with the greatest kindness and hospitality. With him were his three young daughters, fourteen to eighteen years old, very good looking, and passably educated; two young sons; and a brother-in-law, Captain Bibby, officer in the British service who was aide-de-camp to General Fraser[22] at the Battle of Saratoga and whose wife had died lying in a few months before. The girls are Miss Mary, Miss Nancy, and Miss

[21] Half Way House stood, until 1902, at the corner of Atlantic and Alabama avenues in Brooklyn. It was owned by a man named Howard who was forced to serve Howe's army as a guide through Jamaica Pass, allowing the British to get behind the Americans, prior to the Battle of Long Island.

[22] General Simon Fraser was a Scottish soldier who accompanied Burgoyne and was mortally wounded at Bemis Heights.

Eliza; they are of the loveliest disposition and of particular application to letters, especially Miss Nancy. In the company of this pleasant group, we spent the evening very well entertained. At ten o'clock the next morning the entire group sallied forth in two sledges (except the ladies, as it was too cold) to see Hempstead Plain, about six miles from Jamaica. The ground was covered with snow, and I can assure you that when I extended my vision upon this plain, it seemed to me a great lake, for in many places it forms the horizon and its surface appears as level as that of the sea; it is said to be twenty miles long and more than seven wide. We proceeded four miles farther to visit two leading families, one the wife and sons of Colonel Ludlow, the other the wife and daughter of Judge Ludlow, in a handsome and very pleasant country house, where they fully enjoy the peaceful country life.[23]

Three or four miles farther is Success Hill, at the summit of which is a small lake (Success Pond). The latter is always filled with water, contains much fish, and has extraordinary depth. From this hillock there is the most pleasing view; in one glance one sees the sound, the ocean, and the lands of Connecticut.

At three o'clock we returned to Jamaica and spent the rest of the day sociably at the side of a good fire, in military and literary conversation. After breakfast the next day, Mr. McEvers and I took the sledge and ventured forth again, this time to Rockaway, twelve miles from Jamaica, in the southern part of the island. The roads are extremely level and also pleasant, for everywhere one sees agriculture, habitations, waters, and small forests. At three o'clock we were on our way back, having traveled more than thirty miles in two hours and a half without tiring the horses in the least.

The next day I returned to New York, for the extreme cold did not permit many excursions through the countryside and, in truth, made me long for the shelter of my comfortable lodging in

---

[23] Colonel Gabriel Ludlow was in the Third Battalion of DeLancey's Brigade. Judge George Duncan Ludlow, member of a wealthy merchant family, was appointed to the Supreme Court of New York in 1769. Believed to be Loyalists, both were attainted and their estates ordered confiscated.

the city. After breakfast, while the sledges were being prepared for the trip, Captain Bibby and I visited some encampments, built by the British troops which had been garrisoned in this area, about a mile from the town on the slopes of near-by hills. The huts are still there, built with the greatest skill; the chimney is of loose rock, without any kind of mortar, and the rest is of some kind of wood and palm. So well protected are they that they can withstand the harshest winter, perhaps better than the houses in the city, and each can hold forty to fifty men, and if necessary, one company.

At twelve o'clock we started out in our carriages, accompanied by my young comrade, Jack McEvers, our generous host, old McEvers, and one of his sons. Two hours later we reached the neighborhood of Brooklyn, where we stopped to inspect the fortifications built by the British for the purpose of holding onto that position (even if the enemy made himself master of the rest of the island). The ground being very elevated and directly opposite New York, they could force the enemy to abandon said city as long as they controlled this position. New Fort, the principal fortification, is a very well constructed parallelogram with four bulwarks, spacious moat, solid storehouse, well water, and barracks; it can very easily shelter a garrison of 1,600 men. Two or three more positions, built with equal judgment and intelligence, serve as outposts. Likewise one can see there the lines and remains of the American entrenchments, which the British wanted to attack in 1776. In the night, Washington withdrew with his entire army to New York on the ferry, leaving the British completely deceived and certainly averting an irremediable fall. Here also are the Heights of Guana, where, two days before, the British completely defeated and captured the American Generals Sullivan, Lord Stirling, and Odell, who on the orders of Putnam[24] fought tenaciously, on the twenty-seventh of August, with 6,600 men against the 22,000 commanded by General Howe.[25] At three

24 Israel Putnam was in chief command at New York before Washington's arrival and during the defeat in the Battle of Long Island.
25 These were John Sullivan of New Hampshire; William Alexander of New

o'clock we boarded the ferry and, availing ourselves of a fair moment on the East River to avoid the floating ice, made the crossing in a quarter of an hour.

Long Island is considered by New Yorkers the Hesperia[26] of America, and one cannot deny that the surface of the region, its roads, waters, cultivation, forests, etc., give it the appearance of a delightful garden in the summertime. The quality of the land, its products, etc., are very similar to those of Jersey. (The memorandum I received from Colonel William Floyd[27] and Mr. Gilston, persons of education and unquestionable veracity, is proof of this.) The island is about 140 miles long and 9 to 15 wide. Its fruits are very good, and among them stand out the Newton pippin apple, considered superior to every fruit of its kind in the world. Its population, I am assured, comes to 30,000 persons, and it contains 90,000 head of cattle and 100,000 sheep.

On the twentieth of February I set out on another foray, this one to West Point, with the intention of seeing this celebrated place and the neighboring areas, scenes of military actions in the recent war.[28] At two o'clock in the afternoon, provided with letters of recommendation given me by Governor Clinton, my friend Colonel Hamilton, General McDougall, Mr. Parker, etc.,

York, who assumed the title "Lord Stirling" without authority; and Jacob Odell. Sir William Howe had become commander in chief of the British forces in 1775. The three American generals were captured in 1776 in what is commonly known as the Battle of Long Island.

26 Hesperia, or "the western land," was the name given to Italy by the Greek poets and, sometimes, to Spain by the Romans.

27 Floyd was a member of the Continental Congress, signer of the Declaration of Independence, and member of the House of Representatives (1789–91).

28 The Hudson River figured strongly in military planning because it was the natural invasion route south from Canada. West Point was one of four places in the Hudson Highlands which were fortified during the Revolution. Between 1778, after Sir Henry Clinton had retreated to New York, and 1780, Fort Putnam, Fort Arnold (later Fort Clinton) and a number of redoubts were built. A great wrought-iron chain, with a protecting log boom, was stretched across the river at this point to block the passage of British ships. After the failure of Benedict Arnold's plan to hand West Point over to the British in 1780, the area was never threatened. In March, 1802, it became the home of the United States Military Academy.

I started out in my sledge, accompanied by Cornet Taylor.[29] At three o'clock we reached the country house of Colonel Robert Morris, ten miles from New York, one of the handsomest and most pleasing of its type that I have seen in America, as much for its location as for the neatness and taste with which it was built.[30] Two miles farther are Land Hill and Laurel Hill, where we stopped and climbed up to Fort Washington, situated on the former, where I had the pleasure of viewing again the famous British lines I have mentioned. Three miles ahead we crossed Kings Bridge, and traveling another mile, we arrived at Courtland House, where we were very well received and were lodged for the night by the wife of the General and her two younger sons.

Early in the morning we sallied forth and, covering the distance of fourteen miles over extremely broken and hilly ground, reached White Plains,[31] where we had breakfast in a small tavern, the only house remaining there, and then proceeded to visit the posts and positions of the American and British armies that operated on said ground in September, 1776. Still there are the remains of the batteries and trenches which protected the American army of twenty thousand when General Howe wished to attack it with a force of twenty-two thousand. On the right is Chatterton Hill, where the American General McDougall was attacked and defeated by a superior British force, forcing him to withdraw behind the lines, and one and one-half miles farther on are the mountains of North Castle, through the slopes and ravines of which flows the small Bronx River. Here the American army took up its second position, and one can still see the remains of the trenches which covered it. Considering all the circumstances, the first posi-

---

[29] George Clinton was governor of New York from 1777 to 1795 and from 1801 to 1804; Alexander Hamilton was Washington's aide and became a close friend of Miranda; Alexander McDougall took command at West Point after Arnold's treason; Mr. Parker was probably Daniel Parker (see note 15 above); Taylor was a British officer and Miranda's fellow traveler (see note 76 of Part Two).

[30] This is possibly the house now known as the Jumel Mansion, between 160th and 162nd streets.

[31] See note 19 above.

tion of the American army was extremely weak, and the British should have defeated it before or during its attempt to change position; but this is not the first opportunity that escapes General Howe nor the first accident which, through his fault, saves Washington and the American army from absolute ruin. The second position was advantageous and judiciously occupied, and an attack then would, perhaps, have been imprudent on the part of the British.

Four miles farther is another small river, the Sawmill, over which there is a wooden bridge, and one mile farther the small town of Tarrytown, on the North River. On the highway near Tarrytown is a large tree marking the spot where Major André[32] was arrested by three young, rustic militiamen, an incident that produced so much clatter afterwards. From here they took him to New Salem, ten miles distant, and thence to West Point, ten miles farther on. Nine miles from Tarrytown is New Bridge, a well-built wooden structure over the Croton River, the waters of which are quite abundant. Here we ate middlingly in a rural tavern and, following our route on a road that is everywhere broken, hilly, and covered with rocks, at sunset reached Peekskill, a village of some twenty or thirty small houses on the North River ten miles farther on. Here we came upon a mediocre tavern and a most comical scene between a squire of the locality, a justice of the peace, and a drunk who thrust himself into the tavern and insulted them in a thousand ways. Nobody dared to restrain or throw him out, notwithstanding said insulted personages comprised the police of the town and manifested a desire to do so.

The next day we continued our journey over the ice of the North River, the surface of which had the appearance of a very polished and handsome lamina. The ice must have been two feet thick, and the snow on top of this one and a half feet; we did not have the least misgiving about danger, for, although it has broken

---

[32] Major John André was appointed by General Clinton to negotiate with Benedict Arnold for the betrayal of West Point to the British. He was captured by Americans while returning to New York City in civilian clothes, with the negotiation papers in his boots, and was hanged as a spy.

many times in those places where the wind introduces itself between the surface of the water and the mass of ice, the way was already so beaten with the multitude of sledges which came and went on the river that there was no basis for the least care. I assure you ingenuously that this entire spectacle seemed to me one of the strangest one can see in nature. Both shores of the river are extremely elevated and the surface of its waters quite extensive, so that to look at the height of the mountains when one is traveling on the river, or, on the other hand, to observe from the heights the carriages on the ice, is a magnificent and extraordinary scene: the objects look so small in the midst of these majestic strokes of nature that the sledge and horses seemed to me the plaything of a child drawn by a pair of lap dogs.

At ten o'clock in the morning we arrived at West Point and directed our steps to the tavern there, without anybody investigating or caring to know who the newly arrived strangers were—one of the most pleasant circumstances enjoyed in a free country. How many formalities would have been necessary in France, Germany, etc., before we would have been permitted to enter said post! At eleven o'clock, after a second breakfast, Mr. Taylor and I went to visit the commander of the post, to whom we presented our credentials and who received us with the greatest hospitality and attention, obliging us to take lodging in his own house. The day was serene and the cold somewhat tempered, and, taking advantage of the occasion, we immediately went about our military visit, starting with the magazines of arms, munitions, etc. In these are kept some twenty thousand infantry muskets of French make (with their bayonets and leather straps), artillery munitions, partisans, sabers, etc., not in the best state of cleanliness, arrangement, or neatness. There I also saw the painted model of the medal of the Society of the Cincinnati.[33] But what is truly worthy of admiration and examination is the famous chain[34] that served to cut off entirely the navigation of said river, which it crossed from Fort Clinton to Constitution Island, which

---

[33] A fraternal organization of Revolutionary officers; see note 74 of Part One.
[34] See note 28 above.

reduces the width of the river here, forcing one to pass through a channel seventy fathoms deep and little more than half a mile wide. The links of this chain are of ordinary shape, but of a thickness so considerable that I do not know how they were able to keep it over the water. Joined to the iron at intervals were thick beams, serving to support it; so that the tide, in rising and falling, should not make much impression on the beams and break the chain, the greatest care was taken that they should be so placed as to present their points to the current. By means of these and four sturdy capstans fixed on both banks, the chain was kept taut over the surface of the water; it is said some grapnels also helped to support it, but I do not conceive their utility for that purpose, with a bottom so deep. It cannot be denied that this machine is an exertion of the genius, industry, and bold spirit of the people who produced it! Its cost is said to mount to seventy thousand pounds, and had the King of Spain paid for it, doubtlessly it would have been more; but I do not think it cost them the tenth part of this sum.

From here we went to the main fortification, Fort Clinton (named after the colonel who commenced its construction), situated opposite Constitution Island in an elevated spot which completely dominates the channel of said river and the near-by grazing batteries erected for the protection of the chain. Its enclosure is compact more than anything else, and its construction and design are of common merit. The American General Duportail,[35] a former captain of engineers in France who transferred to the Continental service at the beginning of the revolution, is the author of this work. Deposited there is an artillery train of 160 pieces of all calibers with munition cars, limbers, etc., the major part of which was taken from the English at Saratoga and Yorktown. (At the suggestion of General Knox,[36] they have put an inscription on every piece taken from the enemy so that one can

[35] The Chevalier Louis le Bèque Duportail was a French engineer who became an American major general in November, 1781.

[36] Henry Knox organized the American artillery service. He was commander at West Point in 1782 and secretary of war from 1785 to 1794.

read the spot or area where it was taken, thus creating more monu-
ments to their glorious triumphs—without any cost whatever.)
Among them also are four small pieces of ancient manufacture,
their caliber about four, which, together with two old naval mortars, comprised the entire artillery train with which the American
army began contesting the independence of this continent; the
people of Boston removed them from that city covered in hay-
carts.

From here we ascended the near-by mountain which commands
Fort Clinton and the plain in which are located the main buildings, that is, the quarters, the house of the commander, store-
houses, etc.; there I saw Fort Putnam (also takes its name from
the colonel who began its construction), which follows Fort
Clinton in solidity and strength, although it is much smaller, and is
the work of the American General Kosciusko,[37] a Pole by birth,
who came to this continent at the time of the revolution. A series
of mountains which mutually dominate each other make these
positions seem very precarious defenses, to which one adds that
the productions of art in fortifying them are neither ingenious nor
of much soundness. Imperfections in this fort were still being
corrected when the war ended, and one sees a million yet to be
corrected. If any one of the surrounding forts deserves the name
of key to the position, it is this; but in my best judgment it is the
first step for withdrawing consecutively without much difficulty,
unless an effective army oppose it. Forts Wyllys and Webb
(which also take their names from the officers who started to
build them) are nothing but redoubts, dominated successively
by some other one or by a near-by height.

Having finished the visit of all these positions, we retired,
around three o'clock to the house of the commander, Colonel
Hull,[38] who gave us a good meal. In the evening we enjoyed the

[37] Thaddeus Kosciusko was appointed colonel of engineers in the Continental
army on October 18, 1776. He was in charge of fortification construction at
West Point during 1778–80 and became a brigadier general on October 13, 1783.

[38] William Hull had a distinguished career, serving with Mad Anthony
Wayne at Stony Point. Near the end of the war, Hull was made inspector general
of the army for the West Point area. Washington appointed him lieutenant

company of the ladies of the garrison, who, because of the novelty of foreigners, came to have tea with Mrs. Hull.

The next day, after breakfast, we resumed our military visit, in the company of the larger part of the officers of the garrison, who heartily wished to join us, and, ascending the mountain with no little difficulty and toil, for it is quite high and perpendicular and was covered with snow and ice, we reached Points No. 1, 2, 3, and 4, in a circumference of five miles around the entire post. These are still more redoubts, the ramparts of which can barely support light artillery. A series of commanding grounds surrounding this post have produced such a number of weak advance works that the higher parts, which ought to be the strongest, are the weakest.

Our visit this day ended at a wooden blockhouse on the river, very well built and the most advanced work in that part, and at three-thirty, not a little tired, we reached the lodging of Major of Artillery Doughty,[39] who gave us a very good meal. In the evening we drank tea and had supper at the house of the artillery commander, Major Bauman,[40] who likewise treated us very well.

Early the next day we crossed the river in a sledge and visited the fortifications on Constitution Island, which consist of three strong redoubts (very well built and located in dominant places) protecting the great chain and the passage of the river in that spot. We made an observation there: cutting the ice in the middle of the channel, we found it to be two and a half feet thick. We crossed the river to the location called the Ferry and, ascending a mountain extremely high and difficult of access, visited North and South Forts, medium redoubts located in very dominant places; from them an immense prospectus over vast lands and the North River is revealed. Both fortifications are the work of the engineer Duportail and in my opinion could not serve for much more than discovering the approach of the enemy.

colonel of an infantry regiment, and he was stationed there during the winter of 1783–84, but was second in command.

[39] John Doughty was the commander of one of two companies of artillery sent from West Point to occupy New York in 1783.

[40] Sebastian Bauman was the commander of the artillery on the occasion mentioned in the previous note.

At the foot of these heights and two miles from West Point is the house of General McDougall (formerly of Colonel Robinson), and here we alighted at three o'clock. His son the Colonel, at the time the only one there, gave us a very good meal; certainly the best apples I have ever tasted, I ate there that day (called pippins, and those of this area are very special). In said house General Arnold and his wife were living when he escaped, his ignominious treachery having been discovered through the capture of Major André. When darkness came, the entire retinue returned to West Point, where the other subaltern officers honored us with a very decent meal.

West Point is the most advantageous position that could be selected to cut off the navigation of the river, because, in addition to the narrowness of the latter at that spot, the turn it makes forces every vessel to shift sails and consequently reduce its speed, at which time the obstacles and batteries already mentioned can destroy it very easily. An attack upon the post by land would have been of more probable success, but, as the army always maintained such a position as to be capable of coming to its aid in case of necessity, this was not possible either. The location is extremely romantic and majestic in the higher parts. Butter Hill, contiguous to it, rises twelve hundred feet above the surface of the river. One also sees from West Point the Catskill Mountains, the highest in this part of the continent.

Among the ingenious things I noticed here among the artillery were two cannons, of about eighteen, from which the English had removed the trunnions,[41] as they commonly did with heavy artillery taken from the Americans; the latter fitted both out, putting on one supposititious trunnions by means of a large iron ring introduced through the mouth and made fast in the corresponding place with its trunnions joined, and inserting the other halfway in a block of wood and then placing it upon a gun-carriage, where it performed its service like all the others. How much the human spirit and industry can discover when necessity requires it!

[41] Trunnions are the projecting pivots used to swivel or turn a cannon.

Early on the twenty-sixth, after a light breakfast, we started out on our return to New York by way of Jersey, with the intention of seeing the Passaic cascade. The officers of the garrison were so civil and courteous as to accompany us, out of respect, as far as Stony Point. Colonel Hull, Mr. Pierce (the paymaster general),[42] Major Gibbs,[43] Major Doughty, Mr. Taylor, and I accommodated ourselves very well in two sledges and went down the river over the ice, like lightning. Five miles from West Point, on the west bank, are the ruins of Fort Montgomery and on the opposite bank, the extremity called Anthonys Nose, upon which had been fixed a chain in order to cut off the navigation of the river, protected by said fort, the loss of which resulted in the Americans' forming the idea of fortifying and establishing West Point.[44]

Continuing our Laplandish route over the ice, we arrived at Verplancks Point, seven miles farther down, where we went on land. Going about two miles, we reached Kings Ferry,[45] opposite Stony Point, where there is a redoubt, capacious and very well built (perhaps the best I have ever seen of its kind), called Lafayette. Also in this vicinity is the encampment the American and French armies occupied in 1782 upon their withdrawal from Virginia, after the capture of Cornwallis, etc.

I will not forget to record an anecdote which took place here,

[42] John Pierce of Connecticut was appointed paymaster general in January, 1781.

[43] Caleb Gibbs of Massachusetts was in Jackson's Continental (or First American) Regiment.

[44] Fort Montgomery, with Fort Clinton a mile south and Fort Independence across the river in the shadow of Anthonys Nose, guarded the highland passes, while the afore-mentioned chain stopped traffic on the river. These forts, undermanned because of the demand for troops to fight Burgoyne, were attacked in October, 1777, by the British fleet under Sir Henry Clinton. The defenders were forced to flee; the chain was cut and the British continued up the Hudson to Kingston, but upon learning of Burgoyne's surrender, they returned to New York Harbor.

[45] During the Revolution, Stony Point and Verplancks Point were connected by Kings Ferry, the main water link in the east-west military line of communication between New England and the Middle Atlantic states. This ferry moved Washington's troops to Trenton and later to the decisive Battle of Yorktown.

worthy of immortality. A farmer, owner of the land near Crown Point on which the French had their encampment, made his application to them for the rent. The officers paid no attention to the pretension and did not even give a satisfactory answer; seeing this, the republican rustic withdrew from the scene and went in search of the sheriff. And see you here these two poor peasants coming without a single weapon in their hands, but rather with the palladium and authority of the law, determined with heroic firmness to arrest the French General M. de Rochambeau[46] in front of his entire army for the damages and rent. The General was effectively detained by the sheriff and instantly paid the amount owed to the poor rustic (some ten or fifteen pesos was the entire sum), with which the proceeding ended. How is it possible that under similar protections the most arid and barren countries would not flourish? And that the most pusillanimous and abject men would not within a short time be honest, just, industrious, wise, and brave?

From Kings Ferry we crossed the river over the ice, with no slight misgiving, for in some places the water penetrated and the ice was known to be quite thin, but comforting us were a good guide we had in front and a stick in the hand to support ourselves should our feet open a large hole. So we all crossed on foot, sending before us the sledge and horses for greater safety. The river in this spot is something more than a mile wide. In a poor tavern there we found some fresh fish (just caught in the river through a hole made for this purpose in the ice), from which we asked them to prepare us something to eat while we visited the place.

Stony Point is on the west bank of the North River, exactly in front of Fort Lafayette, and is by its shape and location one of the most advantageous positions for fortification that nature has formed.[47] It completely commands what ground there is within

[46] Jean Baptiste Donatien de Vimeur, Comte de Rochambeau, commanded the French force sent in 1780 to aid the Americans. He joined Washington's army at White Plains in July, 1781; later became a marshal of France.

[47] Stony Point is a rocky bluff that projects into the Hudson. Held by the British, it was stormed and captured by twelve hundred Continentals under General Wayne on July 6, 1779, in one of the most daring raids of the war.

the reach of cannon and by its configuration naturally flanks all the avenues by which it can be attacked. So with very little help from art one can erect there the strongest fortification that can be imagined. At present there is only a small fort of earth and wood there, which was what the Americans reduced it to after having taken it and ruined its fortifications; but one still sees very distinctly the lines, moats, etc., of these as they were built by the British, and I assure you ingenuously that, having examined them well and meditated upon the matter, I cannot conceive how the operation of the capture was effected, and with such little cost. The garrison consisted of eight hundred well-regulated troops, a number sufficient for its defense. We should not resort to the subterfuge of saying they were taken by surprise, knowing that the advance posts gave the alarm in time and fired upon the attacking American parties. The strength of the latter amounted in all to twelve hundred men, selected and led by General Wayne. The orders were for no one to load his musket and to kill the first who should retrograde, for the idea was to attack and assault it with the bayonet alone. One soldier insisted on loading in spite of the foregoing orders, and the officer present killed him instantly with his spontoon,[48] which example, severe and very worthy of praise, contained disorder and gave success to the enterprise.

The losses were sixty dead and forty wounded on the part of the British, thirty dead and seventy wounded for the Americans. I obtained the details of the entire action on the very ground from Colonel Hull, who attended it in person and possesses, in addition to the qualities of a military man and good soldier, considerable education, judgment, and veracity. These circumstances leave me in no doubt that this was one of the most brilliant feats of its kind one can find in military history. Our military investigation completed, we returned to the tavern, where we found the meal we had ordered already prepared, with the addition of potatoes, good butter, and abundant cider. Our appetites were well disposed and so we ate grandly, in the country style. Soon afterward we took to the road, for it was already two o'clock. Our friends and com-

[48] A short pike formerly carried by subordinate officers of infantry.

panions recrossed the river, to take their sledge (which had remained in Fort Lafayette) and return to West Point; Mr. Taylor and I took ours and continued our journey to Passaic Falls.

About two miles farther on, near the riverbank, is the house of Mr. Smith,[49] where Major André stopped off and held his first conference with General Arnold; it is quite capacious, new, and of good architecture. Three miles farther on we found the small town of Haverstraw, situated exactly on the bank of the North River, where we noticed an enormous quantity of firewood; this was to be sent to New York whenever the ice should desist and permit the navigation of the river, because so great a shortage was being experienced there that a cartload of firewood was worth twenty or thirty pesos. We continued seven miles to Clarkstown, which has about fifteen houses in its vicinity; here we stopped to give food to the horses and warm ourselves a bit, for the cold pressed upon us like a demon. As darkness came, having traveled seven miles farther, we reached Orangetown (some call it Tappan, from the name of the district), the inhabitants of which are contained in sixteen houses. We spent the night in a Dutch inn there.

Here one can see the position where the American army was encamped in 1781 when the unfortunate André was hanged. I have seen the room where he was imprisoned, people who gave him assistance, and the site of the execution. His body was buried at the foot of the gallows, and his sepulcher remains there, with two ordinary flat stones without inscription or mark indicating the least remembrance of his fame. I do not doubt, having examined the matter thoroughly and gathered the most authentic information, that the plan of the project which led him to the mentioned punishment was his production entirely, based on the intimate friendship he had formed in Philadelphia with Mrs. Arnold (then Miss Shippen), which channel seemed to him, and without doubt was, the most suitable for managing the conspiracy. The result revealed very clearly that he did not lack ability for closet machination and intrigue, but at the same time lets us know

[49] This was Joshua Hett Smith.

he was not the man for its execution, for he did not have that presence of mind which is indispensable for handling critical moments. The way Arnold played his role (that is, knowing through a letter that André had been arrested, he escaped, without the loss of a moment, from the midst of all his enemies, over a million hazards) forms a quite singular and characteristic contrast of the temper and spirit of both men.

At eight o'clock, having breakfasted, we continued our route over a very pleasant road on the edges of the Second River; these stretches are the best populated and most delicious in this part of the globe. Ten miles ahead we came to Paramus, of the same population as the preceding town, and continuing seven miles on an equally pleasant road we arrived at the small town of Footway Bridge, named after a bridge there over the Passaic River. Here we stopped at a middling tavern and, allowing for time in which the horses might have something to eat in preparation for our trip to the cataract, my companion and I visited a no less curious phenomenon: "The Child With The Big Head," whose name is Peter Van Weetle. His body and limbs correspond to a boy six years old, but the head is so monstrous it seems to be that of a giant; doubtless it is about as large as three heads of ordinary men, and the greater enormousness is in the upper part.[50] His complexion is very white, and he has golden hair, blue eyes, and delicate appearance; the beard is full, and he has never permitted himself to be shaved (a servant girl cuts it with scissors). From being always recumbent, for he cannot support himself in any other way, the right side of the face is disfigured. When he was born, his family informed me, he showed no such imperfection, although the bone was open from the right eyebrow to the brain; but in a few days it was already noticed that the head was growing excessively, and thus it continued growing until he was ten years old, when nature, it seems, finished its work. At the time I saw him, he was twenty-eight years old and had never had serious ill-

50 The man undoubtedly suffered from hydrocephalus. In congenital cases the ventricles of the brain are greatly dilated by an excessive amount of cerebro-spinal fluid; the skull is thin and usually much enlarged.

ness. He eats and drinks everything grandly, without being subject to indigestion, notwithstanding he never ceases lying in his cradle, for it is impossible for him to move or support the head with his body. He enjoys good humor, seems to be of a peaceful and happy nature, likes foreigners to visit him, and converses with considerable rationality. He told me he knew people and had friends in almost all the countries of Europe except Spain, for which reason he was all the more pleased to know me; also, that his trips upon the earth had only reached two miles (in a change of home his family made), but that those below would perhaps be of greater extension! He appears to be completely resigned to his fate, which is certainly a remarkable thing!

From there we went to see the falls, half a mile up from the bridge. The water falls a distance of about sixty-five feet, and the width of the river in that spot is about eighty varas.[51] There is also a cavern there, called "The Chimney" because of its shape. There is no doubt that the cascade is quite high, wide, and worth seeing, but it has absolutely no prospectus, for it falls into a narrow crevice which the rock forms. So it cannot be seen from the front nor horizontally; when you examine it from above, you have almost a right angle, and if you go to the other side of the river to take a horizontal point, the angle is extremely sharp. Therefore, the idea the imagination presents pleases more than that which the sight procures. This inspection concluded, we returned to the town to eat, and at two o'clock in the afternoon set out again for New York. After seven miles of very good and pleasant road, we came to the small town of Aquackanonk; six miles farther on, a marshy ground called Schuyler Swamp, which produces cedar, a proper wood for the construction of ships, etc.; four miles farther, the town of Bergen, which contains about eighty houses. Continuing two miles, around five o'clock we arrived at Paulus Hook. At the ferry house here, I met the most insolent and knavish innkeeper I have known in all America or, better said, the only one. Although I had arrived with enough time to board the boat

[51] A Spanish and Portuguese unit of measurement. It is of variable length but is usually about thirty-three inches.

and proceed to New York to sleep there, as was my plan, on account of something, I do not know what, he overheard my servant saying as to the passage of the horses, he signaled the boat to leave while I was in the act of paying my fare in the ferry house, and left me there that night in order to extract from me the charges of the inn in the morning. I do not know in truth how I had the patience to endure this great cheat![52]

As I have already mentioned, the entire region of Jersey is highly cultivated, very well populated, and through its condition and amenity, taken all together, is one of the most delightful lands my eyes have seen.

26. We glanced at the famous position which the gallant Colonel Lee (an American officer who was then twenty-four years old) attacked with four hundred men, surprising the British garrison of two hundred regulars, spiking the artillery, taking several prisoners, and withdrawing with all success.[53]

[Here occurs a gap in the diary.]

May 28, 1784. At five-thirty in the afternoon, I set sail from Albany Pier, New York, on the sloop *Schuyler*, Captain Willet, for Albany. The passengers were two Frenchmen, three American men, and two American women of fairly good manners and not unsociable. With a lazy wind from the south we went up the North River and passed several delightful and very well situated country houses, outstanding among them those of Mr. Lespenard, Mr. Montier, Mr. Eliot, Mr. W. Bayard, Mr. Oliver DeLancey, etc.[54] The wind having changed to the north, we cast

[52] Miranda was here the victim of a well-known trap. The innkeeper, who also managed the ferry, was notorious for deliberately leaving passengers stranded in order to force them to stay at his inn.

[53] This refers to the attack by Light-Horse Harry Lee on Paulus Hook. See note 5 above.

[54] Leonard Lispenard (*sic*) was a member of the state assembly, the Stamp Act Congress, and later governor and treasurer of King's (Columbia) College. Andrew Elliot (*sic*) was royal collector of customs in New York and lieutenant governor. William Bayard was a former assemblyman, later attainted as a Tory. DeLancey was a Loyalist during the Revolution, serving as an officer with the British.

anchor in Tappan Bay, thirty-six miles from New York, at seven o'clock in the morning.

➳ *29.* We remained here the entire day, with the sole recourse of our small society and some books, for the wind was blowing too strongly for us to venture to disembark for a walk on land.

➳ *30.* The wind having calmed a bit, we set sail at four o'clock in the morning and, aided by the tide, arrived at eight o'clock at Haverstraw, four miles farther on, where it was necessary for us to drop anchor again, the wind having increased too much. Around nine-thirty most of us went on land and took a good walk. The Frenchmen and I ate in a poor but clean tavern, and I had an adventure with a shepherdess in the manner of the shepherd Phido, but with greater success.[55] . . . The wind having fallen and the tide rising in our favor, we set sail at four o'clock in the afternoon. At the setting of the sun we were off Stony Point and Fort Lafayette, helped by the tide, for the wind was adverse; thus we passed Peekskill and finally reached Horse Race, where we anchored at eleven o'clock, six miles up river from where we had set sail.

➳ *31.* At seven-thirty in the morning we set sail with a lazy wind from the north and at ten o'clock anchored about a mile farther up, in front of a beautiful cascade created by nature on the east bank. We disembarked to take a walk with the ladies and in the shade of the trees had a colloquy somewhat gallant and amorous. At four o'clock we set sail with the current and at the setting of the sun passed Fort Montgomery opposite Anthonys Nose. At nine o'clock we passed by Buttermilk Falls, one mile from West Point on the west bank, and by all the works of this post, Constitution Island, etc., having traveled seven miles. Here we came upon a fresh wind from the south, with which we soon

---

[55] This is a reference to a work by the Italian poet Giovanni Battista Guarini, *Il Pastor Fido: or the Faithful Shepherd* (1590). The English translation was printed in London in 1633. In the original poem, love did not run smoothly.

View of Newbrunswick New Jersey. Sketch by Davis, 1820.

From Princeton, Miranda went on to New Brunswick, shown here, Woodbridge, and Elizabeth, noting that New Jersey "is commonly called the Garden of America."

NEW YORK.

"A trip to Kings Bridge on the island of New York was my first sally into this region," wrote Miranda. From here, he made other "forays."

reached the spot they call Blowing Hole (for the reason that the wind always blows here extraordinarily). This point is the limit of the Highlands, six miles from West Point. Three miles up river on the east bank is the town of New Windsor, and a little before the chevaux-de-frise, in front of Polopels Island, of the same type as those on the Delaware. Here we were becalmed, and with the tide and a light wind we continued, passing the town of Newburgh about two miles farther, exactly on the bank, and two miles farther on the opposite bank, the town of Fishkill, where we anchored at three o'clock in the morning.

June 1. At eight o'clock we set sail with a lazy wind from the south, passing the town of Poughkeepsie, twelve miles up river on the east bank; at eleven, Davis Store, Livingstons Store, Duers Distillery, Shenks Mills, North's Store, and various other buildings on one or the other bank. Here we drank the river water, exceedingly good and drinkable. Continuing up river, six miles farther on the west bank is Devoes Ferry; farther ahead, Esopus Island;[56] eight miles ahead, Esopus Creek; ten miles farther, Mudlane Island (to the left of the river, in the interior of the continent, are the high Catskills, part of the Allegheny Mountains); two miles farther, Red Hook Landing and Island; one mile farther, Tory Livingston House,[57] on the east bank; on the same bank two miles farther, Widow Livingston House and Manor;[58] four miles ahead, West Camp and East Camp, two small towns opposite each other on the banks of the river, founded by Germans; four miles up river, Livingston Upper Manor and House; four miles farther, Catskill Landing Place; four miles farther, Claverack and Lansingburgh Landing Places, the former on the east, the latter on the west bank; eight miles farther on the east bank, the remarkable

[56] In 1615 a Dutch trading post was established here and named Esopus. The site is near present Kingston, New York.

[57] This was probably Philip John Livingston, High Sheriff of Dutchess and manager of "rebel estates" in New York under the British.

[58] Margaret Beekman Livingston was the wife of Judge Robert R. Livingston, who died in 1775. The house was known as Clermont or as Lower Livingston Manor House.

Kinderhook Landing Place;[59] nine miles up river, Coeyman's Overslaugh, a bar which no vessel drawing more than nine feet can pass; nine miles up river, Upper Overslaugh, another bar, which at high tide only has seven and a half feet of water; here we cast anchor at two o'clock in the morning, because it was dark and we could not see the pickets which serve as marks.

June 2. At four o'clock in the morning, the day already bright, we set sail and half an hour later tied up at the Albany wharves three miles up river on the east bank. Half a mile from Albany is the house of Mr. Henry Cuylar,[60] large and of good architecture; on the opposite bank and almost in front is that of General Schuyler,[61] better in every respect. In the northern extreme of the town, also on the river, is another famous house (not as well situated as the two previous ones, but larger), belonging to Mr. Stephen Van Rensselaer.[62] After disembarking, I took a long walk through the city in the company of Dr. Eliot, one of the passengers, and then obtained lodging at the Hollenbake Inn.

[Two loose fragments of the diary are inserted here.]
... The Shakers, nine miles from Albany, their founder Mrs. Lee, a prostitute who came to America with the army of Burgoyne.[63] They pretend to speak all the languages and to profess the purity of

[59] Kinderhook was settled by the Dutch and long retained a strong Dutch atmosphere.

[60] A landed aristocrat of Albany.

[61] Philip J. Schuyler was a prominent citizen of Albany and a general in command of the Northern Department during the war. He was one of the first two senators from New York. His home, *The Pastures*, is of Georgian Colonial style and is now a state museum.

[62] Descendant of a patroon and owner of a large estate near Albany. He also was founder of Rensselaer Polytechnic Institute.

[63] Ann Lee, an English religious mystic, was founder of the Shaker Society in the United States. She joined the Shaking Quakers, or Shakers, in 1758 and came to this country in 1774, making a settlement at what is now known as Watervliet, New York. There is no evidence of any connection with Burgoyne or of her having been a prostitute. The latter accusation was probably because of her preaching against marriage, although she also opposed sexual intercourse as well. The refusal of the Shakers to bear arms caused them to be considered pro-British, and Ann Lee was arrested for treason in 1780 but released.

Christianity. A general confession is indispensable for admission and is usually performed in front of the entire congregation. I went to see them in the company of Mr. John Lansing, Major Sill, and Mr. Edward Livingston.[64] The house, or site, is called The Gate of Heaven and they refer to themselves as The Sons of God.

. . . Schoharie, a delightful location forty miles from Albany. In the winter of 1779–80, a flock of parrots appeared there (something that has never been seen on this continent), and the house near the spot where they appeared was the first which the enemy burned shortly afterwards. Here is ground for superstition. . . .

3. At three o'clock in the afternoon I left Albany, with my servant, on two very good horses rented for two pesos daily. The weather was very good and the road so pleasant that it was with the greatest delight I continued my journey on the banks of the North River as far as the spot where the Mohawk River joins its waters, about seven miles from Albany. From here I traveled over the banks of the Mohawk towards Cohoes Falls,[65] five miles farther up, where I arrived at five o'clock. The grasses of the fields exuded such an aromatic odor, the forests presented a sight so fertile, the grains and other crops appeared so beautiful and luxuriant, and the land was so rich that I thought I was in Puerto Rico, Cuba, or part of our American continent. The entire region is middlingly populated, and proportionately there is sufficient agriculture, but the inhabitants seem to be poor. The women commonly walk without shoes, and the number of Negroes is large. The latter and the whites speak Dutch generally, so that the traveler imagines himself in the middle of a Dutch colony.[66]

[64] John Lansing was military secretary to General Philip J. Schuyler; Major Richard Sill of Connecticut was aide-de-camp to General Alexander, Lord Stirling; and Livingston had a distinguished career as a member of the House of Representatives, mayor of New York, secretary of state, and minister to France.

[65] Once a seventy-foot torrent about which Thomas Moore, the Irish poet, wrote a poem in 1804.

[66] He was in a former Dutch colony; the Dutch established Fort Nassau near Albany in 1614. The first major Dutch settlement in this region came in 1624, prior to their occupation of Manhattan, and their language and customs long prevailed in the area, despite its seizure by the British in 1664.

When I saw this very famous cascade I confess it surprised me and gave me such contentment as few objects in nature have produced in my spirit. The height of the falls is about 40 varas, and the width about 220, but this is not all that forms its beauty: the play of the waters among the irregularities of the rock and the harmony, union, and aggregate of the whole give it an air of majesty and symmetry exceeding what the mind can conceive without having seen it first. Various other effects contribute to embellish the object; one of them is the rainbow the rays of the sun form in the particles of water floating in the atmosphere thereabout. Having examined all this very well and admiring more each time the land on the banks of this river, the most fertile and luxuriant region of all North America, I rested a little in a house nearby, where two country girls gave me the freshest water to drink and very good conversation. It is a peculiar thing that almost all the inhabitants of this region speak both Dutch and English!

At seven o'clock in the evening I arrived at Half Moon (the river forms exactly this figure there) on the banks of the North River, where I took lodging at the home of the widow Pepples. Here I had very good tea, supper, etc., and a conversation with the daughter of said widow, about sixteen years old, to whom I offered to send some books from New York.

4. At seven-thirty in the morning I sallied forth, continuing on the west bank of the North River. At four miles are the mills for sawing wood called Funday's Mills, and three miles farther the stream they call Stillwater, or Palmer's Mills, the former because here one begins to feel the rapidity of the current of the river, the latter for some large mills for sawing wood, like the preceding ones. It is incredible the quantity of sawed wood one sees, all the distance from Albany, upon this river on rafts, by means of which they transport the wood to New York at very little cost.

Three miles farther are Bemis Heights. On these heights, where the American army was camped when Burgoyne was defeated, one can still see the batteries the Americans had very judiciously built on their right to prevent the British army from forcing its march by the road along the riverbank;[67] also the whole entrenchment of the field and the redoubts on the left, which offered an equal degree of impossibility to the British army for attacking there as for forcing its march forward. The entire terrain is the most advantageous and adaptable to an encampment of twenty thousand men one could imagine, so that with very little work they were protected from whatever attack the British might have attempted. About a mile and a half farther on is the position of the British army, without trenches, works, advance redoubts, etc. The field was very feebly entrenched (from this we know that they regarded their enemy with contempt), but the advance positions were very well built, in large number, and provided with immense artillery, although the terrain was not very advantageous. All these works are still quite complete. One can see the effects of the terrible fire which supported the actions of the nineteenth of September and the seventh of October; there is a tree which has eighteen or twenty injuries from shot, and there is

[67] The British plan was to occupy the Hudson-Champlain Valley and cut the rebellious Colonies in two. Burgoyne's army was to move south from Canada and make contact with the forces of General Sir William Howe in New York City. Burgoyne made his move without knowledge that Howe had gone to Philadelphia. To stop Burgoyne's advance, General Horatio Gates, upon the advice of Kosciusko, entrenched at Bemis Heights. On September 19, 1777, the Americans, led by Benedict Arnold, attacked Burgoyne's army at Freeman's Farm. Despite heavy losses, the British held. On October 7, Gates struck a force led by General Simon Fraser, who was mortally wounded. Arnold, relieved of command and in violation of military discipline, led an attack that caused the British to fall back. The Americans surrounded the British at Schuylerville, and Burgoyne surrendered on October 17. This victory, called Saratoga, was primarily responsible for the French decision to enter the war on the side of the United States. Arnold suffered a wound in his left leg which caused its amputation and almost cost his life. He was promoted to major general after the battle. Because of his later treason, there is now a monument on the battlefield bearing the likeness of a cannon, a left boot, a major general's epaulet, and the inscription: "In memory of the most brilliant soldier of the Continental Army, who was desperately wounded on this spot . . . winning for his countrymen the decisive battle of the American Revolution and for himself the rank of major general." Arnold's name is nowhere on the stone.

hardly one tree in all that area which did not receive some such military marks. Likewise one can see the battery and great trench the brave Arnold, mounted on his horse, assaulted, as a result of which he was wounded in the leg and the horse killed by a cannon ball, obliging him to retire; also the spot where General Fraser was mortally wounded, where Burgoyne had his tent, etc. As all this happened in the midst of a thick forest and as nobody passes through there, it is so well preserved that any intelligent person can form from it a full picture of the event. Mr. Bemis, whose house and lands are right there and who knows all this ground like the palm of his hand, was pleased to mount his horse and show me everything with the greatest individuality. When we returned to his house, we were so tired from this military investigation that I think he will never forget it.

At one o'clock in the afternoon I took the horses and continued my journey on the bank of the river. At one and a half miles is the large, remarkable Vernor's House;[68] one and a half miles farther, Ensine's House, where I halted to eat and rest until five o'clock. Four miles farther are the sawmills called Vanvaghten's Mills; two miles farther, Fish.

[Here occurs a gap in the diary.]

[68] Martha Vernor was the manager of a tavern, near Albany, that was formerly called King's Arms.

PART FOUR

Connecticut and Rhode Island

☆☆☆☆

CONNECTICUT AND RHODE ISLAND

July 24, 1784. At twelve-thirty in the day we set sail from New York on the sloop *Friendship*, Captain Bradley, for New Haven. At two o'clock, the wind and tide adverse, we anchored in Newtown Creek, three miles from New York. We went ashore and took a walk until five, when we returned on board. At nine o'clock that night we had stormy weather, but soon afterwards it cleared, and at twelve-thirty, the wind changing to the southwest, we set sail.

25. At one o'clock in the morning we passed Hell Gate, the Charybdis of this sound,[1] and, continuing our navigation with the same wind, seven hours later were fifty miles from New York. With the clearest weather we arrived at New Haven at three o'clock in the afternoon. We disembarked immediately, finding the streets without a soul in them (everybody was in church), and in the company of Mr. Austen[2] I took lodging at the Coffee-House of Mrs. Smith.

At five o'clock I went to hear a celebrated preacher from Boston, Mr. Murray, whose system is universal salvation. The gathering was extremely large, and his eloquence simple and pleasing.[3]

Afterwards I went to visit the president of the college, the Rev-

[1] Hell Gate was the name given to the narrow channel between Astoria (Queens) and Ward's Island. Dangerous rocks and tidal currents gave it a bad reputation among sailors. Charybdis was a whirlpool off the Sicilian coast, personified by the ancients as a female monster which sought the lives of unwary sailors.

[2] Probably John Austen of New York.

[3] John Murray was originally a follower of the Wesleys, but in 1760 he accepted the doctrine that Christ had atoned for all and that eventually all would be saved.

erend Dr. Stiles,[4] for whom I brought some letters of recommendation, but he was out of town. I had tea with his family (wife and four or five daughters) and at nine o'clock returned to my lodging, where I spent the rest of the evening reading the admirable history of Philip II by Watson.[5]

26. The weather was extremely rainy, so I passed the morning indoors reading of the deeds of the Duke of Alba[6] and his malicious sovereign, Philip II. In the afternoon President Stiles called on me, and in his company I went out to see the college. With the tutors Russell and Meigs[7] I visited the classes in algebra and optics, observing that these sciences were explained to the students in the most simple and natural manner. From here we went to the class in Hebrew, the professor of which is the President himself—still preoccupied with some pedantry. We then visited the chapel for prayers, which lasted half an hour, and, afterwards, went to the room of the tutors, where we had a glass of wine and bandied college pedantries until ten o'clock in the evening, when I retired to my lodging.

27. I have spent the morning seeing something of the town and talking with Mr. Shipman,[8] whom I had met in New York. In the afternoon I went to the house of the President and went through all his memorandum books, which contain various curiosities and information.

New Haven Thermometer

	Heat	Cold
At most	100	10 below zero
Commonly	65 to 75	14 to 22 above zero

[4] Ezra Stiles, a clergyman, was president of Yale (1778–95) and professor of ecclesiastical history. He also taught Hebrew, theology, and the sciences. In his own diary, Stiles referred to Miranda as "a learned Man and a flaming Son of Liberty."

[5] Robert Watson, *History of the Reign of Philip the Second, King of Spain* (London, 1777).

[6] Fernando Alvarez de Toledo, Duke of Alba, was the cruel Spanish general sent by Philip II to suppress the revolt in the Netherlands in 1567.

[7] Matthew Talcott Russell was a tutor at Yale between 1782 and 1786; Josiah Meigs was also a tutor and later clerk of the city of New Haven.

[8] Elias Shipman was a member of the common council at New Haven in 1784.

The number of students in the college is 260 and there have been as many as 270. The number of houses in this city, including all sizes, is 440 and of inhabitants 3,322.

Three Regicides[9]

Edward Whaley	*ob.* at Hatley
William Goffe	at Narving
John Dixwell	at New Haven

In the cemetery, or churchyard, of this city is the following inscription referring to the last:

I. D. ESQR

DECEASED MARCH YE 18. IN YE 82d.

YEAR OF HIS AGE. 1688.

In the afternoon the President and I saw from the college tower a burial, conducted in the processional manner these people use, men and women intermingled in a very numerous gathering.

Afterwards we went to see the library and the philosophical collection. The former is nothing special: two or three thousand volumes, among them one that is curious indeed, written in Latin before the introduction of the press and the contents of which are passages of the Scripture, with some very poorly drawn figures of the Old and New Testaments. An electric pneumatic machine, a telescope, some globes, some other bagatelles of natural history, and a kind of wooden armillary sphere, in which is revealed the movement of the stars and planets, comprise the collection. In this room there are also four or five old pictures of the founders and benefactors of the college.

28. I spent the morning writing letters to my darling S—a and various friends in New York.

In the afternoon, in the company of Mr. Shipman, Captain Powell, and various other persons, I went to see the cave in which, it is said, one of the regicides mentioned above lived for a period

[9] These were three of the judges who condemned King Charles I to death, later fleeing to this country in fear of vengeance by Charles II. Whaley was Cromwell's cousin. According to a questionable local legend, all three were buried behind Center Church, New Haven.

of seven years to avoid persecution by the commissaries sent by Charles II of England to these parts. This cave or, better said, hollow is two and a half miles from the city, in the brow of a small mountain, quite craggy and hidden.[10] Here we remained awhile, made some punch with the apparatus we had brought for this purpose, and returned to the city with the setting of the sun. We stopped at a mill for another swig of the punch and discovered that the miller was a captain of light cavalry in the Continental army and the servant (named Smith) a preacher, man of very good judgment, college educated, and possessing a very good command of Greek and Latin.

29. I have spent the morning writing my diary and taking a walk through the city in the company of Mr. Shipman and Captain Wooster (son of the famous American general).[11] I saw the house in which General Arnold lived for a long time (confiscated and sold when he deserted)[12] and the City Hall, which is capacious and in good taste, and then went to have dinner with Captain Wooster, Major Willis,[13] Mr. Charles Chauncey (famous lawyer), General Parsons,[14] etc., at the house of the first. The meal finished, we went over to the college, where the preceptors were waiting to take me to the declamations which the students presented publicly—an excellent way of accustoming them to public speaking and giving grace to their gesture and expression.

In the city archives we examined the famous Blue Laws.[15] These are contained in three volumes of folio manuscript, beginning with the first act of assembly in 1639, in which the

[10] The cave is located on the summit of West Rock near New Haven.

[11] David Wooster, a major general in the Connecticut militia, was mortally wounded in action at Ridgefield, Connecticut, in 1777.

[12] Benedict Arnold was born in Norwich and moved to New Haven at the age of twenty-one. Operating as a druggist, bookseller, and importer, he became a person of importance in the city.

[13] Probably John Willis, sometimes spelled Wyllys.

[14] General Samuel H. Parsons of Middletown, Connecticut.

[15] A reference to the strict laws governing morality and observance of the Sabbath in the New Haven colony. They became famous in 1781 when Samuel Peters, a Royalist refugee, published a *General History of Connecticut*, containing many so-called "laws."

foundation of this city was decreed. Then follow various resolutions of the great court: a husband who kissed his wife in public on a Sunday is punished with a fine and lashes, another for drinking the health of others on a Sunday, others for playing and dallying with girls, another for having frequent suppers and company in his house. Such was the fanaticism and way of thinking of these people a century and a half ago.

We had tea with Miss Arnold, the sister of the General, who has lived in this city for a long time and is respected by all. Her brother supports her from England.[16] She is a woman of close to forty years of age and has a genteel and pleasant manner and middling education and information. We had supper at the home of Captain Wooster and in the company of various persons of the area conversed until midnight, when each of us retired to his lodging.

30. At noontime Major Willis and I, together with two servants, started out on a journey in two chaises, our good friend Captain Wooster having arranged everything. But the horses were so poor and the road so gravelly that it was with difficulty we arrived at two-thirty in North Haven, eight miles away, where we were given a mediocre meal. We left at four o'clock and with much trouble we were able to reach Hubbard House, thirteen and a half miles from the preceding, where we had tea and supper and spent the night.

The region is highly populated in all parts, and the agriculture appears to be in very good state. The country houses generally are large and of good outer appearance, but on the inside are ordinary and dirty.

31. At six o'clock in the morning we sallied forth, had breakfast in Worthington, seven miles away, and before ten o'clock arrived in Wethersfield, six miles farther on. Here I took lodging at the inn of Mr. Elijah Wright, and my companion Willis went on to Hartford. The day was hot and I did not leave

---

[16] A short time after his treason, Arnold went to England, where he died in 1801.

the inn until the afternoon. At six o'clock I went to see Joseph Webb, Esq.,[17] for whom I brought letters, but he was not home, and I left them for him at his store. I did find Colonel Chester[18] at home and had tea and supper there; his attention and politeness obliged me to take lodging at his home during my stay here. Mr. Webb came in the meantime, we had supper together, and he invited me for dinner the next day. We spent the evening sociably.

August 1. Sunday, and consequently church. At ten o'clock, in the company of Colonel Chester and his wife, I went to the Meeting House, which is quite capacious and clean. The service lasted until twelve o'clock, by reason of its being the Day of Sacrament. I had dinner with Mr. Webb, and at three o'clock we returned to the church. Owing to the gathering's being more numerous and splendid than in the morning, the girls combed and dressed themselves better for this occasion. (The church is the only place where they can present themselves publicly and be seen, because as for walks or theaters, may God grant them these.) They sang their psalms and antiphonies very well. A music teacher instructs all the young ladies and young men at his house, and afterwards everyone takes his book to the church, they form three choirs in the upper gallery, and, under the direction of said teacher, acting as choirmaster, they sing in a very good musical tone, although without organ or any other instrument of accompaniment. The composition of the music, as well as the singing, is the most solemn and ecclesiastic I have heard until now on this continent.

The service ended at four-thirty, and I went to have tea at the home of Mrs. Webb, which lady and her family are extremely gracious and hospitable. Later we climbed the steeple of the church, which is quite lofty and reveals a highly pleasing and handsome prospectus of these environs and the Connecticut River.

---

[17] Webb operated a tannery and was owner of a fine house. He entertained General Washington, and his home was used as the General's headquarters for a time.

[18] John Chester, a prominent citizen of Wethersfield, was a member of the legislature (1778–80) and a justice of the peace.

After we came down, I went over to the burial ground and read various of the countless epitaphs on flat stones, in the manner of the region. From them one infers this place is highly salutary, for the age dates are quite high, and among them I counted more than twelve between eighty and ninety years of life.

That evening we returned to the church to enjoy the musical rehearsal which once a month the singers and the teacher present in order to review together the psalms, etc., they have studied. This lasts something more than an hour. Afterwards I retired to my lodging, tired and glutted with church up to the eyes.

2. I have spent the morning reading indoors, for the heat has been so excessive that it is impossible to go out anywhere. At noontime we had the company of the curate, Mr. Marsh, his wife, and various other individuals with whom we conversed jovially and merrily about writing, etc. After tea I took a walk with the young Mr. Chester, brother of the Colonel, through the meadows about a mile from the center of this town on the riverbanks. These meadows are covered with water for a height of twelve feet during the swells of the river, at which times the inhabitants are compelled to remove their fences to prevent them from being carried away. The river does not demonstrate more width here than about fifty varas.

3. This morning has been equally hot, so I have spent it indoors with books. A somewhat damaged tooth began to incommode me so much with the impress of the heat that it would not let me sleep, eat, etc. I called the doctor, who at four o'clock in the afternoon took it out, in the presence of various ladies who wished to see the operation. The pain was effectually alleviated shortly thereafter, and in the company of the young Chester I went to the tanneries of Mr. Webb, which are very well built and make the best cordovan and sole leather in all this continent. The master is English, a man of high ability in his profession. Were the owner, who as it is receives a large profit, able to obtain here sufficient leather, this would be one of the richest and most flourishing manufactories in the universe. (Later I saw some prod-

ucts of this factory, which surpass all others I have seen, and I persuaded myself that nothing of this sort could be made better. What a treasure it would be for Caracas or Buenos Aires!) From there we went to the home of Mr. Webb for tea, in the company of several ladies, etc.; we remained until nine, when I went home with the family of Colonel Chester.

4. The morning being extremely hot, I have spent it writing my diary and reading the history of the region. At one o'clock I dined very sociably with Mrs. Chester, Miss Parsons (a very lovely character), and Miss Hill. Colonel Chester had gone to attend to the gathering of his harvests, and the young man to a fishing party, to which I was invited, but it did not seem to me that the heat and other circumstances could produce in me the expected pleasure.

At six o'clock in the afternoon the Boston stage arrived to take me to Hartford, four miles away, and I sallied forth, in the company of some Hartford ladies. The road was good and also beautiful, studded with country houses, innumerable fruit-bearing trees, and luxuriant fields, forming the most pleasant rural scene imaginable. At seven o'clock we arrived in Hartford, and I took lodging at the home of Mr. Murray.

5. At six o'clock in the morning we left Hartford in beautiful and moderate weather. A young girl thirteen or fourteen years old, my servant, and I were the only passengers. We arrived shortly after seven o'clock at Windsor, a small town of about sixty inhabitants, where we had breakfast. An hour later, we continued twelve miles farther to Suffield, a similar town; here we halted to feed the horses. Finally, after crossing the Connecticut River on a barge, we arrived at Springfield, in Massachusetts. I will not forget to mention that the spirit of republicanism is such in this region that the coachman sat down with the rest of us at the table, and it was with no little difficulty that I arranged for my servant to be fed separately. This entire road from Wethersfield is replete with country houses and fruit trees on both sides, so that it seems more a street handsomely decorated

STATE STREET, ALBANY,
1805.

Miranda disembarked at Albany on June 2, 1784. "I took a long walk
through the city," he recorded, "and then obtained lodging at the
Hollenbake Inn."

Phelps Stokes Collection, The New York Public Library

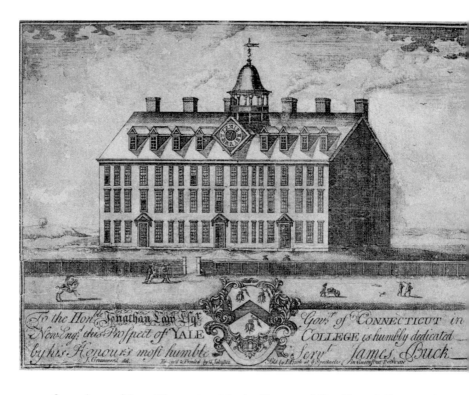

Stopping at New Haven to visit the Reverend Dr. Ezra Stiles, president of Yale, Miranda sat in on the latter's class in Hebrew.

in the rural style than anything else. The road is good enough, and the land fertile and nourishing.

In the afternoon I took a walk through the town, which must have about two hundred houses, and in the evening returned to my tavern, the Coffee-House. At eight o'clock I heard the church bell ringing and informed myself that it was to call the towns-people to the singing school, held twice a week in the courthouse. I went there and found a teacher seated in the higher place, direct-ing twenty or thirty girls and about sixty young men, who with their music books and their candles were seated around him, forming a choir and singing psalms and antiphonies in the manner of Wethersfield. Some of the girls seemed to me good looking and gave every appearance of being from the most decent families. It is a singular thing that the women surpass the men so much in dress and manner!

6. The morning has been beautiful, and I have spent it partly reading and partly looking at the church, which is quite capacious and in good taste. From its steeple one sees the whole town and part of the Connecticut River, a highly pleasing and handsome perspective. In the sepulchral inscriptions there is nothing in particular; most of them are almost ruined, as the ceme-tery does not have a fence and so the hogs have bored through all of it.

After dinner I met Captain of Artillery John Bryant, who has the badge of honor of being minus his right arm, having lost it when one of his own cannons at Fort Montgomery burst. He is the commander of the magazines, foundry, and other installa-tions at the arsenal here, all of which he showed me.[19] Two wooden warehouses contain seventy-five hundred muskets of French make, some ancient weapons of the same type as was used when the war began, about ninety bronze artillery pieces (also of French make, except for ten or twelve cast right here), two thirteen-inch mortars, four or six twelve-inch cannons, some howitzers and miscellaneous artillery, and carriages, limbers, etc.

---

[19] An arsenal was established at Springfield early in the war.

The powder is kept in a brick warehouse, and the good maxim of opening the doors on clear days so that the powder may be better ventilated is practiced. In another wooden warehouse are a furnace for metals and foundry molds, built with intelligence and great simplicity. On the river there is a small mill for boring the pieces. Other wooden buildings here are barracks, housing ten men, a corporal, and a sergeant assigned to guard duty (and, during the war, some officers). There is not a single palisade or entrenchment to protect this arsenal, such was the confidence of these people even in the midst of war. Reprehensible notwithstanding! In another warehouse they prepared and stored the explosives, fuses, cartridges, etc. The commanding officer told me that twenty-four pieces had been cast here and that this was the principal arsenal during the war. The location is a height adjoining the town, its summit a spacious level ground, with the advantage of having a river at hand for the operations which might present themselves.

When darkness came I returned to my lodging, but on entering noticed a large gathering in the so-called "Café"[20] (a cup of this beverage has never been drunk there), so I went to a corner of the room and sat down in a chair, observing for more than an hour and a half the different groups, individuals, and conversations my ears and eyes could penetrate. Finally I became tired and went to my room to read a bit, but around ten o'clock heard such an extraordinary noise that I thought they were trying to demolish the house. I informed myself of the cause and discovered that part of the coterie of the Café had drunk something more than a sufficient amount and insisted the door be opened to them again, and it was deemed necessary to give in to this to avoid having them knock the door down.

7. I spent the early morning, which was quite pleasant, writing my diary and around eleven o'clock returned to Hartford on the same stage and by the same road. We crossed the Connecticut River on a barge and at one-thirty arrived in Suffield, where

[20] From the Italian or French word for coffee.

we all ate together, *including the coachman.* (One cannot exaggerate how beautiful and delightful this entire road is at this time of year!) We left Suffield at three-thirty and two hours later arrived at Windsor, where we stopped in order that the horses might be fed. Through curiosity I entered the little store of the landlady and found her young, not bad looking, and very entertaining. She had a book in her hand and gave it to me when I asked for it with politeness. The discovery that it was Rollin's[21] *Ancient History* induced me to ask her who were, in her sincere opinion, greater men, the ancients or the moderns? Unhesitatingly, she said the latter were and that, in her opinion, Franklin was superior to Aristides.[22]

We left soon afterwards and, as night came, reached Hartford, where I took lodging at the inn of Mr. Murray. Presently I went to see Major Willis, who lives at the home of his brother the Colonel, and not finding him there left a card for him with the number of my lodging and returned immediately to rest from the hardship of the trip.

∼∼∼ *8.* This day, being Sunday, was dedicated to church. At ten o'clock I encountered my friend Major Willis, who was on his way to church, and we went on together. The congregation was somewhat smaller than usual because of the rain; nevertheless it is well known to be neither so numerous nor so genteel as that of Wethersfield. The church is dirty and in bad taste. The men dress with the greatest carelessness and do not put so much as a grain of powder on their heads. The women dress with less grace and taste than one sees in other parts of the region. The service ended, having lasted only one hour, I returned to my lodging, where I read until it was time for dinner. This matter of inviting people, endearing the foreigner, promoting society, etc., is still very remote in this great city, capital of the famous state of Connecticut!

At four o'clock my friend Willis came and we went to see the

---

[21] The author was Charles Rollin.
[22] Probably Aristides the Just, Athenian statesman.

famous poet John Trumbull, author of the poem "McFingal," "The Progress of Dulness," and other works in the [Hudibraico] style, which bring him unbounded honor.[23] He is a young man, thirty-two years old, with the greatest vivacity in his expression and frank, gracious conversation. We had a long literary talk, in which he revealed a considerable knowledge of English and Latin literature, but very little of French. Here I remained with the greatest pleasure until seven o'clock, when I took a chaise and with my servant returned to Wethersfield. I arrived there at eight o'clock (four miles), spending the night at the home of Joseph Webb, Esq., who treated me with the greatest hospitality and courtesy, just as did his brother, Captain Webb, his wife, and his sister, all of an amiable character.

9. This morning after breakfast I returned to my former lodging, the house of Colonel Chester, and was received with the kindness and affection reserved for a son. We all went to eat at the home of Mr. Webb and afterwards to the public library, which is now being formed and contains only about three hundred volumes, but I will dare to wager they have been read more than all those the library of the Escorial[24] contains. At five o'clock I returned to the home of Mr. Webb, where I met a large gathering of ladies who had come to drink tea and, also, Mr. Trumbull and his family, who had come from Hartford to pay me a visit. We had a delightful conversation, literary and political (in this matter one cannot make jokes), which lasted until nightfall, when he left with his wife, etc. The rest of the company retired later on, and I in the company of Mrs. Chester went to my lodging.

Next door to Webb's house is that of Silas Dean,[25] who in 1776

[23] John Trumbull, a lawyer and poet, was the author of "McFingal" (1782), a satire of British mistakes during the Revolutionary period, and "The Progress of Dulness" (1772–73); a leader of the Hartford Wits. "Hudibraico" designates mock-heroic or burlesque style similar to that of Samuel Butler's *Hudibras* (1664, 1678).

[24] Escorial was a royal palace near Madrid, Spain.

[25] Silas Deane (*sic*), a wealthy merchant, was leader of the revolutionary agitation in Connecticut. He was appointed commissioner to France by the Continental Congress in September, 1776.

had been sent to France as commissioner to handle the affairs of this continent, etc. His brother, whom I also met, lives there.

~~~~ *10.* After breakfast I said farewell to my good friend Colonel Chester and his delightful family and at eleven o'clock set out for Middletown with Mr. Webb, who wished to accompany me in his phaeton to that town. Four miles away is Rock Hill, which commands a pleasing view of the neighborhood and town of Wethersfield, the Connecticut River, etc. Five miles farther on and about three before Middletown, we passed over a height named Upper Houses,[26] where there is the most beautiful and delightful view imaginable of Middletown, the river, farms, fields, etc. At twelve o'clock we arrived, by a very pleasant and extremely populated road, and I obtained lodging at Brewer's Tavern (Mrs. Smith). Mr. Webb and I then went to visit General Parsons, who received me with the greatest hospitality and kindness and invited us to stay for dinner, but we could not, having already contracted to eat at the tavern. In the afternoon we called on Mr. Shaler[27] and then took a walk on Upper Street, which commands part of the town and the river. After tea at the home of General Parsons we took a walk in "The Grove," where the townsfolk are wont to gather at sunset for a stroll. In passing, we came to the homes of General Sage and Major Otis,[28] to whom General Parsons introduced me and in whose company we walked until nine o'clock, when they accompanied me on my return to the tavern.

In this town there are various distilleries where rum is made from molasses brought from the Antilles. This branch of industry is practiced throughout the state and provides a very high profit. Revealing the spirit, energy, and industry of these people is the

[26] The part of Middletown north of Little River was known as Upper Houses, until incorporated as the town of Cromwell in 1851, to distinguish it from the southern section, now Middletown, known as Lower Houses. Middletown was once an important West Indian shipping port and from 1750 to 1800 was rated the wealthiest town in Connecticut.

[27] This was Nathaniel Shaler, or Shalor, as it was sometimes spelled.

[28] General Comfort Sage was also a member of the legislature. The major was Jonathan Otis.

fact that when they could not obtain molasses during the war, they distilled the juice of cornstalks and from this made whiskey.[29]

~~~~ *11.* The morning has been quite hot, and I have spent most of it reading indoors. In the afternoon I went with a party, formed for the purpose, to see the lead mines about two and a half miles from the town. At five o'clock, General Parsons, General Sage, Major Otis, Mr. Shaler, Captain Hamlin,[30] and I boarded a vessel, arrived in a matter of half an hour, and made punch (for which purpose we had brought all the necessary instruments and ingredients) in the pure republican manner, which stands out in this state more than in any other. After having savored the punch copiously, we marched up the hillock where said mine is located. There we examined the passages and excavations where the mines had been worked, a mill, and a lead-smelting furnace, now almost in ruins owing to the abandonment of this work before the war. The enterprise was begun more than thirty years ago and after a period of assay, during which the output did not pay the costs, it was given up. One of the miners who had been employed from the beginning, a Dutchman, still lives in that vicinity and showed us various rocks taken out of the mine with many chunks of lead in them and informed us very minutely of said particulars, etc.[31] On our return, there was more punch, dried fish, and cheese, in the republican manner, and around seven o'clock we disembarked and immediately headed

[29] The manufacture of rum was important to all of the New England colonies and played a major role in the West Indian trade. In what was sometimes called the "triangular trade," West Indian molasses was brought to New England to be distilled into rum, which was then taken to Africa and used in the purchase of slaves. The slaves were then brought to the West Indies and there exchanged for more molasses, and so on. Something of the importance of this product can be seen in the fact that in 1780, Congress asked Connecticut to supply 68,558 gallons of rum for use of the Continental army.

[30] This was probably Nathaniel Hamlin, a ship captain.

[31] Lead mines existed about two and one-half miles south of Middletown. In 1776, Captain Samuel Russell was appointed to oversee their operation, and in 1777 the Connecticut legislature voted two hundred pounds of gunpowder for their use.

for The Grove to see the people gathered, but not a solitary soul was there and so we went to visit the owner, who lives right there in a house of moderate capacity and taste. (His name is Philip Mortimer[32] and he is considered to have the largest fortune in the town, seven thousand pounds, or about twenty-four thousand pesos fuertes. Coming from Europe with a small capital in linens, he established in this very town a cordage plant and with his assiduity and frugality amassed the mentioned fortune. He is of an advanced age and persists in thinking of death in a manner almost incredible, as is common in those who bind themselves to this mania. People of complete veracity and knowledge assured me, when I inquired into the fortune of Mortimer, that in all the state there are not two fortunes which come to ten thousand pounds and very few in the neighboring ones that exceed this figure.) So our intention to see the assembly of people in the mall remained a wish, for no one came, notwithstanding the weather was beautiful. We retired, and I went to my lodging to read and meditate.

↝ *12.* Early in the morning I went to see a ship on the river that was ready to take horses and oxen to the Windward Islands.[33] The system of transportation is one peculiar to the region, and without doubt experience has proved it the best, for in a ship of fifty to eighty tons, forty to seventy horses are carried with the greatest safety. All the animals are placed on one side and the other of the deck, covered with a light roof, which gives them shade, protects them from all discomfort, and permits the seamen to walk about overhead and work the ship. Only very rough weather can incommode them and put them in danger, in which situation they would suffer even more between decks.

I then went with General Parsons to see the church, a small but clean building; from its steeple there is a pretty view of the city and the river. We also went to the two meetinghouses, which likewise are small and are in bad taste, and then retired to the house

32 In 1781–82, Mortimer was justice of the peace for Hartford County.

33 The exporting of cattle to the West Indies was a well-established trade originating shortly after settlement.

of Parsons. Here I had a drink of punch (the customary refreshment of the entire region, for lemons and sugar are even more abundant here than in the Islands, owing to the commerce done with them) and then took my leave, as I planned to go to New London, for which he gave me letters of recommendation, with fine expressions of friendship and affection. Middletown is, because of its location, one of the most pleasing towns that one would want to imagine and the best in my opinion, for this reason, of the ones I have seen in this state. It has very good houses and a considerable population, as can be seen in the attached memorandum[34] given to me by General Parsons, a person of the greatest veracity and information.

At one o'clock I boarded a small boat, and we set sail with a loose and contrary wind, but with the tide in our favor. The passengers were three women, a country man, myself, and my servant. They were certainly very good people and entertained me immensely with their simple and curious conversations. At six o'clock we anchored at Knowles's Landing Place, disembarked, and took a walk. I visited a large still and apparatus for making rum and then took lodging at a middling tavern there, for the boat could not set sail until daybreak. (Vessels cannot navigate at night without taking the risk of running aground at every moment, the river being narrow and shallow.) The landlady talked to me much about the French army on its passage through here on its way from Providence to West Point and about other curious histories, which, together with the milking of the cows at sunset, entertained me that afternoon. I spent the evening reading the life of Philip III by the noted historian Watson,[35] until eleven o'clock, when I went to bed.

~~~~ *13.* At four o'clock in the morning the boat came for me, and I boarded immediately. With a small, favorable wind and the tide, we went as far as Potapogue, seventeen miles away,

[34] This has not been found.

[35] Robert Watson, *History of the Reign of Philip III, King of Spain* (London, 1783).

where through the carelessness of the Captain the ship ran aground at three o'clock in the afternoon. Not being able to set sail until the next day, I went ashore. Among the various small vessels being built on the banks of this creek, there is one the burden of which struck me as highly extraordinary (about nine hundred tons). Asking about it, I was informed that it had been there since before the war; the owner and the builder had had an argument at that time, the work had been discontinued, and now, the timbers being rotten, no one would pay a guinea for it.

I took lodging in a very bad tavern, the only one there. The landlady found that I was rather gloomy and said to me, "Fellow, it seems to me that you are perplexed, as if the company does not please you. My husband will come shortly and will entertain you." When darkness came, I took my cane and hat and went for a walk. The place seemed to me extremely poor. Presently I returned to the tavern and talked a bit to the promised husband. He bored me very soon, and I spent the rest of the evening with my favorite Watson.

14. At five o'clock in the morning the boat came for me. We set sail with a favorable wind and tide and at nine o'clock arrived at the town of Saybrook (seven miles farther down), located on the western side of the Connecticut River and in the vicinity of its mouth. Here lives an individual by the name of Silliman, a native of the region and a saddler by profession, who has fashioned a machine composed of two punts and two wheels and operated by a horse, on which he goes up and down the river twice a week far above Middletown. Persons of veracity assure me that a single horse rows this machine at the rate of two miles an hour, as much as six or eight men rowing together can do.[36] Another individual invented a machine called *The Turtle*, when the British attacked New York with a naval force. Submerged,

---

[36] In my efforts to identify Silliman, I reached the conclusion that apparently half the citizens of New England were experimenting with boat propulsion at this time. The only Silliman in Saybrook, according to the 1790 Census, was Thomas.

it could reach and attach itself to the hull of a ship and, when a great quantity of powder it carried was ignited, it would burst in the air. The happenstance that the ship, apparently the *Asia*, against which *The Turtle* was launched (from Paulus Hook) was lined with copper resulted in the harpoon's not being able to penetrate the hull, and so *The Turtle* went past the ship; but the English sailors who, discovering that bulk, went to examine it, not knowing what it was, paid for their curiosity with their lives, for the powder ignited and blew them up. The inventor, Bushnell, studied at the college of New Haven and now lives near Potapogue.[37]

Both of these inventors are alive and have not even received the thanks of their country. Long live Democracy!

At ten o'clock we continued our journey with a fresh wind and favorable tide and disgorged into the sound. Coasting along the shore of New London County and passing Black Point, we entered the Thames River, the mouth of which is spacious and without a single bar. From here we immediately saw the city of New London, where we arrived shortly after noontime. The banks of the river are covered with houses, and one can hardly travel three miles without seeing some vessel being built on the banks. It is a pity the channel is so narrow and the bars and bottoms so shallow, because commerce will always have to be handled in very small vessels.

Presently I disembarked, took lodging at the New London Coffee House (quite indifferent) and in the afternoon went to visit Mr. William Stewart, for whom I brought letters.[38] He was not at home, but I drank tea in the company of his wife, who is an extremely lovely person and has good manners. Afterwards I visited Mr. Joshua Coit and Mr. Amasa Larned, for both of

---

[37] David Bushnell was inventor of *The Turtle*, an early type of submarine torpedo boat. It was wooden, could be propelled by one man on a treadle, and carried 150 pounds of gunpowder and enough air for a thirty-minute voyage. It was used in an unsuccessful effort to blow up Admiral Stirling's flagship, *Eagle*, near Governors Island on September 6, 1776.

[38] William Stewart of New London was a prominent merchant and shipowner.

whom I also brought letters, and at ten o'clock returned to my lodging.[39]

~~~~ *15.* Sunday, and consequently church, Mr. Coit accompanying me. The service was led by a young Presbyterian clergyman who had neither art nor part for being a preacher or minister; he was brief, and this was the best feature of the service. The congregation was neither numerous nor very decent. The building is extremely old, quite small, and located on the most elevated spot in town, so it looks more like a wooden blockhouse than anything else. One needs more than a little fervor or curiosity to climb up to it in the month of August at ten o'clock in the morning.

Afterwards Mr. Coit, Mr. Larned, and I took a walk around the town, and at two o'clock I went out with Mr. Stewart to have dinner at the home of his brother-in-law, Mr. Winthrop,[40] who had invited me the preceding day and who owns the best house in this city (and perhaps in the entire state). His wife, who is very lovely and has fine manners, two sisters, and Mrs. Stewart were our company. After dinner we walked a bit on the neighboring heights, which command a pleasing view of the bay, the sound, Gardiners Island, Long Island, etc., and then came down for tea. Mr. Winthrop showed me an accomplished picture of the Indian chief who in 1630 first discussed lands, etc., with the English in this state; a collection of some twenty of his family and ancestors, who for a long time held the government of this province (among these pictures, particularly outstanding is a very good group of three children in the style and coloring of Rubens); some very ancient gold and silver coins; and a miniature of Charles II, a gift of that sovereign to one of his ancestors. At nightfall we took a long walk with the ladies, returned for supper, and at eleven o'clock retired to our lodgings.

[39] Coit was a Harvard graduate (1776), a member of one of the first families of New London, clerk of that probate district, and member of Congress (1793–98). Amasa Learned (*sic*) was a Yale graduate (1772) and a member of Congress (1791–95).

[40] This could be one of several Winthrops, such as John Still or William. The family was probably the most prominent in Connecticut.

~~~ *16.* I spent the day writing and reading and at four-thirty boarded a packet for Norwich. On the eastern bank, five and a half miles up, is Gale's Ferry, a sort of landing place, and three and a half miles farther, on the western bank, is Mohegan, or Pomachaug, a very spread-out, miserable hamlet of Indians. The fifty to sixty families there are middlingly well dressed and have their corn plantings in the Indian manner, without fence or division whatsoever. The state assembly has forbidden them to alienate their lands and houses without its cognizance, and this is the reason these few inhabitants still subsist.[41]

At eight o'clock that night, after an extremely pleasant passage (good conversation and flowing punch), we arrived at Chelsea, or The Landing, where I obtained quite indifferent lodging at the tavern of Mr. Clement.

~~~ *17.* The next day I readied myself to go visit General Huntington,[42] for whom I brought letters, but discovered that he lived two miles from my tavern, because although all this area is known as the city of Norwich, the center proper is that far away. I rented a chaise and, traveling on the highway (which is bad), arrived there at noontime. His wife received me with considerable rusticity. When the husband, who had been to the store and the farm, arrived, I presented the letter to him, and he showed some civility. Finally, it was necessary to stay for dinner, at which we were joined by the children and a sister-in-law of General Moore from New York. The meal was taciturn, circumspect—as is the character of the General—and not very abundant, so it was soon over, after which we went for a walk. We visited the church and courthouse (poor buildings) and from there went to the cemetery to read the sepulchral inscriptions, among which I saw only four or six with ages past eighty and very few of seventy. Afterwards we climbed a rocky height next to the church and from there

[41] These were descendants of the Mohegan Indians, once under the great Chief Uncas. There is still an Indian community there, but it is no longer a government reservation.

[42] General Jedidiah H. Huntington was a Norwich merchant; commissioned brigadier general in 1777.

saw perfectly the town and part of its vicinity. A powder store-house had been built in that spot, and when the war ended an un-known individual (thus revealing his good sense) set it on fire, to entertain himself. (Luckily it contained only twelve barrels.) All the glass of the church and neighboring houses was broken and many buildings were damaged from the force of the explosion.

Returning to the house, we had tea, in almost as formal and circumspect a manner as the dinner and in the company of eight or ten ladies of the family (as numerous here as the Livingston family in New York) who had gathered no doubt to see the foreigner. When night came I returned in the chaise to my lodg-ing, tired and in truth worn out from the dryness of the women and the austerity of the General, who resembles Washington not a little in this respect. He gave me the following particulars:

Houses, in the entire district	1,000
Inhabitants	7,300
Houses in this city and The Landing	200
Churches in this city and The Landing	3
Ships sailing each year for the Islands	12
Press	1

18. At nine o'clock in the morning I set sail and went down the river Thames in the same boat that had carried me up-stream, two lady passengers greatly amusing me with their con-versation. At noontime we arrived at New London, and I went to my tavern and rested. After dinner I went to see a Catalan named Gabriel Sistaré, who is established here and had come to visit me soon after learning that I was in the town. He is about fifty-five years old and completely coarse and ignorant, even for a Catalan. About thirteen years ago he arrived here with his ship in very bad condition, en route from Havana to Cádiz. The cargo of sugar, so he says, he sent to Spain and the money stayed with him. As a result he bought one of the best houses here and took a mistress (notwithstanding he is married in Spain), from whom he has seven children, as wild as their father and as dirty as their mother. From another side he seems to be a man of good heart, though a beast through and through; the house and the furniture, though very good, indicated his breeding and his low way of thinking. I asked him if he knew of any other fellow countryman established on this continent, and he answered there was only one, a Galician named José Antonio Linares,[43] who is married in this state. So see you here in substance the samples of the Spanish nation for these people to form a criterion of our character, manners, customs, etc.: in this region, Sistaré and Linares, and in the other, Miralles and Rendón. Long live the damned government!

Tired of looking at this savage, I went to the house of Mr. Stewart, where I drank tea and had an extremely pleasant time. That evening, accompanied by Mr. Winthrop, I visited his wife (daughter of Mr. Marston of New York) and sisters, in whose gracious society we had supper and conversed until eleven o'clock. Later, at the tavern, I had an argument with my landlord, because notwithstanding a formal stipulation he had put another guest in my room; thank God he was not put in my bed, according to the custom of the country!

19. At six o'clock in the morning Mr. Stewart and I visited Fort Griswold,[44] on the east bank across from the city. It is in substance a medium-sized field fortification with four bulwarks, built without a grain of intelligence, with a good, solid storehouse and barracks made of boards. Arnold captured it with British troops in a sudden attack and needlessly lost some officers and troops; he abandoned it a few hours later, leaving the artillery, etc., in the same state he had found it. Arnold could have obtained the same results from this undertaking, for all he accomplished and took out of the city, had he not paid any attention to this fort. The other positions were not tenable and were abandoned by the inhabitants at Arnold's approach.

[43] There is a record of a Juan Antonio Linares who refused in 1754 to return to Spain because of debts owed there.

[44] This was a fort commanding the entrance to the Thames River. It was held by Lieutenant Colonel William Ledyard and 150 militiamen. After the fall of Fort Trumbull at New Haven, Griswold was attacked by British troops under Benedict Arnold. On September 6, 1781, the fort was stormed and Ledyard and most of the defenders were killed in a virtual massacre.

At seven o'clock we retired for breakfast, and afterwards I returned to my tavern to write and read. At three o'clock I went to Mr. Stewart's house, where I had dinner in a large company. Later I went to see a ship laden with horses and cattle, about to sail for Guadalupe. Its burden was one hundred tons, and it carried fifty horses and oxen, besides ewes and rams, in the manner I have described above. Upon the same light roof covering the animals, were bales of hay for maintaining them. The heads of the animals were turned toward the center of the ship, where they were fed and watered. Afterwards I went with Mr. Coit to see the town library; although there are not more than two hundred volumes in it, these were well selected. We returned to the house of Mr. Stewart for tea, and at eight o'clock I retired to my tavern to read.

20. At six o'clock in the morning I was called on by the captains of two ships, one headed for Rhode Island and the other for Long Island. After considering the matter, I decided upon the latter so that I might visit Dr. and Mrs. Gardiner,[45] from whom I had received a very polite letter of invitation the day before. My baggage was put on board, and at seven o'clock I set sail with Captain Clark Truman, a great babbling liar, with a fresh, favorable wind. The company consisted of two young businessmen from New York, and although both behaved themselves with decency, one was the most insolent ignoramus I have ever seen. At noontime we dropped these two off, with their horses, at Oyster Pond Point, opposite Plum Island, twenty-two miles from New London, and at one-thirty I disembarked at Shelter Island, eight miles farther.[46] The owner of a miserable hut there, Mr. Fery, generously offered me what he had; he gave me horses and accompanied me to my destination, the house of Mr. Derin,[47]

[45] Dr. Nathaniel Gardiner was a pioneer in education on Long Island. In 1784 he opened the first incorporated academy in New York State—Clinton Academy.

[46] Shelter Island was settled in 1652 by Quaker refugees. It is now a summer resort.

[47] Henry P. Derin was a pioneer in wool production on Long Island.

two miles farther on. The good old fellow, so afflicted he could barely leave his bed, got up and received me with his eldest son; the rest of the family came in from a walk at nightfall. After the family had prayed together, Mr. Derin retired to his room and the rest of us had supper. Dr. and Mrs. Gardiner joined me for a while after the meal, and afterwards we all retired to sleep. I confess I was rather tired.

21. After breakfast I took a walk with the Doctor. This island has about two thousand acres, ten or twelve landowners, and very good forests for firewood, lumber, etc. From the heights there is a complete and beautiful view of Gardiners Bay, Gardiners Island, Connecticut, etc. The British squadron under Admiral Graves[48] stayed in this spacious and secure bay for a long time to observe the French fleet when the latter was at Newport. On my return to the house I read for the first time the book entitled *Magnalia Christi Americana—Or the Ecclesiastical History of New-England by the Reverend Cotton Mather, M.A.,*[49] which Parson Huntington of Middletown had presented to me. This book is one of the most curious and authentic documents one can imagine of the fanaticism and mistaken way of thinking which at that time (eighty-six years ago) prevailed throughout this continent and is a worthy companion of the extraordinary Blue Laws of New Haven!

We dined in the American style of the countryside, and afterwards I took a chaise, accompanied by Dr. Gardiner and the young Mr. Derin, to the ferry, about two miles from the house. Here we took the boat and going against the tide for three hours reached Sag Harbor, three miles away, at eight-thirty in the evening. At ten o'clock we arrived at East Hampton, where Dr. Gardiner's house is, and had a very good supper, his excellent abode repairing somewhat the fatigue of the journey.

---

[48] Thomas Graves was in command of a British fleet operating against the Americans in 1781. He was defeated by a French fleet under Comte François Joseph Paul de Grasse on September 5, 1781.

[49] Cotton Mather, pastor of North Church, Boston, published this book in 1702. It is a curious mixture of fact and fiction.

22. Sunday, and therefore church. An extremely dull and wearisome sermon detained us until twelve-thirty. A poor young man, who had been married a few months and had received a son before the nine, brought the child to be baptized. The preacher refused to administer this Sacrament until the father confessed publicly his sin. So see you here this poor fellow in front of the entire congregation declaring loudly that he had covered his wife before marrying her. I have never in my life suffered greater shame. What barbarity![50]

After church we returned to the house and had a pleasant time in the company of Dr. Sage and Miss Gardiner, the sister of my friend the Doctor. After dinner the ladies went to church, and shortly thereafter we went for a ride in the chaise through the environs of the town. The agriculture and population are in very good state, and there is I-do-not-know-what in the character of the inhabitants of this part of the island that makes it more analogous to that of the people of Connecticut than anything else. This town has about one hundred houses and a public library of about two hundred volumes, ancient theological books for the most part. We returned for tea and in the same gracious company spent the rest of the evening.

23. After breakfast the Doctor and I set out for Sag Harbor in order that I might take the ship supposed to sail to Newport. We arrived around nine o'clock and just when we thought everything was ready, discovered not only that the Captain (though he had promised us otherwise) was not yet thinking of setting sail but also that he would not go directly to Newport (as he had also promised)! So I had to go to the terrible inn there to await the juncture. In the interim I amused myself by examining very carefully the ships, crews, and instruments for whale fishing, which are prepared here and generally go to the coasts of Brazil for the fishing. The ships are brigantines of about 160 tons. Their crews are in large part Indians, who are the most capable harpoonists and are generally named boat officers.[51] In

[50] Public confession of sins was not an uncommon practice at this time.
[51] This fact is reflected in Herman Melville's *Moby Dick*. New Englanders

the performance of their work they behave with circumspection and decency, without ever getting drunk or committing any irregularity during their employment. Through this we see that these beings are as apt for everything as anyone else and that the man who acts with innate prudence has a superior character to risk. The instruments are harpoons and ropes, to wound the whale; spears, to kill it; and tackle, to raise it on board, in pieces. Near the small mast is a brick oven with two boilers, where they melt the fat and the brains of the whale and then barrel the products, calling the first oil and the second spermaceti. In the hold are firewood, barrels of earth to repair the oven, etc. See here an exertion of human industry and spirit! I am assured that every year during the war about four hundred ships sailed out of this neighborhood to go whale fishing.

I spent the rest of the day reading.

24. No ship going to Newport having availed itself, I have spent the morning writing. At eleven o'clock Dr. Gardiner, his wife, his friend Mr. Hunting, and two young ladies from Shelter Island, all on their way to East Hampton, arrived, and we ate together. Afterwards they continued their journey, but I could not join them as I had given my word to Mr. Guilson and Mr. L'Homedieu,[52] old New York acquaintances, to go in the afternoon to their houses, four and seven miles from here, respectively. After dinner, Squire Guilson, Squire L'Homedieu, and I set out for the house of the first, where we drank tea and had supper in society. It is a singular thing the state of simplicity and even scarcity in which these people live, their small and miserable houses, without ornament or the least comfort, and, at the same time, the lofty ideas that dwell in their minds! The first of these squires was a member of the Assembly, and the second of the Senate in New York; notwithstanding, their houses and furni-

had been engaged in whaling in South Atlantic waters before 1776. Sag Harbor was one of the most famous Long Island whaling towns.

[52] Ezra L'Hommedieu (*sic*) was a member of the Continental Congress, an experimental agriculturalist, and "father of the University of the State of New York."

ture appeared to be those of unfortunate people. Squire Guilson has, nevertheless, some books, among them the curious collection of the English poets by Mather Byles.[53]

25. After breakfast we returned to Sag Harbor, in search of a ship for Newport, and, finding none, had to be patient. The day and night were spent reading, for this town is the worst imaginable.

26. Neither ship nor society, so we had to resign ourselves to books completely. A Captain Latan came that night and allowed to me that his ship would leave in the morning for Newport. God grant it!

27. In the expectation of embarking I arose early and brought my diary up to date. It is now nine o'clock and the ship has yet to appear. The worst is that an ague, which has been menacing me for days, is increasing here considerably. In the afternoon, in the company of Dr. Gardiner, I visited Mr. and Mrs. Jacob Conkling.[54] Afterwards I went home, to read until bedtime.

28. The wind being contrary today, we could not embark. Reading, and more reading. In the evening I was entertained watching the sailors wrestle and tumble—proper exercises for men as robust and healthy as these whale fishermen. I paid my bill that night to Mr. William Davall, the landlord. His miserable tavern is called the Sag Harbor Coffee-House, despite the fact one could not find a cup of coffee there, even as a medicine.

29. At six o'clock in the morning we sailed with a lazy wind, crossing Gardiners Bay, where the English squadron had

[53] Mather Byles was an American Congregational minister, essayist, and poet. The work mentioned here has not been identified. Most likely it refers to his work, *Poems on Several Occasions* (1744), some verses of which are addressed to English poets. However, he wrote at least two long poems that may have led to Miranda's confusion: *A poem on the death of His late Majesty King George, of glorious memory. And the accession of our present sovereign King George II to the British throne* (1727) and *On the death of the queen. a Poem* (1738).

[54] Probably Jacob Conklin (*sic*), a local hero for having once been kidnaped by and escaping from the notorious Captain Kidd.

ridden at anchor watching the French fleet at Newport. We arrived at Newport at midnight, after passing Gardiners Island, Fishers Island, Block Island, Montauk Point (where there is yet an Indian village of about fifty families), Judith Point and, at eleven o'clock, the Newport Lighthouse, five miles from the city.

~~~ *30.* Before six o'clock I went ashore to find an inn and called at Mrs. Almy's and others. These, I discovered, were full of persons sick with agues who had come here from the South (especially Charleston) to recover their health.[55] Finally I obtained lodging at the inn of Robert Lillibridge, near the City Hall, paying for my room and board four pesos fuertes (how cheap!) and for that of my servant three and a half (how disproportionate!). After breakfast I went forth to deliver some letters of recommendation. My first visit was to Christopher Champlin, Esq., and his daughter Miss Peggy Champlin, one of the beauties of the region; to them I gave letters from the Sears family.[56] They received me with the greatest affability and warmth. In the company of Mr. Champlin, I went to see Miss Nancy Hunter (another of the graces of Newport), for whom I also brought letters from the Sears family and who, together with her mother, received me with the greatest kindness, promising me that her sister Miss Peggy Hunter, the famous beauty of Rhode Island, who at the time found herself indisposed, would make an effort to come down and see me the next day.[57] I showed my gratitude for their kindness, as was proper, and took my leave, returning to the inn for dinner.

[55] By mid-eighteenth century, Newport had become a mecca for families from South Carolina, Georgia, and even the West Indies, who came to spend the summer to escape the heat and such diseases as malaria.

[56] Peggy Champlin had the honor of being George Washington's partner at the French Ball, March 7, 1781. The Prince de Broglie said of her: "Miss Champlin had beautiful eyes, a sweet mouth and perfectly shaped face, fine figure, pretty foot, and an air altogether attractive." She became the mother-in-law of Oliver Hazard Perry, hero of the Battle of Lake Erie (1813). The Champlin house is still standing. The Sears family was probably that of Isaac Sears, merchant of New York.

[57] The Hunter house also still stands and is one of the most celebrated residences in Newport.

In the afternoon I visited Mrs. Greene, who lives in the section called "The Point" and to whom I delivered letters addressed to her husband (he is in South Carolina).[58] She received me with generosity and kindness. We drank tea, and I remained there in good society until eight o'clock. She is one of the women of most ingenuous manner and festive spirit I have known in this country.

There was a mob here yesterday, owing to the arrival in the afternoon of the British frigate *Mercury*, Captain Stanhope, with a sailor on board who was a native and resident of Boston and whom the English had forcibly put on board and obligated to serve from the time of the evacuation of New York.[59] Said Captain is married in this city and came ashore after the frigate anchored; the mob surrounded his house, demanding the sailor, who remained on board. The Captain gave his word of honor to turn him over the next day, after which the disturbance ceased. When the man disembarked this morning, the court examined him and, finding the imprisonment he had suffered on board to be unjust, freed him. For lack of sufficient reason (they did not harm anybody), it has not been possible to punish the *caudillos* of the mob. Thus this entertainment came to an end.

The air here is so healthful and pure that I, who found myself attacked by an ague acquired in Sag Harbor, no sooner had put my foot on shore than I began to feel better, and the fever, which was wont to attack me irremediably every day, has not returned. The British and French armies here during the war,[60] so I am told, not only recovered completely but when they embarked left not a single invalid in the hospital. Thus this island justly deserves the title they gave it of "The Paradise of New England." Its lands would also be beautiful and pleasing if besides being completely

58 The reference is to the wife of Nathanael Greene, famous general and commander of the southern army. In gratitude for his services, both South Carolina and Georgia gave him grants of land. The family rented the Tillinghast house in Newport in 1783.

59 An early example of impressment, an issue that continued a grievance for many years after independence.

60 The British occupied Newport from December 8, 1776, to October 25, 1779; the French came in July 12, 1780.

cultivated, as indeed they are, they did not lack the ornament of trees and forests, which the armies entirely destroyed during the war, giving an air of aridity to all the countryside just as one sees in La Mancha of Castile.[61]

~~~~~ *31.* After writing some letters to New York I went to see Miss Peggy Hunter, who, keeping her sister's promise, came down to see me, and I had the pleasure of a long visit with her. She invited me for tea that afternoon, and I accepted gladly. At three o'clock I went to the house of Mr. Champlin for dinner, and in the company of his family we ate very pleasantly and sociably (a delicious, if frugal, meal certainly!). At five o'clock he and I went to have a look at the town and bay from the steeple of the British church,[62] which is quite high and commands a large prospectus, but the horizon was overcast and so we had to leave our observations for a better occasion. Instead we visited the interior of said church, which is pretty and spacious and has in addition a good organ.

At six o'clock I went to have tea with Miss Hunter, in whose delightful company I remained until eight o'clock; we spoke French and a bit about literature, but too little to form an opinion. I then went to see Dr. Newman, for whom I brought a credential letter. Finding him at home, I presented the missive, and he offered to introduce me in a good and sure place. We drank a cup of grog and, after he had given me a pamphlet of his cures and discoveries, left the house and went for a walk, which led to the temple of one of the best nymphs, where he left me well recommended. After he had gone, we directed our steps to the altar and there consummated a solemn sacrifice to Venus. At ten o'clock I returned to my lodging and read until bedtime.

~~~~~ *September 1.* I wrote my diary and afterwards went to

[61] La Mancha, an elevated plateau in New Castile, is the locale of *Don Quixote.*
[62] This is undoubtedly a reference to Trinity Church. From the first it was under the jurisdiction of royal authorities. During the Revolution, many of the members were Tories and the King's arms adorned the church. The organ to which Miranda refers was a gift of Bishop Berkeley in 1733. It was surmounted by the crown of England with a bishop's miter on either side.

see some ladies and acquaintances, among them John Malbone, Esq.,[63] for whom I brought a letter and who received me with kindness in a large house he owns in the southern part of Main Street. At three o'clock I went to the house of Mrs. Greene for dinner. Here I found a large company of ladies and gentlemen from Charleston, South Carolina, of the immense number here convalescing and recovering their health. Good Lord! What a contrast between their color and complexions and those of the local citizenry! We dined and drank tea in the company of these presumptuous ladies and gentlemen, and I enjoyed the jocose and entertaining conversations of Mrs. Greene, Dr. Senter, her brother Captain William Littlefield,[64] etc., until nine o'clock.

2. The day has been cloudy and somewhat rainy, so I have spent part of it reading indoors. At ten o'clock I walked to the southern part and observed the cattle and sheep grazing in the neighboring meadows. Their size certainly is larger than that of all the others of the same species I have seen on this continent. (This quality is attributed to the pastures of this island, which are more nutritious than those of any other place; a young ox or sheep brought here from Connecticut immediately grows and fattens more.)

Returning, I went to see my nymph, and we made another solemn sacrifice to Venus. After a few visits, I had dinner. In the afternoon I had tea with Miss Champlin and her mother; their company was so gracious and so instructive in matters relating to the character, procedures, and way of living of the French during their stay here in the army of Monsieur de Rochambeau[65] that I remained there until nine o'clock. Afterwards I visited Dr. Senter and engaged in literary conversation until eleven o'clock.

3. In the morning I examined the sepulchral inscriptions

---

[63] John was probably the son of Godfrey Malbone, one of the most successful eighteenth-century merchants and slave traders.

[64] Littlefield was a Rhode Island officer during the war.

[65] On July 12, 1780, General Jean Baptiste de Vimeur, Comte de Rochambeau, and 5,088 men arrived in Newport.

in the great cemetery in the northern part of the city. Among them was not a single age of one hundred years, very rare ones of eighty, and a few of seventy, from which one infers that in the most healthful regions the age of man does not increase! From here I went to see a garden, one mile from the city, belonging to Mr. John Malbone. The location is extremely pleasant and commands a very advantageous view of the bay, islands, and surrounding countryside. The house was completely destroyed by a fire which accidentally started in it; from what the ruins reveal and the inhabitants say, it must have been the most elegant building in the entire state. The garden is extensive and well laid out, with a pretty bath and many excellent fruit trees, but is completely neglected. For nine pennies one can enter it, walk wherever one wants to in it, and take all the fruit one wishes. About half a mile away are two very dominant, contiguous heights, called Tonomy Hill, where there is a spacious and well-constructed fort, with a redoubt covering the second height and under the command of said fort. Both structures were built by the British and are extremely strong. This fort likewise commands one of the most delightful and extensive views of the bay, city, and surrounding country one would want to imagine. The so-called "lines," now in ruins, are half a mile from the city and compass it from one end to the other, cutting the island (hardly more than a mile and a half wide here) into two pieces. Here the British faced Sullivan when he besieged them in 1778 and repulsed him.[66]

At three o'clock I returned to my lodging for dinner. Afterwards I took a walk to The Point, delivered a letter from New York to Jacob Rodrígues Rivera,[67] a Jew of character and honesty, and, not having found Mrs. Greene at home, went to have tea with

[66] General John Sullivan of New Hampshire was leader of the American forces which on August 28–29, 1778, attempted to drive the British from Newport. The move failed, primarily because of lack of support from the French fleet.

[67] Jacob Rodrígues Rivera, a prosperous merchant, arrived in 1745 with a group of refugees from the Spanish Inquisition. He is credited with introducing the spermaceti (a type of tallow, taken from the head of sperm whales, used in making candles) industry to the Colonies.

Mrs. Champlin and her daughter, whose society and lovely manner are more pleasing to me every day. I remained there until ten o'clock, when I went home.

⟜ *4.* At nine o'clock in the morning I took my chaise and went for a tour of the island. I started out on the West Road, which is good enough, but full of loose stones which make traveling unpleasant. At five miles there is a country house, *Redwood House,*[68] with its garden. Here I saw a belvedere, for drinking tea, built with the greatest taste and elegance and the best work of its kind I have seen. The house and the rest are nothing special. Half a mile before this is the house where General Prescott was surprised in bed and made prisoner by the Americans.[69] A short distance from the garden is Redwood Hill, where one sees a fortification, product of the retreat of Sullivan; this hillock commands a handsome perspective.

Four miles farther on is Burington's Hill, where there is another small redoubt, and contiguous on the right is an extensive fortification (work of the French) on Butt's Hill, a highly dominant spot, although I do not understand what purpose it serves there. Two miles farther on is Bristol Ferry, where I made a halt at a small but clean tavern. Here I ate and spent a good while in conversation with the landlady and her family, who are extremely good people and reveal (as do all the people of this island) great cleanliness, hospitality, and good countenance in general. The distance from here to the continent is barely a mile, but a ship of large burden can pass; the strait at Howland's Ferry, about two miles to the east, is not more than a quarter of a mile wide, but deep enough for the same ship to pass.

The road on the eastern side was much better and allowed me

---

[68] The country house of Abraham Redwood, the Quaker philanthropist who in 1747 gave five hundred pounds sterling to start Redwood Library.

[69] General Richard Prescott was commander of the British forces in Rhode Island. On July 9, 1777, Colonel William Barton, with forty men, surprised the General in bed and spirited him away, undressed. He was later exchanged for General Charles Lee. For Miranda's version of the raid, see the entry for September 7.

to complete the tour of the island. Three miles farther on is New-town, consisting of six or eight houses, where the troops of Sulli-van had a skirmish during their withdrawal; the British gained control of hard-by Quaker Hill and in the end had to allow the Americans to continue their retreat, having suffered no small loss. Quaker Hill (receives its name from a Quaker church there) commands every other height on the island and also a view, more extensive and delightful than one can imagine, of the channels, bay, islands, and surrounding countryside. I continued on this delicious road, stopping at several houses of laborers in order to observe their character, customs, etc. I can assure you with all ingenuousness that neither more generous and affable simplicity nor more delicate and beautiful complexions have I seen in any part I have visited.

Nine miles farther on I arrived at Southwest Point (a sort of island joined by a small throat of sand to this island), where there is a tavern called Slocum's House. Many people come here to eat and others to drink tea. I had tea and amused myself for a while with the simple conversation of this family and with the beautiful view of the ocean and near-by places.

Returning to Newport by the beach road, I saw the "maiden-head" fishermen[70] at work. With nets, they haul these fish out in large numbers, without further ceremony put them in barrels, throw layers of salt on them, and ship them to the Antilles,[71] where they sell very well as food for the plantation Negroes, etc. There is not even a shed to cover the catch, so it stands there without shelter in all weather. There have been days when as many as eight hundred barrels of these fish have been caught on these shores, such is their abundance. The number of barrels exported annually is large, as are the profits, but I have not been able to determine the amounts with certainty.

At seven o'clock I arrived at my inn, drank tea, and then went to the house of Dr. Senter, in whose company and that of another

[70] This is probably a reference to menhaden, one of the most plentiful fish on the Atlantic Coast.
[71] The islands of the West Indies.

Quaker, Dr. Easton,[72] I spent the evening in literary and political conversation.

〜〜 5. Sunday, and consequently church. I went first to the Presbyterian, its building indifferent and old. At the Anglican church I remained for the entire service, celebrated with great dignity, the organ accompanying the singing of the psalms and the good taste of the building and the elegance of the gathering (certainly not large) giving a majestic air to the religious ritual. (This is the only place in all this continent where a decent foreigner arriving at the church is not offered a seat by the others.) When it was over, I climbed the steeple to see the beautiful prospectus it offers of the town, bay, and vicinity, which was certainly delightful, for the horizon was quite clear.

When I came down and entered the cemetery, I saw this inscription among others:

ci-gît
Charles Louis D'Arzac
de Ternai.
Chevalier de l'ordre de Saint Jean de Jerusalem,
ancien gouverneur general des isles de France,
et du Bourbon, Chef d'Escadre des Armees na-
vales de S.M.T.C. Commandant l'Escadre
Francaise envoye en 1780. au Sucours des
Etats-Unis de l'Amerique.
Mort le 15. Decembre 1780, agé de 57. ans.[73]

I visited Mrs. Hunter and at three o'clock went to the temple of the Quakers, in whose company I remained for two hours, without anybody speaking a single word. I entertained myself all this time by examining slowly the dress and the countenances of

[72] Probably Nicholas Easton, descendant of a prominent family.

[73] Chevalier de Ternay (1722–1780) retired from the French naval service about 1772 with the rank of brevet *chef d'escadre*. After the French alliances of 1778, he took charge of a squadron at Brest and was commander of the fleet that brought Rochambeau. His epitaph reads: "Here lies Charles Louis D'Arzac de Ternai. Knight of the order of St. John of Jerusalem, former governor-general of the Isles of France and Bourbon, Commodore in the Naval Forces of his very Catholic Majesty. Commander of the French Squadron sent in 1780 to the aid of the United States of America. Died December 15, 1780, aged 57 years."

the female concourse and I can assure you with all ingenuousness that neither more simplicity, cleanliness, and taste in the first nor more natural and simple beauty in the second can be imagined. I am firmly persuaded that the coloring of Rubens and the carnations of Titian can never imitate what nature offers here in the hue and the beautiful complexion of these simple Quaker women, who have not a grain of powder or drop of oil on their persons. Suddenly we all stood up, shook hands, called each other "friend," and went our separate ways. I visited Dr. Senter, with the intention of taking a naturalist's walk, but it began to rain, and so we returned to his house, where we engaged in literary conversation, mixed with cups of tea. (Mrs. Hunter had invited me for tea, but I relinquished my place to the courtiers.) Afterwards I went to visit Mrs. and Miss Champlin, in whose pleasant company I stayed until ten o'clock.

6. Around eleven o'clock we started out on a visit of the fortifications in the bay. First we saw Rose Island, with a battery of some thirty cannons; then Brinton's Point, with a fort in ruins and some batteries of not much importance (also a country house, which at a distance appears to be very good but not close by); and Goat Island, with a fort and batteries, which can mount forty cannons. D'Estaing[74] crossed and recrossed these last two positions, with fifteen ships of the line, without receiving great damage, and silenced some of said batteries. The other was built later by Monsieur de Ternay. The three positions form a triangle and combine to impede entrance to the bay, but in my opinion the intent is, rather, to deceive. The intent of Monsieur de Ternay was for these three batteries to protect his squadron in an attack, but his own position indicated distrust.

From Goat Island one has the most complete and advantageous prospect of the city one can find. At two o'clock we returned to the mainland, and at four I went with Dr. Senter to see a rock, or piece from a mountain, fissured and separated from end to end

[74] Comte Jean Baptiste Charles Henri Hector d'Estaing sailed into Newport Harbor in July, 1778. After an inconclusive battle and storm, the fleet went to Boston. He died on the guillotine in 1794.

(by some sort of earthquake, naturally), two miles from the city, by the seashore, and commonly called Purgatory. Its height is about fifty feet and its width sixty. The fissure is three or four feet wide. The sea enters through its base and runs the entire length of the crack. Its most peculiar aspect is that one part is smooth and compact like a fine wall, and the other irregular and wavy as if it had been split from another identical piece. We returned by the beach, and here I had the pleasure of seeing a second time the catching, salting, and barreling of the fish I have previously mentioned. There have been days on this beach when the catch has come to eight hundred barrels, such is the abundance. At nightfall we returned to the city, and later I retired to read and drink tea, for I felt somewhat chilly and feverish.

7. I have spent the morning writing my diary, etc. Around four o'clock in the afternoon I took a horse and went to the country house of John Overing, Esq., where General Prescott, the commanding general of the island, was surprised and made prisoner by a band of Americans. The house is small and is about four and a half miles from the city and about three-fourths of a mile from the sea, near Redwood Creek, where thirty Americans, under the command of Colonel Barton, disembarked from three boats. With the setting of the sun they started out, twelve miles away, using oars the entire distance so as not to be observed by the frigates and guard boats posted all around the island. With the help of the night and the Colonel's good management and knowledge of the terrain, they were able to disembark without being observed and approach the house through a cornfield. They deceived the sentinel stationed at the door of the house and removed the Commander in Chief and his aide-de-camp, in nightshirts, through the midst of his entire army and squadron without a single post sensing it, despite the fact there were several between the distances of one-fourth and one-half mile and more than three thousand men in the circumference of one and two miles. This certainly was one of the most brilliant actions of its kind executed in modern or ancient times. The same Negro house servant who

at the command of Colonel Barton kindled the light for the search and one of the guides, who today lives in that vicinity, informed me of the incident. . . . Afterwards I returned to the city, about a mile from which, on the highway, is the handsome Gozzen's House. I entered the Malbone garden, where I took all the fruit I wanted, and drank tea in a house near by used for that purpose. As darkness came I arrived at my tavern.

Finally, I said farewell to all my friends. At the house of Mrs. Hunter I saw two original paintings by Salvator Rosa,[75] certainly very good ones. Miss Betsey Hunter played the harpsichord and sang a few French songs very well; it is a pity such beauty and personal excellence are threatened with loss of sight. This is a lovely and affectionate family. I was told that Mrs. Stora, who is the subject of the adventure the Abbé Robin[76] mentions, lives here (and that Miss Nancy Vernon[77] is a girl of personal merit and education). Later I went to the house of Mrs. Champlin, in whose tasteful and affable company I remained until ten o'clock. She invited me for breakfast the next day.

8. At seven o'clock in the morning I went with Dr. Senter to visit the library. This building is ample, comfortable, in very good taste, and well located (on a height within the city.)[78] It is a shame the British troops treated so badly the collection of books it contained (twelve thousand volumes),[79] because one knows from the remains that they were select (among those left are the works of Bayle, Bolingbroke, Hobbes, Hume, Descartes, Plato, Cicero, Sallust, Boerhaave, and various other philosophers

[75] An Italian painter (1615–1673).

[76] Claude C. Robin, a French chaplain with Rochambeau. In an account of his American experiences he mentions a love affair between a French officer and a matron of Newport.

[77] Nancy was probably the daughter of William Vernon, a wealthy merchant and shipowner, who played a major role in the organization of the American navy.

[78] This was the Redwood Library. In addition to the £500 gift of Redwood previously mentioned, the people of Newport subscribed £5,000 to erect a building. The Crown and Dean Berkeley also gave books.

[79] When the British left in 1779, they took the town records, sacked the library, and carried off many books and some church bells.

and classics, ancient and modern). God preserve you for ignorance! Three or four hundred volumes are all that remain.

I had breakfast with Mrs. and Miss Champlin and remained in
their pleasant company until ten o'clock, when the packet sum-
moned its passengers. My friend Dr. Senter and Mr. Champlin
accompanied me to the pier. A memorandum the latter gave me
indicates inadequately the number of the inhabitants and the decline of the town. (The poor man is a pedant and knows very
little.) The women are generally very good looking, affable, civil,
and dress with taste; the men are dull, barely sociable, careless in
their dress and manners, and without much education. I do not
believe there are three dozen buildings and houses of decent appearance in the entire city; the rest are huts and stalls. On Main
Street, about a mile long and the principal thoroughfare of the
town (in reality there is no other), there are about three stores
which deserve the name, the rest being shacks; all the goods which
together they contain I think could be bought for thirty thousand
pesos.[80] It is a pity that a location so beautiful and advantageous
for commerce is in fact so miserable and decadent. The government is in the hands of the most ignorant part of the population,
known as Whigs,[81] and this in my judgment is the root of all the
trouble!

At eleven-thirty in the morning we finally set sail, with nineteen passengers on board, seven of them women. Fifteen miles
above Newport is the town of Bristol, with about eighty inhabitants, and ten miles farther, on the west bank of the Providence
River, the small town of Pawtuxet. Here the wind and tide turned
against us, and we were barely able to travel two miles. At nightfall we anchored at Fields Point, three miles from Providence.

---

[80] Following the war, Newport went into a financial decline as its commerce
passed to New York and many of the wealthy were impoverished by the depre-
ciation in paper money. The population fell to four thousand as residents moved
to Providence or left with the British army. As late as 1793, there were only six
brick buildings in the town.

[81] This is a term used in both England and America to indicate those opposed
to the King. It was used here to indicate the lower, or debtor, classes, which came
into control in Rhode Island during this period.

The skiff was leaking so badly that it was foundering, the passengers did not even have a blanket to sleep in, and the tide would not be favorable until midnight. Some of the men resolved to set out in the skiff, disembark at said Point, and walk three and a half miles to the city. Six accomplished it, but only by dint of great toil, for by the time it reached land the boat was half-filled with water; the rest of us stayed on board, including all the women. The shouts, sports, and frolics the latter engaged in cannot be described. I had brought my cot and with great difficulty was able to sleep awhile in the morning, thrust into an infernal corner of the cabin, which with so many people in it and so much noise had the appearance of Hell indeed. Finally at three o'clock in the morning, making use of the oars, the ship went the last three miles, and the Captain let the women off at Providence.

9. At seven o'clock I went ashore and obtained lodging at Rice's Tavern, near the City Hall, paying six pesos for myself and three for my servant, weekly. At ten o'clock I went out to distribute letters of recommendation, starting with the Reverend Mr. James Manning, president of the college here.[82] He was away, but his wife received me with the greatest courteousness and assured me that he would be back the following day. I then went to Messrs. Clark & Nightingale, where I found my baggage undamaged and was given a polite reception.[83] Mr. Clark offered to accompany me and we went for a stroll through the town, visiting a young watchmaker, Cyril Dodge,[84] who had made great advances in this art, for example, a watch which without being wound runs constantly. Lieutenant Governor Jabez Bowen, Esq.,[85] was not in town, and therefore I gave the letter for him to Mr. Clark, his son-in-law. We then went to the court, which

[82] Manning, a Baptist clergyman, became head of Rhode Island College in 1765. The school was renamed Brown University in 1804.

[83] Clarke (*sic*) & Nightingale, a shipping firm in Providence, owned one of the principal docks in that city.

[84] Seril (*sic*) Dodge was also the first jewelry manufacturer in Providence, specializing in silver shoe buckles.

[85] He was deputy governor (1778–86), chancellor of Rhode Island College

was in session, and heard the proceedings and arguments until one o'clock, when I retired to my tavern.

In the afternoon I had tea with Mrs. Clark, at whose house I met Miss B. Bowen, various persons from Charleston who have come here to restore their health, and the celebrated Dr. Moyes of Edinburgh, who a short while ago came to this continent in the company of Mrs. Helly, an English widow and businesswoman. The Doctor has been completely blind since he was eighteen months old and nevertheless has acquired a classical education and a variety of accomplishments which are really surprising. He is now about thirty-two years old. His deportment is highly becoming; his person and manner agreeable; his conversation festive, affable, erudite, and occasionally jocose. I advanced some subjects which he discussed with interest, and as a result we bound ourselves up in literary topics until the hour was late, when he retired to his tavern and I to mine.[86]

10. In the morning I wrote my diary and around eleven o'clock started out on a walk with Mr. Clark. After I delivered a letter for Thomas L. Halsey, Esq.,[87] who was away, we went to the eastern part of the town, where Mr. Clark has a still for processing molasses brought from the Antilles. Because of a lack of this substance during the war, the extract of cornstalks was used—to make whiskey. See here how far the industry of these people goes!

We proceeded to Fox Point,[88] an advantageous height, where

(1785), a delegate to the Annapolis Convention (1786), and an outstanding amateur astronomer.

[86] Henry Moyes, M.D., born in 1749, was blinded by smallpox at the age of three. Nevertheless, he graduated from college and, probably at the suggestion of his friend Joseph Priestley, began a career as a public lecturer. He made extended lecture tours of Great Britain and spent two years in the United States, with great popular success. In the United States he traveled as far south as Charleston. Articles by Moyes on galvanic electricity appeared in the *Philosophical Magazine*, VII, 347, and IX, 217.

[87] Halsey was a famous *bon vivant* who reputedly kept live terrapins in his cellar for himself and his guests.

[88] A Revolutionary fort under the command of Esek Hopkins. In 1775 it contained six eighteen-pound cannon and four smaller ones.

there is a battery, or, better said, its outlines. It was built, together with many redoubts and entrenchments in the vicinity of this town, by General Sullivan[89] (for the most part) to resist whatever attack the British might attempt by land or sea, as was expected after they took possession of Rhode Island.

Afterwards I entered the court and had occasion to observe the talents and abilities of the judges and lawyers. The latter are very much superior to the former, as much in ability as in character and dignity, the judges appearing to be so inferior as to degrade the dignity of the tribunal. The reason is clear. There are no salaries of consideration and, therefore, no suitable persons to perform the functions; whereas advocateship produces unlimited business and, consequently, considerable fees.

Among the most outstanding lawyers are Governor James McVarnum, Governor William Bradford, and Mr. Marchant;[90] with them I formed particular acquaintances, and they seemed to me persons of talent and ability. Here republicanism is at its highest point! Governors and generals attending the tribunals with legal documents and records under their arms just as in Europe our law clerks and students do!

In these courts I have noticed that the abuse of innuendo on the part of the lawyers is scandalous; doubtless it stems from the slight character and dignity of those who compose the tribunal.

In the afternoon we had tea with the Misses Bowen, three or four passably good-looking sisters, particularly the youngest. There was much company, but when the tea was over we all went to hear the third of the lectures, entitled "On The Philosophy Of Chemistry & Natural History," being given by Dr. Moyes at the City Hall. In the course of an hour and a half the Doctor presented to a large and very decent gathering a learned and elegant

[89] John Sullivan was captured in the Battle of Long Island but later exchanged. He commanded the American forces besieging Newport in 1778.

[90] McVarnum had also served as an advocate for the Court of Admiralty in Rhode Island; Bradford was former deputy governor and administrator of confiscated estates; and Henry Marchant had been a member of the Continental Congress and was later a federal judge.

discourse on "The Theory of the Fluids," accompanied by various observations and curious experiments, which effectually produced satisfaction and applause in the entire audience. One of the observations corroborating his doctrine is that in Bath, England, the ladies, after dancing and being agitated by this exercise, wet the points of their ears with a bit of *eau de cologne*, thus cooling their bodies and avoiding the consequences of catching a cold when they pass into a colder atmosphere; also, that it is very useful to distribute portions of snow in different parts of the room where one lives in the summer, as thus the air is cooled and becomes more healthful; also, that it is very easy to freeze a man to death in a short time, even in the summer, if, with his clothes wet, he is placed between two doors or in a place where there is an air current. It is certainly a very singular thing that this man, blind from birth, conducts himself and produces these physical operations with so much facility, grace, and effect.

11. In the morning I had a conversation with Governor Hopkins, a man of great character and of the highest respect in this state and brother of the American commodore.[91] He is more than eighty years old; nevertheless, affability, fine manners, and vast erudition mark his conversation and conduct. He was one of the leading members of those that formed the first Congress and had a part in the handling of the most difficult decisions of this great revolution.

I then went to the home of President Manning, where I amused myself reading *The Character of the College*, a very liberal and well-founded document. Afterwards Mr. Clark and I toured the environs of the city in a chaise. The land is extremely poor and sandy; notwithstanding, the industry of the inhabitants is such that a large part is covered with excellent cornfields and, what is

[91] Stephen Hopkins was governor of Rhode Island in 1755, 1756, 1758–61, 1763, 1764, and 1767; member of the Continental Congress (1774–80); and signer of the Declaration of Independence. In 1764 he wrote *The Rights of the Colonies Examined*. His brother was Esek Hopkins, who was appointed commander in chief of the Continental navy on December 22, 1775.

more, fields of very good tobacco,[92] for which we must suppose they fertilize and prepare the earth to a superlative degree.

At five o'clock we attended the so-called Tea Party. Every Saturday afternoon the businessmen and ladies of the town gather at a small country house, three miles away and rented for this purpose, and drink tea and punch until sunset. The costs are paid by a subscription among the men, and they have the right to bring the ladies and strangers of note visiting the city. Here we found twenty ladies and somewhat more men, drank our tea sociably, and then all took a walk, promiscuously, in the vicinity. In a tree near the house were a bar and rope, so that the ladies might swing themselves. After two of them had performed (one was a marvel at this sport), the party ended. Outstanding among the ladies, for her good looks, is Miss Smith (also full of affectation), and, for her fine manners and graciousness, Mrs. Hopkins. We all withdrew, and I was with Mr. and Mrs. Clark until nine o'clock, when I went home.

12. Sunday, and I spent the morning in the Anabaptist meetinghouse. This is the principal church here, as the richest inhabitants are of this persuasion (as were the founders of the town). The building is spacious, but with neither proportion nor taste in the interior. The steeple, 198 feet high, is, however, one of the best proportioned and most elegant I have ever seen. It is made entirely of wood, but its ornaments and the rest are so well executed that it is not inferior to the best architecture of Italy. The congregation was not too numerous; the minister, Mr. Manning, quite indifferent.[93]

From there I went to the top of the college, which is situated in a place sufficiently elevated to view the prospect it commands, but I found that for the most part it is circumscribed by the im-

---

[92] The Connecticut River Valley is still a commercial producer of tobacco.

[93] The Anabaptists were originally distinguished by their opposition to infant baptism. Rhode Island was from its earliest days a stronghold for the Baptists because of the absence of religious restrictions. Manning, president of the college, was the minister of the church Miranda mentions here. The structure, erected in 1775, is still standing.

mediate mountains and that only by the channel of the river can one see Rhode Island and some of the islands in the bay: in no way comparable to those offered by Quaker Hill and other points on said island.

In the afternoon I attended the church, or community, of the New Lights, a small variation of the Presbyterians;[94] the building is so-so, the congregation quite numerous, and the manner of singing psalms similar to that used in Connecticut. From here I immediately went down to the river, where my friend Mr. Manning, in the midst of a large gathering of people, was baptizing a neophyte. The latter was a boy about eighteen years old, dressed in his ordinary clothes, as was the minister. Both entered the water to where it covered them halfway up the thighs, and there the cleric took hold of the boy by the collar and plunged him into the water, first backwards and then forwards, until he was well soaked. The one retired immediately to change all his clothes, and the other only half. Good God! What frauds and fatuities!

We went to the house of Mr. Arnold for tea and had an amusing time in a large group. Among the guests was Miss March, about nineteen years old, whose amiability and good looks are very commendable; likewise, the affability and manner of Mrs. Arnold are highly creditable. From here I went to see that fine old fellow Governor Hopkins, in whose instructive society I remained until I retired.

13. At six o'clock in the morning Mr. Edward Chinn[95] and I set out on a twelve-mile excursion into the countryside to see a foundry for iron cannons and a machine for evacuating water through evaporation, which a certain Mr. Joseph Brown has established and directs.[96] The cylinder is about twenty-four

94 The New Lights were a branch of Presbyterians, usually middle or lower class, who approved of Whitefield's revivalistic techniques. The more conservative wings considered such practices to be undignified.

95 Chinn was appointed by the legislature in 1783 to settle Rhode Island's accounts with Congress.

96 Joseph Brown was a member of a prosperous commercial family, an ama-

inches in diameter and ten feet long, is of iron, and was cast by
Mr. Brown himself. With this machine he can evacuate water in
the mine at a depth of three hundred feet and at the rate of one
hundred gallons per minute. (See here the character of two nations! Whereas in Mexico and all our other dominions in America
we have yet to see a similar machine, nor any other that deserves
the name, for draining our richest mines, which for this reason we
consider ruined, here these apparatuses for drying the ground
from which iron is extracted are fashioned.) The artisan informed
me that its cost amounts to one thousand pounds sterling. In the
cannon foundry, now inactive owing to the peace, twelve
hundred pieces were cast in the course of the past war, principally
for arming corsairs. Mr. J. Brown must be a man of constant
application in the branch of mechanics and ingenious in his work,
but his conversation and manner are vulgar and somewhat dis-
agreeable. At eleven o'clock Mr. Chinn and I returned, leaving
the good Mr. Brown at his machine and disposed to eat with the
carpenters and laborers, as is his custom. In the afternoon I went
to the house of Mrs. Arnold for tea and afterwards to the lecture
by Dr. Moyes entitled "Ignition & The Connection Between
Light & Heat," as delightful and interesting as the preceding.

14. This day I observed a transition of more than thirty
degrees in the course of twenty-four hours. I do not know how
there are constitutions that bear it!

I have spent the morning writing my diary. At two o'clock
I went to the home of President Manning for dinner, where I
encountered the celebrated Dr. Moyes, with whom I had a pleas-
ant and erudite conversation throughout the length of the meal.
This singular man eats only vegetables. Succotash (a food of the
Indians, composed of tender corn with vetches, beans, etc.) was

---

teur architect who designed the Baptist church previously mentioned and several
commercial buildings, a student of mathematics and astronomy, and later became
a professor of philosophy at Rhode Island College, the institution now bearing
the family name. At the beginning of the Revolution, Rhode Island had a larger
iron and steel production than any other colony.

his favorite dish, in fact his only one. I confess it is a tasty and healthful composition. Here I also met Mr. David Howell, a member of Congress and an educated man, beneath the cloak of a simplicity almost vulgar.[97] At four o'clock I proceeded to examine the college with the President. This brick building is quite spacious and located on a height which commands the town of Providence, and from its top one sees the entire bay, the island, and in very clear weather the city of Newport. The library, philosophical apparatus, etc., are still in their swaddling clothes and barely deserve the name; furthermore the President himself is a completely illiterate man. (The attached memorandum was prepared by him and demonstrates the cheapness of the education and the liberality of the institute.)[98] This inspection concluded, I took the chaise with Mr. Clark and went to visit the famous American Commodore Hopkins, who lives two miles from the city. We found him directing and helping in the paving of part of the ground next to his house. Smoking a pipe, he received us with attention and conducted us to the parlor, where we had an hour of conversation. Among other things we talked about Mexico, and he manifested surprise when I mentioned the city of Mexico, insisting there was no such city and that I was mistaken. Such are his geographical accomplishments! His bearing is vulgar and he keeps tobacco in his pocket for chewing, putting in his pipe, etc. His manner, nevertheless, is gentle and pleasant.

The town is located on the riverbank, to the benefit of commerce. There is only one street and it is somewhat more than a mile long. One observes that the houses here are increasing, while in Newport they seem to be decreasing.

That night, on my return to the inn, I had a long conversation with Dr. Moyes, who had awaited me for that purpose. We talked of sciences and arts and in particular of Spanish poetry, about which he is highly passionate. We bound ourselves in special

[97] In 1796, Howell acted as a United States commissioner on the northeast boundary.

[98] The memorandum has not been included here, although it is in Miranda's manuscripts. Manning was a graduate of New Jersey College—with honors!

friendship, and I offered him letters to my friends in Philadelphia and New York. With this we separated, at one o'clock in the morning.

PART FIVE

Massachusetts and New Hampshire

☆☆☆☆☆

MASSACHUSETTS AND NEW HAMPSHIRE

15. AT SEVEN O'CLOCK in the morning I took the stage, an ordinary coach drawn by four horses which goes twice a week to Boston, paying four pesos for my seat. There was a little of everything in the company of six passengers, but one of them, Major Blodger, was an extremely pleasant and courteous person, so that my time in this mishmash was not spent badly. The road is quite good and at this time of year is delightful. Well populated on both sides, with the orchards next to the houses, it looks like a rural street, the fruit hanging in such abundance that we could seize apples from the windows of the coach. Four and a half miles from Providence is the Pawtuxet River, of slight magnitude, over which there is a wooden bridge. Below the bridge it forms a cataract, called "The Falls" and about fifteen feet high. Eight and a half miles farther is Hatch's Tavern, where they gave us a very good meal. When we reached the so-called town of Walpole, we dined at Hiddin's Tavern and afterwards continued on this always pleasant and populated road until we reached Boston, having passed through the following towns or, better said, districts:

	From Providence to Boston		
to	Pawtuxet River	4½	
	Attleboro	8½	Hatch's Tavern
	Wrentham	4½	Mann's Tavern
	Walpole	6½	Hiddin's Tavern
	Dedham	10	Gay's Tavern
	Roxbury	9	
	Boston	2	
		45	miles

At five-thirty in the afternoon we arrived happily in Boston, and I obtained lodging at the private inn of Mrs. Scott, in Scott Court, paying seven pesos for myself and three for my servant, weekly.

16. I had left my baggage in Providence in the care of Mr. Clark with the understanding that he was to send it the following day in a cart, and see you here he made me wait five days before sending it. Having been careless enough to leave my letters of introduction with the baggage, I had to remain incognito all that time (well spent!) during which I read the history of New England by Hutchinson,[1] which although ponderous and without taste is full of authentic documents and good information. After my trunks arrived (the customhouse permitted them to be unloaded on my word alone that they did not contain merchandise), I proceeded to deliver the letters, which were not few, thanks to the graciousness and kindness of my friends in New York.

Governor Hancock,[2] Joseph Barrel, Esq.,[3] Samuel Breck,[4] General Knox,[5] Tris. Dalton,[6] Christopher Gore,[7] General Henry

[1] Thomas Hutchinson, royal governor of Massachusetts (1771–74). The first two volumes of his *History of the Colony of Massachusetts Bay* were published in 1764 and 1767.

[2] Hancock, Massachusetts leader of the Revolutionary movement and first signer of the Declaration of Independence, was governor of Massachusetts from 1780 to 1785 and from 1787 to 1793.

[3] Joseph Barrell (*sic*) was a prominent Boston merchant, member of the Sons of Liberty, selectman, and a pioneer in the opening of the fur trade with the Northwest (Columbia River).

[4] Also a merchant.

[5] Henry Knox was a close friend and adviser to Washington. He took the initial steps that led to the founding of the United States Military Academy and had command there in 1782. He was founder of the Society of the Cincinnati and secretary of war (1785–94).

[6] Tristram Dalton was a member of the Massachusetts Legislature, one of the first senators from Massachusetts (1789), and an aristocratic, scholarly, country gentleman from Newburyport.

[7] Gore was a lawyer, diplomat, and politician. He was governor of Massachusetts (1809–10) and senator (1814–17).

Jackson,[8] Joseph Russell,[9] Dr. Lloyd,[10] Benjamin Guild,[11] John Lowell,[12] James Swan,[13] Thomas Russell,[14] Dr. Aaron Dexter,[15] Dr. Benjamin Waterhouse,[16] Dr. Smith, Mr. Soderstrom,[17] Reverend Joseph Willard (president of Cambridge College),[18] Miss Ruth Dalton,[19] Mrs. Knox, Miss Rooksby Coffin,[20] etc., received me with the greatest warmth and kindness.

I had dinner with Mr. John Livingston,[21] who received me as a friend. The meal concluded, we went to Beacon Hill,[22] the greatest height on the peninsula where Boston is located, commanding an extensive and extremely pleasant view of the bay and adjacent

[8] Jackson was commander of Massachusetts infantry and was especially active in the Rhode Island campaign of 1778 and at the Battle of Monmouth. He served until the end of the war.

[9] Russell was a wealthy merchant, auctioneer, and owner of Russell's Wharf.

[10] James Lloyd was a popular and distinguished physician, surgeon, and one of the first male obstetricians.

[11] Guild was a Harvard tutor and owner of a Boston bookstore.

[12] Lowell was a jurist and legislator, a member of the Continental Congress, and grandfather of James Russell Lowell.

[13] Swan was a member of the Boston Tea Party group, a colonel in the cavalry during the war, and a wealthy land speculator.

[14] Russell has been described by Samuel Eliot Morison as "a sort of marshal of this mercantile nobility."

[15] Professor of medicine at Harvard and corresponding member of the Medical Society of London.

[16] Physician (M.D., Leyden, 1780), first professor of the theory and practice of physics at Harvard (1783–1812), and best known as a pioneer in use of vaccination in America.

[17] Richard Söderström (*sic*) was Swedish consul general.

[18] Willard was president from 1781 to 1804. John Quincy Adams described him thus: "Mrs. Willard is as different in her manners from the President as can be; they form quite a contrast. Mrs. W. is easy and unaffected, and appears not to be made for cerimony [*sic*]. He is stiff and formal, attached to every custom and trifling form as much as to what is of consequence; however, he was quite sociable; much more so indeed than I should have expected."

[19] Daughter of Tristram Dalton, a merchant, Ruth Hooper Dalton was born May 17, 1767, and married Louis Deblois in July, 1789. In his diary for 1788, John Quincy Adams makes the amusing comment that she was "*Miss* Dalton, emphatically so called even by her parents, which is rather unusual."

[20] The daughter of William Coffin of Boston.

[21] Probably one of the New York Livingstons.

[22] So named because in 1634 the General Court ordered a beacon placed there. Later it became the most fashionable residential section of Boston.

country. Afterwards we returned to his house for tea and spent the rest of the evening there.

The next day I took a stroll on the shore with my friend General Knox. Certainly the quantity of wharves one sees indicates clearly the extensive commerce this port has. These stand out among them: Farnum's, Parson's, Governor's, and, above all, Long Wharf, the size and extension of which are magnificent and which exceeds every other work of its kind on this continent. It is 1,700 feet long, 104 wide, and at low tide has 17 feet of water at its head. There are some seventy others, small and large.

We also visited the city hall, called the State House,[23] at the head of State Street. It is a brick building without any grace whatsoever, ample enough for the purpose it was built for, but not to contain the two branches of the Legislature, which meet there now. In the Senate Room are some bad pictures of the leading personages who founded this colony (clerics for the most part) and an engraving representing the Swiss scene in which the Governor obliged William Tell to shoot at the apple on the head of his young son. (From this resulted the revolution through which those happy people recovered their liberty—the idea cannot be less than pleasing to these! And should be so to all humanity.) There are no more ornaments nor cleanliness than one commonly sees in a good European barracks! The Assembly Room is larger, in the same style as the preceding, and full of benches for the representatives to sit on. In the middle, hanging from a chain, is the figure of a codfish in natural size, made of wood, and in bad taste.[24] This idea is an imitation of the wool sacks in the English Parliament. The lower part is a hall, supported by two rows of wooden columns of the Doric order, through which people who have business there and idlers stroll. From here we went to the Court House, located in Court Street. This building is also of brick, but constructed with much more skill than the preceding, although the lower part is lugubrious and dark. . . . The best build-

[23] Built in 1713, it is now known as the Old State House.
[24] The figure of the codfish, which was added in the year 1784, is still to be seen in the Assembly Room.

ing is the church called Kings Chapel;[25] although its exterior is not finished, the interior is very well proportioned and arranged with taste and skill in the Corinthian style. The congregation known as Church of England (the most genteel in this city) meets in this church and also Trinity Church. The pastor of the first is James Freeman, a young man of few accomplishments and less eloquence; of the second, Samuel Parker,[26] a man of pleasing aspect, delicate enunciation, and middling eloquence.

Mr. Breck, who has been very friendly, came for me in his coach, and we went to Cambridge to dine at the house of Mrs. Tracy.[27] Here we found a large circle of ladies, gentlemen, republicans, etc. I was introduced to all of them in due form (a tedious ceremony certainly!), and after dinner we returned to Boston, seven miles away on the isthmus, or "The Neck,"[28] as they call it. The evening was spent in society at the house of Mr. Breck.

Names of the principal ladies I have known and talked to here: Mrs. Hancock, Mrs. Hayley (sister of the famous John Wilkes[29] in England and extremely lovely), Mrs. Bowdoin,[30] Mrs. Amory,[31] Mrs. Knox, Mrs. Brimmer,[32] Mrs. Swan (ostentatious and

[25] Designed by Peter Harrison and erected in 1749. The plans called for a tower that was never built. It is now considered as being the finest Colonial church interior extant. In 1784 it became the first Episcopal church in New England. James Freeman became pastor after the Anglican rector fled.

[26] Parker was for a time after 1776 the only Episcopal clergyman in Boston. Later he became the second Bishop of Massachusetts.

[27] The wife of Nathaniel Tracy, one of the most successful privateers during the war and owner of many merchant vessels. They lived in what is now known as Vassal House in Cambridge. Mrs. Tracy, the former Ann Lee of Marblehead, was considered a handsome and accomplished woman.

[28] Boston was almost on an island, joined to the mainland by a long narrow neck three miles in length and a mile wide at its widest point. It was so narrow and low that at times it was submerged.

[29] Wilkes was an English political reformer and enemy of George III. He favored parliamentary reform and the safeguarding of liberty against ministerial autocracy; he was a champion of Colonial rights during the Revolution.

[30] Probably the wife of James Bowdoin, later governor (1785-87).

[31] Probably Elizabeth Coffin Amory, wife of Thomas. They built a large house, later owned by George Ticknor, at the head of Park Street.

[32] The former Sarah Watson of Plymouth. Her husband, Martin Brimmer, was a businessman engaged in iron manufacturing.

without any education whatsoever), Mrs. and Miss Lloyd, Mrs. Babcock,[33] Mrs. Bulfinch (vain and ridiculous woman),[34] Mrs. Breck, Mrs. Hitchborn (famous for having married her present husband after he accidentally killed, with a pistol, his predecessor in the latter's house; and to all appearance he courted this lady on that occasion, not to say that he was her gallant!),[35] Mrs. Morton (has read a bit and swells with pride about it),[36] Mrs. Barrel, Mrs. T. Russell, Mrs. S. Davis,[37] Mrs. J. Russell,[38] Mrs. Jarvis,[39] Mrs. Lowell,[40] Mrs. Sheaffe,[41] Mrs. Livingston, Mrs. Waldo,[42] Mrs. Apthorp,[43] Mrs. Deblois,[44] Mrs. Cushing,[45] Mrs. Prince,[46] Mrs. Warren (widow of the General, who died gloriously at Bunker Hill),[47] Mrs. Greene,[48] Mrs. Andrews,[49] Mrs. Stillman,[50] Mrs. Cooper,[51] Mrs. Sargent,[52] Mrs. Hall,[53] Mrs. Apple-

[33] Mrs. James Lloyd; see note 10 above and note 95 below. Mrs. Babcock was the wife of Adam Babcock, a Boston merchant.

[34] She was a daughter of Charles Apthorp and married Dr. Thomas Bulfinch, described by a contemporary as having "a good share of very genteel practice" and living "in good style." A portrait of her by Jonathan Blackburn is still extant.

[35] Wife of Benjamin, a prominent Boston lawyer.

[36] Sarah Apthorp, daughter of a wealthy merchant, was the wife of the prominent lawyer Perez Morton. They were outstanding in the social life of Boston and she was locally noted as an authoress. Her portrait was painted by Gilbert Stuart.

[37] Most likely this was the wife of Captain Soloman Davis.

[38] Probably the wife of Judge James Russell.

[39] Mrs. Leonard Jarvis, wife of a Boston and Cambridge merchant.

[40] Possibly the wife of Judge John Lowell of Boston.

[41] This could be either Maria or Sarah Sheaffe; both were wealthy and moneylenders.

[42] Perhaps the wife of Francis Waldo.

[43] Probably Sarah Wentworth Apthorp, mother of Mrs. Morton and member of a wealthy merchant family.

[44] Wife of William, a merchant.

[45] Wife of Lieutenant Governor Thomas Cushing (1780–88).

[46] Shipowner Job Prince's wife.

[47] A reference to Dr. Joseph Warren.

[48] Probably the wife of the merchant David Greene. The family was proscribed as Tories, but their citizenship was restored in 1787.

[49] The wife of John Andrews, a prosperous merchant.

[50] She was probably the wife of the Reverend Samuel Stillman, pastor of the First Baptist Church (1765–1807).

A South West View of Newport.

Miranda found the climate at Newport highly agreeable. "This island justly deserves the title . . . 'The Paradise of New England,'" he said.

Emmet Collection, The New York Public Library

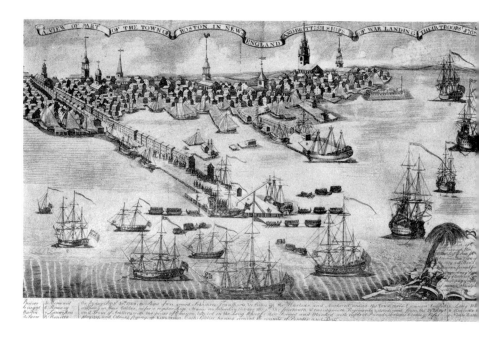

Boston was the scene of many activities and new acquaintances for Miranda. This view, showing British troops landing in 1768, was engraved by Paul Revere.

Phelps Stokes Collection, The New York Public Library

ton,[54] Mrs. Bradford, Mrs. Oliver,[55] Mrs. Williams,[56] Mrs. Dalton,[57] Mrs. Pitts,[58] Mrs. Otis,[59] Mrs. Paine,[60] Mrs. Gore,[61] Mrs. Newell, Mrs. Tudor,[62] Mrs. Head,[63] Mrs. Powell,[64] Mrs. Phillips,[65] Mrs. Hill,[66] Mrs. Blanchard,[67] Mrs. Prentiss, Mrs. Adams, Mrs. Gould, Mrs. Winslow,[68] Mrs. Coffin;[69] Miss B. Deblois[70] and Miss Temple (both pass as beauties today), Miss Lloyd, Miss Hall, the Misses Sheaffe (good looking), Miss Appleton, Miss Warren (beautiful), Miss Stillman, Miss Waldo, Miss Greenleaf,[71] Miss

[51] The wife of William Cooper, town clerk of Boston (1761–1809), merchant, and legislator.

[52] Possibly the wife of Nathaniel P. Sargeant (*sic*), justice of the Massachusetts Supreme Court (1775–90) and chief justice (1790–91).

[53] The wife of Joseph Hall, a lawyer.

[54] The wife of the patriot Nathaniel Appleton. He was also Commissioner of the Continental Loan Office in Massachusetts.

[55] Probably the wife of Judge Andrew Oliver.

[56] This could be the wife of either Jonathan or Thomas Williams, both members of the Boston bar at this time.

[57] Mrs. Tristram Dalton; see note 6 above.

[58] Spouse of John Pitts, Boston selectman.

[59] This might be either the wife of James Otis, Revolutionary statesman, or Samuel A. Otis, erstwhile speaker of the House of Delegates.

[60] Probably Mrs. Robert Treat Paine, nee Sally Cobb. Her husband was an eminent lawyer and judge.

[61] See note 7 above.

[62] Wife of William, lawyer, state senator, and founder of the Massachusetts Historical Society.

[63] Joseph Head was a Boston merchant.

[64] The wife of merchant William Powell.

[65] This is possibly the wife of William Phillips, lieutenant governor (1812–28).

[66] Possibly the wife of lawyer Aaron Hill.

[67] Samuel Blanchard, a surgeon.

[68] Isaac Winslow, Jr., a merchant and distiller.

[69] This was probably the wife of William Coffin. This was an old and respected family.

[70] Writing in 1788, John Quincy Adams said of her: "Miss Deblois has been much celebrated as a beauty; and she may still be called very handsome, though she be as much as twenty-seven. She is sociable and agreeable, though she is not yet wholly destitute of that kind of vanity which is so naturally the companion of beauty. She puckers her mouth a little, and contracts her eye-lids a little, to look pretty; and is not wholly unsuccessful."

[71] Judge Benjamin Greenleaf had four daughters. John Q. Adams courted Hannah in 1788.

Amory, Miss Dalton (the fattest creature I have seen for her age), Miss Paine, Miss Storer, Miss R. Coffin, Miss Watson, Miss Winslow, Miss Adams, Miss Polly Scott, etc.

The women here have very little education, and their diversions are confined to games of circumspection in which society hardly has a place. The married women have a club that meets every Saturday, at which six or eight families gather to eat (often seven miles from the city); when the meal is over, each goes to her home. The unmarried women have tea parties with each other as their only school for manners, customs, elegance, etc., and therefore they are highly deficient in these respects and have a self-preoccupation such as I have never seen. In the winter there is a badly directed Assembly (the hall, although somewhat small, is made with taste and the ornaments are elegant), at which the old and the young dance together, grossly as a rule. It is a very peculiar thing that the list of subscribers has not been offered to any officer of the American army, with the result that not one of them can attend. See here the envy of the mercantile corps and the ingratitude of the people in general!

The men are not better off in point of society. A club that meets on Monday evenings, at which they play cards and partake a little of cold meats from seven to ten o'clock, is all they have been able to invent in behalf of society.

In a word, society is not known yet. Extravagance, ostentation, and a bit of vanity are the predominant features in the character of those that are rich today. A young man who, ten years ago, wore silk stockings and satin breeches or powdered his hair needed nothing more to ruin his character forever; today, not only do they wear all this, but they wear it even when booted and riding horseback. The women, as follows: silks, ribbons, muslins, pomades, and perfumes every day. [The three sentences which follow, in parentheses here, were included in a footnote indicated by Miranda at this point.] (The schools of French dance are on a par with this and are so numerous that even the Negroes have theirs, which they attend twice a week from seven miles away. There is not a mechanic who does not send his daughters with predilection to this important branch of democratic-American education, paying four or five pesos monthly. § The number of coaches is thirty, excluding the multitude of phaetons and chaises.) Since the region does not have a single manufactory of the above-mentioned and by necessity must pay foreign countries for it all, it follows that ruin is unavoidable, and if we consider that the only products with which the region can pay its debts are potash, tar, and codfish, we will not be surprised when the businessman says all the wealth in this capital today can barely pay Europe (England principally) half the current debts! And if this happens in so short a period of time, what will it be in twenty years? Commerce will always be the principal downfall of democratic virtue. . . . This stems from the simplicity and equality of the people!

I have had the pleasure of communicating with the famous republican and very prominent actor in the recent revolution, Mr. Samuel Adams. He is a man of talents and extensive accomplishments in legislation. We had some drawn-out conversations regarding the constitution of this Republic. As for two objections which I raised about this subject, he declared he would meet with me after he had chewed them well. The first was, how is it that in a democracy the foundation of which was virtue no position whatever was indicated for it, and on the contrary all the dignities and the power were given to property, which is precisely the poison of a similar republic? The other was the contradiction I observed between admitting as one of the rights of mankind the worship of the Supreme Being in the manner and form one chooses, without giving predominance by law to any sect, and later excluding from every legislative or representative office the man who does not swear he is of the Christian religion![72] Weighty solecisms without doubt. He gave me much interesting information on the origin, beginnings, and occurrences of the past revolution, favoring me with his conversation familiarly.

[72] Samuel Adams, leader of the Massachusetts Radicals, was a member of Congress, lieutenant governor (1789-93), and governor (1794-97). He helped frame the Massachusetts constitution of 1780. This document, as was usual, set up property qualifications for voting and holding office and barred from office all who did not profess the Christian religion.

James Bowdoin, Esq.,[73] president of the American Academy of Arts and Sciences and former president of the convention when the constitution of the state was drawn up. He is a person of profound accomplishments in experimental physics and has judgment, some erudition, and a quiet manner. I am indebted to him for particular friendship and esteem and, likewise, very interesting information regarding the true origin and events of the past turbulences.

Mrs. Macauley Graham, the celebrated writer of the history of England.[74] I have talked with her particularly, and, although her conversation is not amiable, her society is interesting and amusing, accompanied by fine manners. I owed her particular approbation and friendship.

Dr. Carant, a native of France who came to this continent at the beginning of the past revolution. His vast accomplishments in metaphysics, natural history, and government make him worthy of the title of Wise Man. I am indebted to him for singular fondness and regard.[75]

Dr. Waterhouse, young professor of medicine in Cambridge. Studied in Leyden and afterwards spent a long time in England, advancing himself considerably. These advantages, joined to a singular application, promise an eminent man. He was very much my friend.

General Knox. This man, who from a simple bookseller passed to the militia and from there to the first ranks of the American army, is one of the best informed on the theory and practice of the art of war of the many *caudillos* I have known on this continent, including "The Idol."[76] His manner is very pleasant and his conversation interesting.

[73] A merchant and member of the constitutional convention of 1779. He became governor in 1785. Bowdoin College was named in his honor.

[74] Mrs. Catherine Macauley Graham was author of *History of England from the Accession of James I to that of the Brunswick Line* (8 vols.; London, 1763–83) and *History of England from the Revolution to the Present Time* (Bath, 1778).

[75] Regardless of Miranda's high esteem, I have not been able to identify Carant.

[76] Obviously a disparaging reference to Washington.

Phillis Wheatley, a Negro slave who, as a child, came from the coast of Guinea to this city. Her owner[77] gave her the small beginnings of an education, and see you here that the compositions of Phillis, in prose and poetry, went to press. She went to England and was admired. Afterwards she returned here and suffered the same neglect the talents experience everywhere. She finally married a sagacious Negro named Peters, by whom she had several children, and today is dying in indigence. Here one sees that the rational being is the same in whatever form or aspect. The most cruel laws of forbearance and the enjoyment of the most exalted pleasures are preserved in this Negro being.

Samuel Stillman, pastor of the Baptists in this city, has fluency, much vivacity, and gesticulation, but not much of the accomplished orator.[78]

Parson Murray[79] is the exact opposite of his namesake in Newburyport, so the people call him "Redemption Murray." His system is to prove there is not a single passage in the Bible which says the contrary and that, additionally, it is inconsistent with the attributes of the Divinity to act partially; that the redemption was universal; and that nobody can be condemned eternally. This little doctrine has made its bit of noise; but, in truth, is a marvel at winning sectarians. Such is the power of reason! This generous expositor announces himself with a grace, emphasis, and good locution that attract people amazingly. Had this apostle preached here twenty years ago, his shadow would not exist today! In every country where sects are neither persecuted nor protected the people will live happily and will think with less absurdity on this subject! That fool Freeman[80] ventured to preach a few days ago in

[77] Mrs. John Wheatley.

[78] Became pastor of the First Baptist Church in 1765.

[79] John Murray, known as the "Father of American Universalism," came to America in 1770 and became an itinerant preacher. He was later pastor of the Independent Church of Christ, Glouchester (1779–93), and of the Universalist Society of Boston (1793–1809).

[80] James Freeman, American Unitarian clergyman, first began as reader in Kings Chapel (1782). There he proposed revision of the liturgy to omit certain trinitarian parts, and the revision was accepted by the proprietors in 1785. When

Kings Chapel that the mystery of the Trinity was absurd and the Athanasian Creed[81] apocryphal. In another place they would have burned him! But here they have laughed and the preacher has remained in his pulpit.

On all the avenues and the environs of Boston one encounters fortified works, made by the British and Americans during the siege of this place. Likewise there is an infinity of the most advantageous heights for views and for locating country houses I have ever seen in so short an extension of land; Milton Hill and Dorchester Point are very remarkable.

Here is an anecdote. Last Sunday morning I went for a ride in the chaise to the castle a little below Dorchester Point and since it is necessary to cross a small ferry I asked for the boat, but as it was Sunday they did not wish to send it. Patiently I returned over the same road, quite good and pleasant, and when I was about to cross some low ground, found that with the rising tide there was about one foot of water there. A very decent man approached at that moment on horseback with a woman on the haunches. He came up to me and asked if I could take her across in my chaise, as she was afraid. I told him yes, and with that she jumped off the horse, got into my chaise, and I carried her two miles. She then asked me to let her off and remained there in a house waiting for her husband, who came on horseback some distance behind us. Now who is there in Europe who judges so favorably of the human heart as to deliver thus to a stranger his young and beautiful wife? Nor who so crackbrained as to think it a great sin to cross a river on Sunday?

On various occasions I attended the General Assembly of the state legislative body, where I saw clearly the defects and inconveniences to which this democracy has subjected itself by placing

---

refused ordination by the Episcopal Bishop, he was ordained by the senior warden of the church, and by this act the first Episcopal church in New England was transformed into the first Unitarian church in America on November 18, 1787.

[81] A Latin confession of faith probably originating in the fifth or sixth centuries.

the legislative power in the hands of ignorance. One member recited couplets in the middle of a debate he did not understand. Another, at the end of this debate and after the matter had been discussed for two hours, asked what the motion was so he could vote. And thus it is for the most part, with the result that the most absurd and unjust points have been debated, proposed, and approved in these democratic assemblies throughout the continent. All the influence being given by the constitution to property, the leading members do not have to be the wisest, and the Senators and Assemblymen are generally people destitute of principles and education. One, B–k, was a tailor four years ago; another, M–n, an innkeeper; another, B–n, a porter; another was a smith, etc.

Le Marquis de Lafayette arrived while I was here.[82] I had occasion to talk to him, and he seems to me a mediocre character, invested with that activity and perpetual motion of a Frenchman. Accompanying the Marquis were his aide-de-camp, Le Chevalier de Caraman, a young man completely destitute of accomplishments, and the captain of the frigate-of-war *La Nimphe* (sent to this port to take him to France). The latter, Le Chevalier de Grandchamp, is a man of judgment and education. This trip of the Marquis seems to me one of those legerdemains with which France is wont to wish to delude human nature and which on many occasions have had the desired effect; but to the eyes of those who see well, they are nothing but ridiculous political farces. These simple people, inexpert as yet in politics, have made excessive and absurd demonstrations (even the smallest hamlets, like Marblehead) as "The Hero" passes from one town to another, with the speed of a Roland,[83] to receive their praises. While I was here there also arrived a certain Monsieur le Comte de Broglie with his wife, a young American [*del Cabo francés*].[84] Going from this port to France, they had been shipwrecked, whereupon

82 The French war hero returned to the United States in 1784 to great acclaim.

83 A French hero of romantic tales of the Charlemagne era.

84 Broglie was apparently the nephew of Victor François, Duc de Broglie, a soldier in the Seven Years War. The material in brackets is a geographic description, "from Cape Francés," and may refer to Cape Francés in southwest Cuba.

an American ship rescued them and took them to Providence. They say he is a nephew of the marshal of the same name.

Dr. Waterhouse and I set aside one day to visit the University of Cambridge. We started out at eight o'clock in the morning and crossed the Charlestown Ferry in ten minutes. (This ferry is the best regulated I have seen. There are four boats. Two are constantly in motion taking the people who arrive across, and hardly do these touch the dock but the others depart, even if there are no passengers.) Taking a chaise on the other side we undertook our literary excursion towards Cambridge, about four miles away.

In passing by Bunker Hill, I could not do less than stop and look into this important military affair, with the aid of both an American officer who had been in the action and of the original information I had acquired. The event did not occur in the place mentioned, as is generally thought, but on a height closer to the landing place of Charlestown, called Breed's Hill.[85] This is the site the Americans were fortifying when the batteries on Copps Hill started firing on them and the British troops disembarked to attack. The location of said position is quite accessible from all sides and not extraordinarily advantageous, from which I infer that the effect was produced principally by *surprise*. That is, the British troops, confident in the advantages of their numbers and discipline, marched to the enemy with the presumption that on their approach the latter would abandon their positions and flee; far from this, they let them come close and, with a deliberate and well-aimed discharge, destroyed the formation and threw them into confusion. The same troops formed again and despite the loss renewed their attack instantly and took the position at bayonet point. The Americans withdrew as best they could through the narrow isthmus formed by the small peninsula on which Bunker Hill and the others are located. The advance American troops in that locale protected their withdrawal, curbing the reach of the enemy. Bunker Hill is about a mile from Breed's Hill and although it was later fortified strongly, for it commands all the neighboring heights, this was done by the

[85] Miranda is correct: the battle took place at Breed's Hill.

British to hold on to that peninsula. What difficulties will there not be, therefore, in posterity, when its Polybius,[86] traveling in order to write with truth and prudence the history of this military action, encounters the contradiction between the name of the position and that of the event, unless a monument erected now for immortality on the very spot clears up this doubt?

We then proceeded to Cambridge and there, in the company of some tutors (the President was not at home), visited the college. The quarters of the tutors and of the students are middlingly comfortable and without taste or ornament. The library is well arranged and clean. It contains some twelve thousand volumes,[87] English generally, although not badly selected. The room or cabinet of natural history hardly deserves the name: a few things of that sort placed there in a disorderly manner (among them a monstrous tooth of those extraordinary carnivorous animals found here, larger than the elephant and not known to us, according to what the society of London has declared about the presence of the skeletons found in various places on this continent and sent to England for that purpose). Afterwards we went to the so-called Philosophical Hall. It is a spacious room, well proportioned and decorated, with pictures of the principal benefactors of the college, some engravings by Copley (a native of this city),[88] and a marble bust of Lord Chatham,[89] a work of middling merit. The key to the philosophical apparatus could not be found, and, it being mealtime for the students, we descended to the refectory, where we all ate quite frugally: a piece of salt pork, potatoes, cabbages, a bit of cheese with the bread, and cider. As scholars are wont to rush through their meals, our repast was soon concluded. . . .

We returned the following week to examine the rest of the College. With Professor Williams,[90] a man of science and judg-

[86] Polybius was a Greek historian and author of some forty books.

[87] The library, some five-thousand volumes, burned in 1764.

[88] John Singleton Copley was a famous portrait painter. He was born in Boston in 1737 and moved to London in 1775.

[89] William Pitt.

[90] Samuel Williams became professor of mathematics and natural philosophy at Harvard in 1780.

ment, we visited the philosophical apparatus, which is without doubt very good and quite complete for its purpose. They lack nevertheless an observatory, for which reason the astronomical pieces are scattered in one place and another. Afterwards we climbed to the top of the building, from which there is a beautiful prospect, and not having more to see, we went to the house of the President, who had invited us for dinner. We ate in his reverend company, and I made them a present of a silver medal engraved in Mexico by Gil[91] to commemorate the founding of the Academy of National and Public Law, which they much esteemed. . . . This establishment seems to me better calculated to form clerics than capable and educated citizens. It is certainly an extraordinary thing that in this college there is no professorship whatever of the living languages and that theology is the principal professorship. The manner of dressing, presenting oneself, being polite in company, etc., are branches to which not the least attention is paid, and therefore the exterior of these scholars is the most slovenly I have ever seen in those of their sort. The President is unsociable, austere, and of an unbearable circumspection.[92]

Boston is happily situated for commerce. Its streets, although not very straight or wide, are spacious enough and all are paved. Among them the best are State, Common, Court, Marlborough, and Cornhill streets. The houses are middling; although in general they are perhaps not so good as those in Philadelphia and New York, the number that are spacious and elegant is much greater (more than thirty). These stand out for their advantageous location and pleasing view: the homes of John Hancock (the governor), James Bowdoin, William Phillips,[93] William Vassell,[94] Josiah Doure, Mr. Sherburne, Dr. Lloyd,[95] etc., on the brow of Beacon Hill.

[91] This medal was engraved by G. A. Gil and struck off in Mexico in 1778.
[92] See the description by John Quincy Adams in note 18 above.
[93] There were two men named William Phillips active at this time. One died in 1804 and the other in 1827.
[94] William Vassall (sic) was born in the West Indies. He became a sheriff, a mandamus counselor, and a Tory.
[95] Dr. James Lloyd invited Miranda to lunch on October 18, 1784.

The market is not the cleanest, but is quite abundant, particularly in fish, the delicacy and variety of which are remarkable. Strolling through the cemeteries of this city with my friend General Knox and reading the multitude of sepulchral inscriptions, I noticed that the longeval were not very numerous in this region. An inscription by the famous Dr. Franklin[96] deserves to be transcribed, for its manner and simplicity:

Josaiah Franklin

&

Abiah his Wife

lie here interred.

They lived lovingly together in Wedlock

fifty-five years.

and withaut an Estate or any gainful employement

by constant Labour & honest-industry

(with god blessing)

maintain'd a large family confortably

and brought up tharteen children & seven

grand children

Reputably.

from this instance reader

be encoraged to dilegence in thy calling, &

distrust not Providence.

He was a pious & a Prudent man,

She a discret & vertuous Woman.

their youngest son,

in filial regard to their memory,

Places this Stone.

J.F. born 1655. died 1744.

A.F. born 1667. died 1752.

The names of some more persons whom I have known here particularly: Mr. Morton,[97] Mr. Hitchborn,[98] Mr. Cushing,[99]

[96] The reference is to Benjamin Franklin. There are errors in Miranda's transcription, but the stone still stands in the Granary Burial Ground.

[97] Perez Morton was a member of the house, speaker, and attorney general.

[98] Benjamin Hitchborn was a noted lawyer.

[99] This could be either William, chief justice of the Massachusetts Supreme Court (from 1777) and later in the U.S. Supreme Court (1789–1810), or Thomas, lieutenant governor (1780–88).

Mr. Jarvis,[100] Mr. Babcock,[101] Mr. Roach, Dr. Bulfinch,[102] Mr. William Deblois,[103] Mr. Brimmer,[104] Mr. Barrett,[105] Mr. Gardiner (chief justice),[106] Mr. Tudor,[107] Mr. Saint John (French consul in New York), Mr. Freeman,[108] Mr. Winthrop,[109] Mr. Benjamin Cutler, Mr. Joseph Scott,[110] Mr. Sullivan (lawyer),[111] Mr. Simpson,[112] Mr. Foster,[113] Dr. Eustis,[114] Mr. Hews[115] (lawyer), and Mr. Erving.[116]

I went to visit the laboratory of a young portrait painter named Savage, who has come here from the neighboring hills.[117] His intuitive faculties must be considerable, for without further schooling or knowledge he has drawn some items with great dexterity and has portrayed the likenesses of some persons very

[100] Leonard Jarvis, a Boston and Cambridge merchant.

[101] Adam Babcock was also a merchant.

[102] A physician, Dr. Thomas Bulfinch.

[103] William Deblois was a Boston merchant.

[104] Martin Brimmer was a Plymouth manufacturer.

[105] Samuel Barrett was active in politics, a merchant, and commissioner of Loyalist estates.

[106] Although not chief justice, this was almost certainly John Gardiner, who was born in Boston, educated at the Inner Temple in London, practiced in England, was appointed attorney general of the island of St. Christopher, and came to Boston after the peace of 1783. He delivered the Fourth of July speech in Boston in 1785.

[107] William Tudor was a lawyer, commissioner of bankruptcy, and state senator.

[108] James Freeman, a minister discussed earlier.

[109] James Winthrop, librarian for Harvard College (1772–87).

[110] A Tory merchant.

[111] Probably James, brother of General John Sullivan; governor, 1807, 1808.

[112] Probably Judge Joseph Simpson.

[113] Bossenger Foster, a distiller.

[114] William Eustis served as a surgeon during the war, practiced in Boston, and was secretary of war (1809–13), minister to Holland (1814–18), and governor (1823–25).

[115] This may have been George Robert Twelves Hewse (sic), who claimed to have been a member of the Boston Tea Party.

[116] This was probably John Erving, member of a wealthy Tory merchant family.

[117] Edward Savage, an engraver and portrait painter, was virtually unkown at this time. He was born in Princeton, Massachusetts, in 1761. He did, among others, portraits of George and Martha Washington.

well. If he goes to Europe and continues in the great schools of art with the same application, he will perhaps become an eminent man. He is now about twenty years old.

The famous Mr. Samuel Adams gave me the most exact calculations of the finances, expenses, and economic regulations of this state at the present time. The obligations contracted by the state since the beginning of the past disputes (for at that time it was just extinguishing, fortunately, the debt contracted in the previous [French and Indian] war, when Canada was conquered), exclusive of the national debt, amount to £1,500,000, the interest on which, at 6 per cent, comes to £90,000 annually. Add to this the Civil List, £13,270 (44,233⅓ pesos), and you have the amount the state must pay annually, exclusive of the sixth part of the national debt, or 7,000,000 pesos. For this it obtains annually about £50,000 through the duties called imposts and excises. It makes up the rest with taxes, which for this reason are extremely large at the present time. The "faculty" item[118] is as arbitrary as it can be, for it is purely a voluntary computation or suspicion. Would it not be better to entrust this secret, as is done in Holland, to the honor and conscience of the businessman and have each put in a public box that which in truth is just for him to pay, and no more?

Civil List

	Salaries
Governor	£1,100
Lieutenant Governor, perquisites as Captain of the Castle, for from the first employment he receives nothing	400
9 Counselors, 8 shillings per day (150 days)	540
20 Senators, 7 shillings 6 pennies per day (100 days)	750
140 Representatives, 7 shillings per day (100 days)	4,900
Chief Justice	350
4 Puisne Judges, 300 each	1,200
Attorney general, by grant, about	300
Sheriff, from his fees	———
Extraordinary expenses, for committees, etc.	1,200

[118] This was a tax on faculty or ability and was meant to supplement other taxes.

Secretary	300
Treasurer	300
Clerk of the House of Representatives	100
Clerk of the Senate	100
Clerks in the Secretary's, Treasurer's, and Senate Offices	300
Messenger of the House and Senate	130
Messenger of the Governor and Counsel	100
Members of the Congress (2 generally), 33 shillings per day each one	1,000
President of the University of Cambridge, by grant (although with all his perquisites his income amounts to £400)	200

$$\overline{(44,233\tfrac{1}{3}\ \text{pesos fuertes})\qquad £13,270}$$

With my friend Mr. Morton I went to the country house of his father-in-law, located in the hamlet of Braintree. The owner, Mr. James Apthorp,[119] received us with great kindness, as did his wife and two very good-looking daughters. After a sociable meal we took our phaeton back to Boston, stopping on Milton Hill to pay a call on General Warren, who had invited us when we passed by in the morning. We had tea and spent more than half an hour in the company of the General and his wife, who reveals great acuteness and knowledge.[120] This country house used to belong to Governor Hutchinson,[121] whom John Adams called "The Machiavellian Politician on Milton Hill." With the broad and beautiful view it commands, this location is certainly one of the most delightful one can imagine.

When night came we continued our journey, and I confess the cold was enough to paralyze us, especially while crossing the Neck of Boston. (So great is the multitude of carriages entering and leaving through the Neck that there have been days when their number reached twelve hundred.) So what I report here does

[119] A wealthy merchant and father-in-law of Perez Morton.

[120] James Warren was a political leader and paymaster general of the Continental army. His wife, Mercy, was a sister of James Otis, author of political satires, verses, plays, and a history of the American Revolution.

[121] Thomas Hutchinson, last royal governor of Massachusetts.

not surprise me, namely, that a carter who attempted last year to cross it in the nighttime was found in the morning frozen, together with his oxen.

Here is an anecdote worth the trouble, and true. Mr. Gorham,[122] distinguished member of the Congress and recently speaker in the assembly of this city, set out in 1783 for England with the humble and extraordinary purpose of asking for alms with which to rebuild Charlestown, burnt during the attack on Bunker Hill. Does not this argue indecorous submission on the one hand and on the other the superior estimation of generosity and benevolence in which they hold the Anglican nation? Why do they not go to their illustrious French allies to test their charitable and generous disposition?

The bank of this capital has stopped lending money until the ship of Captain Callahan[123] sails for England, for they fear that all specie will leave the region and they will be left with paper only. A ship does not leave this port for England that does not carry from fifty thousand to eighty thousand guineas in specie (I have seen four in the time I have been here), which clearly proves how excessive the balance of trade in favor of that nation is, to the ruination of this.[124]

This information was given to me with exactness:

Houses	1,718
Churches, or temples, of all beliefs	17
Inhabitants of the city	14,640
Inhabitants of the state	450,000
Articles of commerce the region produces: codfish, whale oil, potash and pearlash, furs, lumber of all sorts, linseed	
Vessels built annually	8

[122] Nathaniel Gorham was a member of the Continental Congress, president in 1786, a delegate to the Federal Convention, and a signer of the Constitution.

[123] John Callahan was captain of the *Neptune*, which plied between Boston and London.

[124] The guinea was an English gold coin issued from 1663 to 1813 whose value was set at twenty-one shillings in 1717. Being outside the British mercantile system, the states had a very unfavorable balance of trade in relation to England.

Commercial vessels belonging to this port (120 frigates and brigantines, 80 sloops and schooners)	200
Newspapers, weekly	7
Ships of all sorts leaving this port yearly	1,100

October 15, 1784. At three-thirty in the afternoon I embarked at Winnisimmet Ferry[125] (one and three-quarters miles wide) and in a matter of a quarter of an hour crossed to that part of the continent in which Charlestown is located, passing on the left the beach where the English disembarked their troops (in seventy boats) at the time of the attack on Bunker Hill, or, better said, Breed's Hill. Along with a woman, a girl eight years old, and four men—people who seemed to be of good manners—I mounted the stage there. The road is not very bad, although stony, and the terrain quite poor as far as the eye reaches. At five o'clock we halted at Newell's Inn,[126] had a cup of tea, and in a quarter of an hour were on our way. The road is not so stony from here on. At seven o'clock we arrived happily in Salem, and I obtained very decent accommodation at Goodhue's Tavern.

16. In the morning I went to see William Wetmore, Esq.,[127] for whom I brought a letter of recommendation, and he received me with great kindness and politeness. We climbed the near-by heights, called Gallows Hill because the witches were hanged there in times of crass fanaticism,[128] and from there saw the entire town and bay, a beautiful view certainly. We descended and walked through the town, the principal street of which

[125] For north-country folk the nearest point of mainland was Winnisimmet (now Chelsea). Consequently the General Court enacted a subsidy to encourage a ferry route between Boston, Charlestown, and Winnisimmet. This was the first in New England, and probably North America.

[126] Newell's Inn was the most ancient tavern in Lynn and one of the most celebrated in the country. Situated at the midway point on the road from Boston to Salem, in a picturesque spot within sight of the sea, for over a century it was the favorite resting place of travelers. From Governors Bradstreet and Endicott to Presidents Washington and Adams, it counted among its guests many of the prominent men of the time.

[127] Wetmore was the leading Salem attorney and later a judge.

[128] Nineteen persons accused of witchcraft in 1692 were hanged on Gallows Hill and at least two died in prison.

A Prospect of the Colledges in Cambridge in New England

Highly educated himself, Miranda took advantage of every opportunity to visit American institutions of higher learning. Harvard was
no exception.

Phelps Stokes Collection, The New York Public Library

In Portsmouth, Miranda complained that "there have been more than thirty-one degrees of change in the thermometer in the course of twenty-four hours."

(almost the only one, in truth) is close to two miles long. In passing we saw the City Hall, which is an old, poor building almost completely in ruins (only deserves attention for being the place where the witches were tried and sentenced), and the house of Mr. Darby,[129] a good building and the best in town. We then examined the town archives, where we read something of particularity:—Salem, 1667, County Court, husband and wife for having committed fornication before being married, whipped and fined—others for saying "By God," fined—others for having fornicated simply, whipped and fined—one woman for not attending church, whipped and fined—others for playing cards simply, fined . . . etc., etc., . . . Similarity to the Blue Laws of New Haven.

At nightfall Mr. Wetmore came to my tavern and invited me to sup with him, but I excused myself as I was somewhat fatigued and his house very distant; so we left it at our going together to church the next morning and to Marblehead in the afternoon. But being informed that the stage would leave early the next day, I wrote him an apology, reserving the mentioned sortie for my return.

17. At seven o'clock in the morning I left Salem on the stage, with only two men for company—a very singular thing, because be it in ferryboats, coaches, or packets, there is never a lack of women to incommode you. That it was Sunday was the reason doubtlessly that so rare an accident occurred; nevertheless, one was waiting to be fetched, but through some accident the coachman forgot her. After passing through the small villages of Danvers, Beverly, and Wenham, we arrived at Ipswich, fourteen miles from Salem, where we had breakfast at a middling tavern, and continuing our route through Rowley, another hamlet, and over the Parker River, which permits the navigation of small vessels but handles hardly any commerce, we arrived around two o'clock in the afternoon at Newburyport, a place of importance. The road from Salem is quite good and highly populated with

---

[129] Almost certainly the Richard Derby (*sic*) house built in 1762. He was first in a line of merchant princes in Salem.

houses on both sides and with an abundance of orchards, which make it delightful. The land, which produces pasture, corn, and rye, looks, and is in fact, poor. Nevertheless, such is the industry and spirit which liberty inspires in these people that from a small portion of the lands they obtain enough to maintain their large families, pay heavy taxes, and live in comfort and contentment, a thousand times happier than the proprietaries of the rich mines and fertile lands of Mexico, Peru, Buenos Aires, Caracas, and the rest of the Spanish-American continent.

From Salem to Newburyport

to	Danvers	3
	Beverly	2 ½
	Wenham	2 ½
	Ipswich	6
	Rowley	4
	Parker River	4
	Newburyport	4
		26 miles

At four o'clock we crossed the Amesbury Ferry over the Merrimac River, but with difficulties. It being Sunday, the ferryman did not wish to take us across; finally, after some delay, some friends of his secretly did it, obliging the coachman and us to pay double fares. The religionistic stratagem is not bad!

After passing through the scattered villages of Salisbury and Seabrook, we arrived at Hampton Falls, where we stopped to drink tea and give the horses food. It was almost dark when we renewed the journey, but confident that the remaining road was smooth and very good, the coachman did not exert himself much, and we did not press him. We had traveled a matter of three miles, when see you here the horses suddenly stopped, my servant jumped to the ground, and we found that the coach was on the edge of a very deep hole and that only by the space of half a foot had the wheel not fallen in with all of us turned upside down! With some effort we were able to remove the horses and coach from the danger, obliging the coachman, an ignoramus and frightened to death, to go on. One of my fellow passengers was too unnerved to continue and stayed at a near-by tavern; the other, who knew the road, offered to sit next to the coachman and direct him. With this security I took a nap in the coach, celebrating our escape from the recent danger. At ten o'clock we arrived in Portsmouth, where I took lodging at Stiver's Tavern. After supping very well, I went to bed, to a repose required by the recent agitation. (The seat on the stage from Boston to Portsmouth costs five pesos.)

	From Newburyport to Portsmouth	
to	Amesbury Ferry	4
	Salisbury	1
	Seabrook	1
	Hampton Falls	1 ½
	Greenland	9 ½
	Portsmouth	5 ½
		22 ½ miles

18. I spent the morning writing a bit in the diary and delivering some letters for Joshua Wentworth, Esq.,[130] Colonel Langdon,[131] and Mr. Sheaf,[132] not one of whom was at home. ...

This tavern is not the best possible, but there is nothing better in the town. After dinner, Mr. Langdon visited me and invited me for tea at his house. So I went forth, and Mrs. Langdon received me with great affability and attention. With some company that had gathered there, I spent the evening in society until eleven o'clock, when I retired to the tavern.

19. In the morning Mr. Langdon and I took a walk

[130] Wentworth was a merchant from a prominent New Hampshire family. In 1776 he was a Continental agent and became a counselor in New Hampshire in 1786.

[131] John Langdon was active in pre-Revolutionary agitation, a member of the Continental Congress, naval agent for the colonies (1776), a member of the group that opposed General Burgoyne's march, president of New Hampshire (1785–86), governor (1788, 1805–1809, 1809–11), and senator (1789–1801).

[132] James Sheafe (*sic*) was a Loyalist, a Federalist senator in 1802, and was narrowly defeated for governor in 1816.

through the town and saw the City Hall, or Assembly as they call it, which building is no more than suitable for the purpose. We called on the famous builder, John Peck, for whom I brought letters, finding him in a workshop, near the ocean, where some yards and masts were being built (with great taste and neatness certainly). We had a long conversation concerning his method of construction and the little reward his country had offered him for discoveries so important to commerce and navigation. Mr. Langdon and I then continued our stroll, looking at the buildings of the town, which, except for three or four houses of medium magnitude, are quite indifferent. Never before have I seen a town of this size in which there was greater sadness and loneliness!

At two o'clock I went to dine at the house of Mr. Langdon, who has really treated me with great hospitality. The only company was his own family, including the brother of his wife, a young lawyer about twenty-two years old, in whom arrogance and ignorance shine conspicuously. At tea we had in addition the company of Monsieur Toscain, vice-consul of France in New Hampshire, a man of some education and extremely gentle manner.[133] We spent the rest of the evening sociably, and at eleven o'clock I retired to my tavern.

The weather here is so variable that there have been more than thirty-one degrees of change in the thermometer in the course of twenty-four hours. It must be added that the cold is so continuous that for nine months of the year the inhabitants are forced to maintain fires constantly in their homes. With how many disadvantages these poor people struggle! And how many obstacles their indefatigable industry overcomes!

20. This morning the builder Mr. Peck came to visit me, and we had a long conversation concerning his plan of construction, the principles of which are philosophical, as well as practical and scientific. The shape, says this ingenious artist, is the principal motor of a vessel. The boats towing a whale after it is dead and consequently without movement in itself, find themselves com-

---

[133] Toscan (*sic*) was appointed French vice-consul to Portsmouth in 1784.

pelled, when a strong wind blows, to cut the cable for fear of
foundering through the violence with which the body of the
dead fish drags them, notwithstanding said boats are of the best
construction imaginable. Moreover, he says, in modern construction such strakes have been given to the prows and keels of vessels
that on the exterior they form a multitude of inflected curves not
found in the works of nature (particularly in fish) and consequently the least adaptable to the body of a vessel. This is the
principal foundation of his theory and, I confess, has made a
greater impression upon me than any other on this matter. When
this artist, after immense opposition, was building his first vessel in
Boston, people called it "Peck's Folly," until with their own
eyes they saw, and thus disabused themselves, that it would not
turn over with the force of the sail, as their limited talents had
told them, and was not a folly. This construction combines advantages the other builders and the public in general thought
incompatible, that is, it has the best sail we know, carries more
than another of the same burden, and has less roll than ships of
different construction. He has already built seven since the last
war began, of which I have seen two: *The Empress of China*,
belonging to Mr. Parker of New York, and the *Leda*, belonging
to Mr. Swan[134] of this city. Both combine all the qualities I have
mentioned. This man of genius complains that there is no ship-
yard here in which he can verify certain operations and discoveries
he thinks are very advantageous in theory. After this learned and
very useful conversation we climbed a height about a mile from
the town and had a full view of the entrance to the port, the bay,
and the larger part of the town. The environs of the latter are quite
arid and the ground stony for all its circumference. We descended
to the shore and in a small boat crossed to an island at the entrance
of the bay, upon which there is yet a fort and fragments of artillery for the defense of the channel, which in this part is a quarter
of a mile wide and thus easily defended in time of war. From this
point there is a complete view of the islands interpolated throughout the bay. On one of these, belonging to Mr. Langdon, the

134 This was probably John Swan.

seventy-four-ton ship *America*, which these states presented to France, is being built.[135] (Not having the artillery, rigging, etc., with which to equip it, according to what a satirist of this continent says, the Congress gave the work to Mr. Langdon.) I observed the food which was being prepared in a house there for the workmen building a ship and was amazed at the abundance and magnificence with which the mechanical people of the region are treated. It is not strange that labor comes at such a high price.

At two o'clock I left, and Mr. Peck went to look for Michael Sewall, Esq., a famous lawyer and a man of genius, that I might visit the latter in the afternoon, but it turned out he was away, running around the district with satchels under his arm following the court, in order to obtain the wherewithal to eat and win renown. (I had occasion to meet him afterwards in Boston, and he is the most eccentric character I have known. The most puerile ideas are constantly intermingled with the most ingenious in his conversation.) The same was true of General Sullivan,[136] so I did not have the pleasure of seeing him either. He lives in an indifferent country house fourteen miles from Portsmouth, where he keeps his wife and numerous children completely segregated from society and without giving the latter formal education. He never receives company at his home, and thus there are few that can say they have seen Mrs. Sullivan or the children. May you judge the extravagances of men!

I spent the afternoon and evening in the company of Mr. and Mrs. Langdon, very sociable persons. She is a good-looking girl, married because of pregnancy, as are almost all the women in these regions. He made himself known (he had been the poor captain of a sloop) at the beginning of the past dissensions with England. At the head of a mob of two or three hundred individuals and over the feeble resistance an officer and eight or ten soldiers on guard attempted to make, he took possession of the powder in the

[135] The *America* was presented to France by the United States in September, 1782, to replace the *Magnifique*, which had been lost by accident in Boston Harbor.

[136] John Sullivan resigned his commission in 1779, becoming a member of Congress. In 1786 he was elected president of New Hampshire.

castle at the port entrance. With these munitions the siege of Boston was effected, and the event gave such importance to my friend Langdon that afterwards he was made a member of Congress, commissioned in various matters of importance, etc. The natural course of human affairs![137]

    21. I spent the morning reading a book just published and written with judgment, knowledge, and middling taste, Volume I of the *History of New Hampshire*, by Belknap.[138] Mr. Peck came, and we took a walk by the shore. There can be no doubt that this port is excellent, particularly for ships of burden, because of the depth it has next to the shore. When the French squadron of de Vaudreuil[139] came to Boston in 1782 and the dismantled ships passed there to be repaired, the advantage was seen. The masts and yards fashioned here are the neatest and most perfect imaginable, to which the superior quality of the pine is the principal contributor.[140]

    At two o'clock I went to the Langdon home for dinner and had occasion to talk with His Excellency the President of the state, Nathaniel Folsom, Esq.,[141] who is superannuated and does not hear well. He agreed with me that the constitution was defective in the article which requires one to profess the Protestant religion in order to be a member of the legislature. Mrs. Cushing of Boston and another person were all the company. Because in this town people are not wont to invite each other, society is banished and

[137] Preceding the Revolution, John Langdon was one of the leaders in the seizure of the powder at Fort William and Mary. This was then sent to Cambridge.

[138] Jeremy Belknap, a Congregational minister, was author of the three-volume *History of New Hampshire* (1784, 1791, 1792) and *American Biography* (2 vols., 1794, 1798).

[139] Louis Philippe de Rigand, Marquis de Vaudreuil, commanded one division of De Grasse's fleet at Yorktown in 1781. He was in Boston in August, 1782.

[140] As early as 1671, New Hampshire, no larger than a modern village, shipped ten cargoes of masts.

[141] Folsom was a member of the Continental Congress (1774, 1775, 1777–80), a major general in command of the New Hampshire militia, and president of the New Hampshire constitutional convention of 1783.

every one shuts himself in his house with his wife to enjoy the so-called "domestic pleasures." That is their own affair!

In the afternoon I attended the General Assembly, which had convened to put into effect the new constitution accepted by the people the preceding year.[142] When I entered the chamber of the Assembly, I saw that everybody was standing up and that a multitude of clerics, eight in number, were reading a memorial or address.[143] In this scene was revealed not only the ambition and vanity of the ecclesiastics, but also the simplicity and prejudices of the people, in paying extraordinary respect to some mere members of the republic when they are representing the majesty of the people. This monastic scene concluded, the Assembly adjourned until the next day, and I retired for tea at the Langdon house. There I met two presidents of small colleges in the interior of the region: Mr. Wheelock (Dartmouth College is the institution this fop directs) and Mr. Woodbridge were their names, and if we must judge the institute by the preceptor, there is not little pedantry in said seminaries.[144] After we had listened to their scholastic nonsense for two hours, these gentlemen did us the favor of leaving. Mrs. Cushing and I ate in the company of the family, and at eleven o'clock I went home, to prepare for my return to Boston the next day.

The following memoir gives only a fair idea of the present condition of the commerce, population, etc., notwithstanding it was communicated to me by persons of veracity and knowledge. As for the town, it is quite badly formed and has the saddest appearance one can imagine.

Houses	800
Temples, of all persuasions	5

[142] In October, 1783, the convention announced that the constitution, having been approved by popular vote, would go into effect in June, 1784.

[143] On October 24, 1784, an address by the Congregational ministers of several associations of New Hampshire was presented to the legislature.

[144] John Wheelock was the son of Eleazar, founder of Dartmouth College in 1769. John became president (1779–1817) after the death of his father. Neither Woodbridge nor his "college" has been identified. It was probably a very short-lived venture.

Newspapers, in the state	2
Inhabitants, of the city	5,000
Inhabitants, of the state	90,000
Commercial ships belonging to this port	56
Commercial ships built annually here	30

Articles of commerce the region produces: masts of all sizes, lumber, codfish, whale oil, fine hides.

22. It was with no little difficulty that, for five and a half pesos, I obtained a chaise with a poor horse, and at eight o'clock in the morning I started out. An hour later I arrived in Greenland, where they gave me and the horse very good breakfast. The latter needed it more than I did. At ten o'clock I continued my journey by the same well-populated road I had come. With the exception of a few sandy parts, it is good enough and it is level.

At two-thirty in the afternoon I happily reached the ferry and in less than a quarter of an hour disembarked in Newburyport. I went immediately to the inn of Mr. Davenport;[145] as this was full, he directed me to the private inn of Mr. Merrill, where I found far superior lodging. The fatigue of the road and the cold induced me to stay at home reading the *History of the Progress and Termination of the Roman Republic*, by Ferguson,[146] written with dexterity and profundity.

23. The morning was fine, and I went forth to deliver some letters. I presented one to Mr. John Tracy,[147] who received me cordially, even though stuck in his store measuring salt, a precious article here for being so necessary. Afterwards I took a walk through the town, which consists principally of a street running for a distance of a mile along the Merrimac River. It has numerous good wharves for the loading and unloading of ships, thus giving notice of the quantity of commerce. It is a pity the

145 The inn was built in 1762 by William Davenport, who named it "Wolfe Tavern" in honor of the British general under whom he had served.

146 Adam Ferguson was a Scottish philosopher at the University of Edinburgh. His *History of the Progress and Termination of the Roman Republic* was published in 1782.

147 A merchant, justice of the peace, adjutant general of militia, and member of a shipowning and privateering family.

bar at the mouth of the river is not more than fourteen feet deep
at high tide, since past the bar the depth is more than twenty-two.
The people here seem more animated and occupied with business,
and there is a joyful appearance everywhere. At the same time
I observed a large number of merchant ships being built as far
as the eye reaches on the riverbank.[148] After this long walk I went
to the house of Mr. Tracy for dinner; this building is a quarter
of a mile from the town, in an advantageous location, and well
disposed. There I met a large company of inhabitants of the
region, and before dinner we mounted to the top of the house
to look at the extensive and pleasing prospectus revealed, not only
towards the mouth of the river, the sea, and Cape Ann, but also
towards the interior of the region. We had a good meal in the
American style, with something of the Rousseauan doctrine in
the conversation (Émile appeared at the table);[149] when it was
over, everyone went forth to do some business before the Sabbath
came, for I doubt that the Jews observe more restriction in the
matter than these people. Mr. Freeman,[150] former officer in the
Continental army and a person of fine manners, accompanied me
for a walk in the garden until teatime. With the amiable Mrs.
Tracy and her husband we spent the evening in festive society.

    24. It being Sunday, Messrs. Tracy and Freeman came
for me at my lodging so that we might go together to hear a
famous preacher named John Murray[151] at ten o'clock. We went
to the Presbyterian church, and see you here an apostle who in
the most emphatic tone commences the prayer by entreating God
for the ruin and extirpation of pagans, Mohammedans, Antichrist
(the Pope) and his sectaries, heretics. . . . So that for a moment the

[148] Between 1681 and 1741, some 107 ships were launched from Newburyport
shipyards.

[149] Jean Jacques Rousseau, French philosopher and author, known for his
philosophy that the savage state is superior to the civilized and that government
must rest upon popular will. *Émile, ou Traité de l'Éducation* (1762) was a con-
troversial book that greatly influenced modern elementary education.

[150] Probably Captain Constant Freeman of Massachusetts.

[151] Murray was for several years after 1781 Presbyterian minister in Newburyport. He was so vigorous a patriot that the British placed a reward of five
hundred guineas on his head.

entire universe, except for his flock, was excluded from the Divine Protection! Barbarous! Ignorant! For this reason the people called him "Damnation Murray." He continued in the same tone until twelve-thirty, when he finally stopped braying.

From here we proceeded to visit Mrs. Dalton,[152] who received me with great affability, and afterwards we dined with Mr. Tracy and his family. The meal finished, we examined a sword and a stone pipe, work of the Indians, found last year with the bones of a cadaver by General Titcomb[153] in a forest of his a mile from Newburyport and worthy of being admired for the patience and ingenuity required to execute it without metallic tools.

From the memorial that follows (the best information I could obtain) one may judge the commerce and current situation of said town with confidence. The most conspicuous buildings are the Presbyterian meetinghouse (where the famous preacher George Whitefield, Esq.,[154] is buried) and the houses of John Tracy,[155] Jonathan Jackson,[156] N. Tracy,[157] T. Dalton,[158] and Captain Coombs.[159]

---

[152] The wife of Tristram Dalton, discussed earlier.

[153] Jonathan Titcomb was active in Massachusetts politics, holding numerous offices, and was a major general of militia. He served in brief campaigns with General Sullivan in Rhode Island during (1777-78).

[154] Whitefield was an American revivalist and founder of the Calvinistic Methodists, who split with the Wesleys over predestination. After his death in 1770, he was buried at the Presbyterian church in Newburyport. The church was built in 1756.

[155] This house, on aristocratic High Street, was one of the finest in town and a duplicate of the Jackson house (see note 156 below).

[156] Jackson was a merchant, delegate to the Continental Congress, and treasurer of Massachusetts and Harvard College. His house, still standing and known as the Jackson-Dexter House, was built in 1771 by the wealthy eccentric "Lord" Timothy Dexter.

[157] A brother of John. On his marriage in 1775, his father Patrick presented him with a brick home on State Street. The building still stands. In 1775 he sent out the first privateer from Newburyport. Between 1775 and 1783 he sent to sea some 24 cruisers which captured 120 vessels and 2,225 prisoners. At the same time, he owned 110 merchant vessels. Thomas Jefferson was his guest in 1784, but by 1786, Tracy was bankrupt.

[158] The Dalton house on State Street, built in 1746, still stands.

[159] William Coombs was actively engaged in maritime life until the Revolu-

Houses	375
Churches, of all persuasions	5
Inhabitants	4,109
Newspapers	1
Commercial vessels belonging to this port (approximate)	100
Commercial vessels built each year in this town, Amesbury, and Salisbury	100

Articles of commerce produced in this region: masts, lumber, shipbuilding, potash and pearlash, linseed, New England rum (there are twelve distilleries in the town), codfish, and pitch.

~~~~ *25.* At seven o'clock in the morning I took the stage and started out for Salem. We had breakfast in Ipswich, and I took a walk through this ancient town, one of the first to be established in this part of the continent and which today is almost in ruins.[160] There is scarcely more than small wharves where they load the few ships that arrive. Around three o'clock we arrived in Salem, where I obtained lodging at The Social Club, quite decent and comfortable. The afternoon was cold, and as I was rather tired, I asked for tea and spent the rest of the day reading.

~~~~ *26.* A heavy cold and a tooth-ache attacked me, so I stayed indoors next to the fire, reading as best I could. In the afternoon I felt somewhat better and visited my friend William Wetmore, in whose pleasant company and that of his lovely wife (young and very good looking) I remained until eleven o'clock, when I retired to my lodging.

~~~~ *27.* Around eleven o'clock Mr. Wetmore and I sallied forth in a chaise to Marblehead, four miles distant. The road is

---

tion. An ardent patriot, his last voyage was to obtain a supply of arms and ammunition for the impending conflict; these were turned over to the authorities without compensation. He then became a merchant and the owner of many ships. He served as a member of the Committee of Safety and Correspondence and in the Massachusetts legislature.

[160] Ipswich was incorporated in 1634 and was first known as Agawam. Like most New England towns, it suffered the effects of the Revolution and postwar depression.

very good until one is about to enter this town of fishermen, which is completely surrounded by rocks; upon these the houses are built. The appearance of the place indicates perfectly what it is. The houses are poor, but filled with people, particularly children, whose number is proportionately larger than in any other town I have seen (Mr. Wetmore and I counted five hundred boys playing in the street); nevertheless all are suitably dressed, which shows there is no need at home. As we went down to the shore on the stony and uneven streets, we saw on all sides a multitude of stretchers filled with drying fish (not a small addition to the fishing scene said town represents); likewise a fort built at the entrance of the small bridge there, where the ships take shelter. Presently we returned to Salem, observing for the second time the number of boys in the streets. The women have the reputation of scandalous customs, and it is said around there that Marblehead is remarkable for the many children and people of red hair. In the last war it suffered immensely,[161] but since the peace, recovers its prosperity with great progress. There are two conspicuous buildings in this town besides the church;[162] these are the houses of Colonel Lee[163] and Mr. Hooper,[164] very clear proof that the poor always have to make somebody rich.

Houses	600
Inhabitants	6,000
Fishing vessels, which catch yearly 60,000 hundredweights of codfish	60

We returned at three o'clock and with the Reverend Mr. Barnard,[165] a true antiquary of the town and man of letters, dined

161 During the war the British blockaded Marblehead, and the end of the war found it economically prostrate, its merchant fleet captured or sunk and its fishing fleet rotting at the wharves.

162 Probably St. Michael, erected in 1714.

163 William Lee, an early merchant prince of the town. His home still stands.

164 This house, still standing, was built in 1754 by Robert Hooper, known as "King" because of his great wealth and royal manner of life. The Lee and Hooper houses were both Georgian in style.

165 Thomas Barnard, pastor of North Church in Salem from 1773 to 1814. John Quincy Adams wrote of him: "He gave us two very excellent sermons; and his prayers were admirable, which is something very uncommon."

at the home of Mr. Wetmore. The meal finished, we took a walk through the town, its principal street a mile and a half long, and visited the public library, which contains about 550 volumes of not bad books. The most remarkable buildings (and good ones) are the houses of Mr. Darby,[166] Captain Orne, Mr. Page, Mr. Orne,[167] Mrs. Pickman,[168] and Mr. Oliver.[169] The wharves are numerous and good, but the so-called "flats" prevent the unloading and receiving of the entire cargo, which produces considerable expense for the owners of the vessels. This port has the advantage of not having a bar.

On a small peninsula, or isthmus, protruding into the bay is the spot where the first Europeans established themselves,[170] cutting off communication by means of a moat and palisade for their security against the Indians, and see you here the reason why this place was populated before the commodious and spacious port of Boston! Likewise we saw some ancient houses belonging to those unfortunate families which fanaticism, in its ignorance, immolated for witchcraft.

This town prospered greatly through privateering during the war and does not decline in time of peace. Notwithstanding, the inhabitants are noted for being unsociable (not without foundation), so that there is already a proverb.

Houses	650
Inhabitants	7,000
Churches, of all persuasions	7
Commercial ships belonging to this port	60
Fishing ships (excluding boats, which, together with those in Marblehead, come to 100)	25

[166] Elias H. Derby (*sic*), one of the richest merchants in Salem and a pioneer in the East Indian trade. See also note 129 above.

[167] Mr. Page was probably Jeremiah L., a shipowner. The Ornes were a large and prominent shipping family. The captain was probably Josiah and the other William Orne.

[168] The wife of Colonel Benjamin Pickman, a successful merchant of Salem.

[169] This was probably Judge Andrew Oliver.

[170] Salem was first settled in 1628 by Roger Conant and a group of emigrants. This early settlement has been reproduced in what is now known as Pioneers' Village.

| Ships built yearly | 6 |
| Newspapers | I |

Articles of commerce this region produces:
codfish, lumber.

At nightfall we retired to the house of Mr. Barnard. Here we had tea and, in the company of some erudite persons of the town, spent the evening in society until twelve o'clock, when all retired. The variations in the weather are excessive, and I do not know how the constitutions of these people can endure them.

~~~ *28*. At eight o'clock in the morning I took the stagecoach which goes every day to Boston, in the company of a good woman and two men who prattled furiously. We had breakfast at Newell's Inn and at noontime were at Winnisimmet Ferry. In a matter of a quarter of an hour we disembarked in the city of Boston, and I went to my former lodging, which in truth suited me grandly, and my health now required it.

[A gap here.]

~~~ *December 15, 1784.* At four-thirty in the afternoon we set sail on the merchant ship *Neptune*, 250 tons, Captain John Callahan, and at six o'clock anchored near the so-called Castle,[171] a distance of some three miles. The passengers were Levi Willard, John Reynolds, George Harrop, John Garniss, Herman Goverts, John Derritt, Samuel Dashwood,[172] and Nicholas Gilman[173]— agreeable people and of good manners. Because this ship was carrying a quantity of specie to England, sixty thousand guineas according to calculation, the bank suspended its lending operations, and from this resulted something of a popular convulsion, as one can see from this notice which was posted in several parts of the city: "It is sincerely wish'd the Tory Ship commanded by that noted Smugler Cap. Callahan, would sail immediately as no Bussiness either at the Bank or any where else (of any conse-

[171] Probably Castle Island in Boston Harbor.

[172] An active patriot, buried in Granary Burial Ground, Boston, in 1792.

[173] New Hampshire delegate to the Constitutional Convention, member of the House of Representatives (1789-97), and senator (1804-14).

quence) will be transacted until *she is gone* for Fear of cash being sent off." Poor foundation in truth!

16. At noontime we set sail with a lazy wind from the southeast, and the pilot, Mr. Knox, anchored us at six o'clock in Nantasket Road, eight miles from Boston at the outlet of the bay. (Passing near Castle Island, we had occasion to examine with care this fortification, the key to the port. The batteries are fashioned loosely from green sods and seem very badly cared for; they can mount about one hundred artillery pieces in case of necessity.) From these different points one sees perfectly the Bay of Boston, made beautiful by the number of islands planted throughout it. In all its channels there is sufficient water for merchant vessels, but a squadron would have its difficulties: three fathoms at low tide and this rises ten or twelve feet.

17. With variable winds we remained at anchor the entire day, anxiously. The company behaved itself graciously, and I read much of the history of the Roman republic by Ferguson.

18. Calm weather, until between seven and eight o'clock in the evening, when hard weather came upon us from the northeast with rain and snow. Had we not had good anchors and excellent cables, we would have suffered the fate of a schooner near us, which ran aground on the beach of Hull.[174]

19. The wind continued with much force all night and at seven o'clock in the morning changed to the northwest, whence it continued blowing with diminution until midnight.

We had intended to put to sea this morning, but after hauling up more than one hundred braces of cable and shaking the ice off the sails and cordage, night came, and we had to leave it for the following day.

20. At nine o'clock in the evening we set sail with fresh weather and at midnight passed "The Light-House," which is at the outlet of Nantasket Road. The ship is leaking so badly that it is necessary to work the pump four times every hour.

[174] A settlement near the entrance to Boston Harbor.

25. With a moderate wind from the north-northwest and clear weather we sailed eight miles to the east. At two o'clock in the afternoon we observed a sail off starboard whose maneuvers led us to suspect that it was a pirate. We held a council and readied the short arms we had brought. At nightfall we changed our course somewhat to avoid the encounter, which we succeeded in doing, to the notable joy of the poltroons R—ds, G—s and H—p.

26. The passengers enjoy good humor, and Captain Dashwood continues to give us much laughter with his amusing accounts of amorous intrigues, even though he is more than sixty-two years old and is one of the Presbyterian patriarchs of New England.

27. The passengers in good spirits, each one revealing by degrees his nature and character, which are difficult to conceal when one lives in familiarity for a considerable time. I have read extensively in the history of the Roman republic by Ferguson, a book of much merit.

28. The day was spent reading, and in company with the Captain and two or three passengers who are persons of distinction and reasoning.

30. The ship continues to leak, and this has filled with fear some of our pusillanimous passengers, notably those who profess being most religious.

31. A great wave struck our pilot, Mr. Whitwell, leaving him with a contusion under the eye, which deprived him of his senses. (Fortunately he recovered the following day with a bit of Torlington which I had brought.) What was more extraordinary was that in one of the excessive rolls of the ship the cord of the steering wheel slipped off, and in that first moment of confusion (the ship being without control) behold the poltroon Garniss, carried away with fear, calling everybody to the pumps and communicating such a panic to the other passengers that all expected their final moment. I sprang from my stateroom, where I had been sleeping, and inquiring after the matter immediately

made them see that there was no reason for the alarm. Nevertheless one of them remained so affected that a short time after, there being some impediment in the helm, he gave us a second alarm, shouting, "The saw, the saw!" Although the others gathered anew, I only came to the door of my stateroom.

[From this point, only the most interesting portions of the diary have been included.]

~~~ *January 4, 1785.* The weather cleared, but there remained a deafening swell, which racked the ship, and those in it not a little. One good thing we always had, and that was hot food, a result of the activity and hospitable mode of the Captain.

One pump worked continuously, to keep the ship clear of water.

~~~ *16.* With fresh breezes from the southeast we sailed ninety-seven miles to the east. The weather cloudy with some showers.

The passengers seem in good humor, and there has been no lack of horseplay, productive of coarseness and disrespect. Hume and more Hume for me.[175]

~~~ *18.* Today I finished reading the political and philosophical works of Mr. Hume, with singular profit and pleasure for me; and I began Roberson's history of the reign of Charles V of Spain.[176]

~~~ *February 1, London, England.* At ten o'clock in the morning I disembarked and, taking a hackney coach, crossed almost all of this capital to Pall Mall,[177] where I took lodging at the Royal Hotel. All my baggage remained on board, because

[175] David Hume, Scottish philosopher and historian, author of such works as *A Treatise of Human Nature* (1739), *Essays Moral and Political* (1741–42), and *History of England during the Reigns of James I and Charles I* (1754).

[176] William Robertson (*sic*), Scottish historian and author of *History of the Reign of Emperor Charles V* (1769).

[177] Pall Mall Street was a favorite stopping place for foreigners visiting London during this period.

not having more than the usual clothes and books, it did not seem just to pay more than half a guinea to those scoundrels of guards who were on board the ship. When these finally wanted me to give them more, I became angry and afterwards I regretted it, because it cost me considerable embarrassment and I lost some trifles.

INDEX

Adams, Miss (of Boston): 162
Adams, Mrs. (of Boston): 161
Adams, John: 174, 176n.
Adams, John Quincy: 157n., 161n., 189n.
Adams, Samuel: 163, 173
Addington, Henry, Viscount Sidmouth: xvi
Adison, Captain J.: 12, 16
Agriculture: on Ocracoke Island, 4; in environs of New Bern, North Carolina, 5, 8, 9; in environs of Beaufort, North Carolina, 12; in North Carolina, 15; in environs of Georgetown, South Carolina, 17; in South Carolina, 17n., 32, 34; in Pennsylvania, 64; in New Jersey, 73; on Long Island, 81; in environs of New Haven, Connecticut, 109; in environs of Providence, Rhode Island, 147–48; in environs of Salem, Massachusetts, 178
Ague: *see* Malaria
Alba, Fernando Alvarez de Toledo, Duke of: 106
Albany, New York: 95, 98ff.; houses in, 98; Hollenbake Inn, 98
Alexander, General William (Lord Sterling): 80, 99n.
Allen, The Misses (of Philadelphia): 56
Allen, Mrs. James: 47, 49, 55f.
Allston, Washington: 23n.
Almy, Mrs. (innkeeper in Newport): 132
America (ship): 182
Amesbury, Massachusetts: 188
Amesbury Ferry, Massachusetts: 178f.
Amory, Miss (of Boston): 162
Amory, Thomas: 159n.

Amory, Mrs. Thomas (Elizabeth Coffin): 159
Anabaptists: 52, 148n., 149
Anburey, Thomas: xxxi
André, Major John: 83, 88, 92f.; execution and burial of, 92; abilities of, 92–93
Andrews, John: 160n.
Andrews, Mrs. John: 160
Annapolis, Maryland: 57
Anthonys Nose, New York: 89, 96
Appleton, Miss (of Boston): 161
Appleton, Nathaniel: 161n.
Appleton, Mrs. Nathaniel: 160–61
Apthorp, Charles: 160n.
Apthorp, James: 174
Apthorp, Mrs. James (Sarah Wentworth): 160
Aquackanonk, New Jersey: 94
Archivo del General Miranda, Viajes, Diarios, 1750–1785: viii
Aristides the Just: 115
Armand, Charles (pseudonym of Armand Tufin, Marquis de La Rouërie): 47
Armstrong, Major John: 57
Arnold, Miss (sister of Benedict Arnold): 109
Arnold, Mr. (of Providence): 149
Arnold, Mrs. (of Providence): 149f.
Arnold, Benedict: 81n., 82n., 83n., 88, 92f., 101n., 102, 108, 126; monument to, 101n.; in New Haven, 108n.; death of, 109n.
Anrold, Mrs. Benedict (Margaret Shippen): 48n., 92
Ashley River: 25, 27f.
Astoria (New York City): 105n.
Attleboro, Massachusetts: 155
Austen, John: 105

196

Index

Success Pond, Long Island: 79
Suffield, Connecticut: 112, 114f.
Sullivan, James: 172
Sullivan, General John: 80, 136ff., 146, 172, 182, 187n.
Sullivan (Sullivans) Island, South Carolina: 18, 33f.
Swan, James: 157
Swan, Mrs. James: 159
Swan, John: 181

Tappan, New York: 92
Tappan Bay, New York: 96
Tarboro, North Carolina: 16
Tarrytown, New York: 83
Taucker, Mr. (secretary to Peter John Van Berckel): 51
Taylor, Cornet (British officer): 59f., 62, 82, 84, 89, 92
Temple, Miss (of Boston): 161
Ternay, Charles Louis D'Arzac de: 139f.
Thames River: 122, 125, 126n.
Thibault, The Misses (of Charleston): 24
Thompson, Mr. (owner Indian Queen Inn in Philadelphia): 41
Thorning, Joseph F.: ix, xvin.
Thurber, Captain John: 33n.
Ticknor, George: 159n.
Titcomb, General Jonathan: 187
Tocqueville, Alexis Charles Henri Clérel de: vii, xxx
Tonomy Hill, Rhode Island: 136
Toscan, M. (French vice-consul): 180
Townsend, Miss (of Charleston): 24
Tracy, John: 185ff.
Tracy, Mrs. John: 186
Tracy, Nathaniel: 159n., 187
Tracy, Mrs. Nathaniel (Ann Lee): 159
Tracy, Patrick: 187n.
Trenton, New Jersey: 57n., 72, 89n.; Battle of, 44n., 70
Trent River: 5ff., 10
Truman, Captain Clark: 127
Trumbull, John: 116
Tryon, Governor William: 7
Tucker, Mr. (of Boston): 16ff.
Tudor, William: 161n., 172
Tudor, Mrs. William: 161
Turnbull, Dr. Andrew: 22, 30

Turnbull, Mrs. Andrew: 24
Turnbull, Miss P. (of Charleston): 24
Turner, Mrs. Mary: 71

United States of America: rise of nationalism in, xxiii–xxiv, xxvii; government in, xxiii–xxv; foreign aid to, xxiiif.; social and economic changes in, xxv–xxvi; religion in, xxv; schools in, xxv; Treaty of Paris, xxvi; monetary problems of, xxvi; cessation of hostilities and preliminary treaties with England, xxvii; area of, xxvii; population of, xxvii; settlements in, xxvii; cities in, xxvii; travel accounts of, xxx–xxxii
Upper Houses (Cromwell), Connecticut: 117
Uppsala University: xvii

Van Berckel, Peter John: 44, 50n., 51
Van Bramme, Mr. (Dutch consul in South Carolina): 35
Vankroff, Dr. (of Philadelphia): 45
Van Rensselaer, Stephen: 98
Van Weetle, Peter: 93–94
Vassall, William: 170
Vaudreuil, Louis Philippe de Rigand, Marquis de: 183
Vaughn, Dr. John: 45
Vaughn, Mrs. John: 49
Venezuela: xvi, xx, xxif., xxviiif.; revolution in, xxi–xxiii; Declaration of Independence from Spain, xxii
Vernon, Nancy: 142
Vernon, William: 142n.
Vernor, Martha: 102n.
Verplancks Point, New York: 89
Vining, Mrs. (of Wilmington, Delaware): 59f.
Vining, John: 59, 63
Vining, Polly: 47, 56, 59f., 62
Virginia: xxxi

Waccamaw River: 16; Town Entrance, 16
Waldo, Miss (of Boston): 161
Waldo, Francis: 160n.
Waldo, Mrs. Francis: 160
Walker, Major (of Wilmington, North Carolina): 14

of which *The New Democracy in America* is Number 40, was started in 1939 by the University of Oklahoma Press. It follows rather logically the Press's program of regional exploration. Behind the story of the gradual and inevitable recession of the American frontier lie the accounts of explorers, traders, and travelers, which individually and in the aggregate present one of the most romantic and fascinating chapters in the development of the American domain. The following list is complete as of the date of publication of this volume.

1. Captain Randolph B. Marcy and Captain George B. McClellan. *Adventure on Red River*: Report on the Exploration of the Headwaters of the Red River. Edited by Grant Foreman. Out of print.

2. Grant Foreman. *Marcy and the Gold Seekers*: The Journal of Captain R. B. Marcy, with an Account of the Gold Rush over the Southern Route. Out of print.

3. Pierre-Antoine Tabeau. *Tabeau's Narrative of Loisel's Expedition to the Upper Missouri*. Edited by Annie Heloise Abel. Translated from the French by Rose Abel Wright. Out of print.

4. Victor Tixier. *Tixier's Travels on the Osage Prairies*. Edited by John Francis McDermott. Translated from the French by Albert J. Salvan.

5. Teodoro de Croix. *Teodoro de Croix and the Northern Frontier of New Spain, 1776–1783*. Translated from the Spanish and edited by Alfred Barnaby Thomas. Out of print.

6. A. W. Whipple. *A Pathfinder in the Southwest*: The Itinerary of Lieutenant A. W. Whipple During His Exploration for a Railway Route from Fort Smith to Los Angeles in the Years 1853 & 1854. Edited and annotated by Grant Foreman. Out of print.

7. Josiah Gregg. *Diary & Letters*. Two volumes. Edited by Maurice Garland Fulton. Introductions by Paul Horgan.

8. Washington Irving. *The Western Journals of Washington Irving*. Edited and annotated by John Francis McDermott. Out of print.

9. Edward Dumbauld. *Thomas Jefferson, American Tourist*: Being an Account of His Journeys in the United States of America, England, France, Italy, the Low Countries, and Germany.

10. Victor Wolfgang von Hagen. *Maya Explorer*: John Lloyd Stephens and the Lost Cities of Central America and Yucatán.

11. E. Merton Coulter. *Travels in the Confederate States*: A Bibliography.

12. W. Eugene Hollon. *The Lost Pathfinder*: Zebulon Montgomery Pike.

13. George Frederick Ruxton. *Ruxton of the Rockies*. Collected by Clyde and Mae Reed Porter. Edited by LeRoy R. Hafen.

14. George Frederick Ruxton. *Life in the Far West*. Edited by LeRoy R. Hafen. Foreword by Mae Reed Porter.

15. Edward Harris. *Up the Missouri with Audubon*: The Journal of Edward Harris. Edited by John Francis McDermott.

16. Robert Stuart. *On the Oregon Trail*: Robert Stuart's Journey of Discovery (1812–1813). Edited by Kenneth A. Spaulding.

17. Josiah Gregg. *Commerce of the Prairies*. Edited by Max L. Moorhead.

18. John Treat Irving, Jr. *Indian Sketches*, Taken During an Expedition to the Pawnee Tribes (1833). Edited and annotated by John Francis McDermott.

19. Thomas D. Clark (ed.). *Travels in the Old South, 1527–1860*: A Bibliography. Three volumes. Volumes One and Two issued as a set (1956); Volume Three (1959).

20. Alexander Ross. *The Fur Hunters of the Far West*. Edited by Kenneth A. Spaulding.

21. William Bollaert. *William Bollaert's Texas*. Edited by W. Eugene Hollon and Ruth Lapham Butler. Out of print.

22. Daniel Ellis Conner. *Joseph Reddeford Walker and the Ari-*

zona Adventure. Edited by Donald J. Berthrong and Odessa Davenport.

23. Matthew C. Field. *Prairie and Mountain Sketches*. Collected by Clyde and Mae Reed Porter. Edited by Kate L. Gregg and John Francis McDermott.

24. Ross Cox. *The Columbia River*: Scenes and Adventures During a Residence of Six Years on the Western Side of the Rocky Mountains Among Various Tribes of Indians Hitherto Unknown; Together with a Journey Across the American Continent. Edited by Edgar I. and Jane R. Stewart.

25. Noel M. Loomis. *The Texan–Santa Fé Pioneers*.

26. Charles Preuss. *Exploring with Frémont*: The Private Diaries of Charles Preuss, Cartographer for John C. Frémont on His First, Second, and Fourth Expeditions to the Far West. Translated and edited by Erwin G. and Elisabeth K. Gudde.

27. Jacob H. Schiel. *Journey Through the Rocky Mountains and the Humboldt Mountains to the Pacific Ocean*. Translated from the German and edited by Thomas N. Bonner.

28. Zenas Leonard. *Adventures of Zenas Leonard, Fur Trader*. Edited by John C. Ewers.

29. Matthew C. Field. *Matt Field on the Santa Fe Trail*. Collected by Clyde and Mae Reed Porter. Edited and with an introduction and notes by John E. Sunder.

30. James Knox Polk Miller. *The Road to Virginia City*: The Diary of James Knox Polk Miller. Edited by Andrew F. Rolle.

31. Benjamin Butler Harris. *The Gila Trail*: The Texas Argonauts and the California Gold Rush. Edited and annotated by Richard H. Dillon.

32. Captain James H. Bradley. *The March of the Montana Column*: A Prelude to the Custer Disaster. Edited by Edgar I. Stewart.

33. Heinrich Lienhard. *From St. Louis to Sutter's Fort, 1846*. Translated and edited by Erwin G. and Elisabeth K. Gudde.

34. Washington Irving. *The Adventures of Captain Bonneville*. Edited and with an introduction by Edgeley W. Todd.

35. Jean-Bernard Bossu. *Jean-Bernard Bossu's Travels in the Interior of North America, 1751–1762.* Translated and edited by Seymour Feiler.
36. Thomas D. Clark (ed.). *Travels in the New South, 1865–1955:* A Bibliography. Two volumes.
37. John Lloyd Stephens. *Incidents of Travel in Yucatán.* Edited and with an introduction by Victor Wolfgang von Hagen. Two volumes.
38. Richard A. Bartlett. *Great Surveys of the American West.*
39. Gloria Griffen Cline. *Exploring the Great Basin.*
40. Francisco de Miranda. *The New Democracy in America:* Travels of Francisco de Miranda in the United States, 1783–84. Translated by Judson P. Wood. Edited by John S. Ezell.

The New Democracy in America has been set on the Linotype in eleven-point Janson with two points of leading between lines. The Janson design dates from the late seventeenth century and is thought to be of Dutch origin. The original matrices in Germany were used as the models for the modern machine face, which is today regarded as one of our most legible types.

UNIVERSITY OF OKLAHOMA PRESS
Norman

Miranda, Francisco de, 1750–1816.
The new democracy in America; travels of Francisco de Miranda in the United States, 1783–84. Translated by Judson P. Wood. Edited by John S. Ezell. ₍1st ed.₎ Norman, University of Oklahoma Press ₍1963₎

xxxii, 217 p. illus., port., map. 24 cm. (The American exploration and travel series, 40)

Translation of Viage por los Estados Unidos de la America del Norte, año de 1783–84, a portion of Miranda's diary which was begun in 1771.

Bibliographical references included in "Editor's preface."

1. U. S.—Descr. & trav.—1783–1848.   ɪ. Wood, Judson P., tr. ɪɪ. Ezell, John Samuel, ed.   ɪɪɪ. Title.   ✓(Series)

E164.M673   917.4   63–9959 rev